QUESTIONNAIRES AND INVENTORIES

QUESTIONNAIRES AND INVENTORIES

Surveying Opinions and Assessing Personality

Lewis R. Aiken

John Wiley & Sons, Inc.

New York • Chichester • Weinheim • Brisbane • Singapore • Toronto

Library of Congress Cataloging-in-Publication Data:

Aiken, Lewis R., 1931–
    Questionnaires and inventories : surveying opinions and assessing
  personality / Lewis R. Aiken.
       p.   cm.
    Companion volume to the author's Rating scales and checklists.
    Includes bibliographical references and indexes.
    ISBN 0-471-16871-8 (alk. paper) (includes disk)
    1. Psychological tests. 2. Questionnaires. 3. Psychometrics.
  I. Aiken, Lewis R., 1931–   Rating scales and checklists.
  II. Title.
  BF176.A483   1997
  150'.28'7—dc21   96-53659

Printed in the United States of America

10 9 8 7 6 5 4 3 2 1

Preface

This volume is a brief but comprehensive handbook on the design, selection, analysis, and interpretation of questionnaires and psychological inventories.

It is a companion volume to *Rating Scales and Checklists: Evaluating Behavior, Personality, and Attitudes* (Aiken, 1996). Together, the two books represent a valuable resource for constructing, administering, and evaluating the results obtained from questionnaires, checklists, ratings scales, and psychological inventories, and the reader will benefit from studying both volumes. However, the present volume stands on its own and may be studied as an independent treatise on two kinds of data-collection instruments—questionnaires and inventories. The format of the present volume—the number and length of the chapters, the chapter summaries, the end-of-chapter questions and activities, the glossary and the appendixes—are similar in structure to those of the previous book. Terms in italic are defined in the glossary at the end of the book. In addition, while there is some overlap in the methodology and substantive matters discussed in the two volumes, the previous volume places more emphasis on psychology and education, whereas this one strikes a better balance between various applied fields concerned with surveys of practices and opinions and the assessment of individual and group characteristics. Two chapters, instead of one as in the earlier volume, are devoted to instrument construction; an entire chapter is devoted to the topic of data analysis; and another chapter to reliability and validity. Commercially available questionnaires are described in one chapter and standardized inventories are described in another.

As in *Rating Scales and Checklists,* an integral part of *Questionnaires and Inventories* is the accompanying diskette of several dozen computer programs correlated with the text material to aid the reader in designing, constructing, administering, scoring, and evaluating questionnaires and inventories. Although the text can be studied profitably without running the computer programs, the two sources of information complement each other and are best used together. Several of the end-of-chapter exercises provide practice in running the computer programs, which can be used for many other purposes as well.

The book and the accompanying computer diskette are designed primarily for researchers and practitioners in business and the behavioral sciences who use questionnaires, inventories, and related instruments for theoretical and applied purposes such as consumer surveys, epidemiological studies, population studies, psychodiagnosis, and for evaluating the effectiveness of interventions or tryouts of various kinds. The intended audience encompasses market researchers, psychologists, sociologists, educators, and other professionals in health-related professions, legal professions, business, education, the military, and other organizational contexts. The book should serve as a useful supplement to research and measurement courses in business, psychology, sociology, and medicine. Graduate students in many different fields who are planning theses and dissertations in the social, behavioral, and health sciences will also find this book informative and helpful.

The explosion of knowledge and the growth of technology and research methodology during the past few decades have increased the need for information-intensive sources that communicate in a terse but informative style. And like all teacher-authors, I should not like my readers to be mere automata who process and apply what they read without thinking; rather, I hope that they ponder the material, question it, and adapt it to their own purposes. Ideally, this book will serve both as a compact source of information and a stimulus for application, elaboration, and further development of the topics.

LEWIS R. AIKEN

Contents

QUESTIONNAIRES AND INVENTORIES

1

History and Methods of Social and Psychological Investigation

L ike the child in Walt Whitman's poem who asked "What is grass?" we all learn by questioning. From an early age, we are told to "ask if you don't know." Responses to "who, what, when, and where" supply descriptive information, and the how and why questions provoke explanations that allow people to adapt to and change their environments. Answers to such questions satisfy not only our curiosity but provide us with practical information for meeting our needs and expressing ourselves (see Box 1.1).

Everyone asks questions, and some people make a living doing so. Reporters, scientists, and investigators of every stripe develop the craft of questioning as a part of their breadwinning activities. But, not every query evokes a response that provides the desired information. To avoid misunderstanding, a question must be in the correct form, phrased and verbalized in an appropriate way and context so that the listener understands and is encouraged to reply thoughtfully and truthfully.

One of the most famous questioners of all time was Socrates, who frequently responded to a question posed by a student with another question. Believing that his students already knew the answers to many of their questions—that the answers were actually within them

---

Box 1.1
Some Common What, Who, Why, Where,
When, and How Questions

What's your name?
What time is it?
What's for dinner?
Who won?
Who knows?
Who cares?
Why me?
Why did you do it?
Why not?
Where are you going?
Where did you put it?
Where do you live?
When do we start?
When do we get out?
When do we eat?
How are you?
How old are you?
How do you know?

---

waiting to be revealed—Socrates attempted to teach by asking a series of leading, probing questions that stimulated thinking and the gradual discovery of the sought-for answers.

Another teacher who relied on the Socratic method of self-discovery was Sigmund Freud. Rather than directly telling his patients what they should do in order to solve their problems or alleviate their disorders, Freud encouraged them to talk about their feelings and experiences and thereby come to understand the nature and causes of their difficulties and discover ways of resolving them. This *clinical method* also requires adeptness in "listening with the third ear" to detect the subtleties and self-deception involved in much human thinking and behavior.

Many other great teachers and healers have been keen questioners. They realized that the most satisfying, enduring, and even therapeutic answers are those that are discovered or formulated by the individual. Certainly, we are sometimes too quick to ask for information or form judgments when a little more concentration and forbearance, and a greater adherence to the maxims "seek and ye shall find" and "patience is virtue" would lead us to arrive at answers by means of our own resources. But, the day of the Renaissance man or woman is long past, and even highly educated adults today find it necessary to seek guidance by questioning others about numerous matters. Typically, these questions are presented in a face-to-face situation or over the telephone, but sometimes they are posed in a more formal manner by constructing and administering a paper-and-pencil, self-report instrument.

HISTORICAL BACKGROUND

With the advancement of science and technology from the 17th through the 19th centuries, it became possible to make precise measurements of many physical and biological variables. In ancient times, all knowledge was subsumed under philosophy; but during the Renaissance period of European civilization, the physical and biological sciences broke away from natural philosophy and became scholarly disciplines in their own right. The social sciences were a bit slower in separating from philosophy. Until the late 19th century, the study of social sciences such as politics, psychology, and sociology was still considered a part of philosophy. True, many philosophers and other scholars described their observations and thoughts concerning human behavior, but these investigations and analyses were not strictly scientific in the modern, controlled, empirical sense of the term. In fact, philosophers such as Immanuel Kant believed that psychology, which he viewed as based exclusively on subjective phenomena, could never aspire to be objective and, consequently, scientific. During the 19th century, however, empirical studies of mental and social events, and theories pertaining to those events, showed how disciplines concerned with behavior might become scientific.

Quetelet, Fechner, and Galton

The hallmark of science is the precise measurement of the variables of interest. The separation of psychology and other social sciences from philosophy during the last century was greatly facilitated by the development of techniques and instruments for measuring mental and social events. Men such as Adolphe Quetelet, Gustav Fechner, and Sir Francis Galton provided the beginnings of theory and methodology concerned with social and psychological measurement.

In the early 18th century, the mathematicians Pierre-Simon Laplace and Karl F. Gauss conducted seminal research on probability theory that had a profound effect on psychology and other social sciences. Gauss demonstrated that the errors made by astronomers and other scientific observers were describable in terms of a bell-shaped, normal distribution, which came to be known as *Gaussian distribution.* Procedures for computing the arithmetic mean, probable error, and certain other statistics also are attributable to Gauss.

Extending the discoveries of Laplace and Gauss to biological and social data, Quetelet maintained that the common occurrence of a normal distribution of observations made on living things is due to bona fide characteristics of those things rather than to errors of measurement. Quetelet introduced the concept of the "average man" *(l'homme moyen),* an ideal of nature around which there is a normal distribution of approximations to the average. To demonstrate his thesis, Quetelet conducted statistical surveys of birth rates, death rates, marriages, crime, suicide, and other demographic and anthropometric variables in populations. These early surveys marked the beginnings of the systematic collection of *vital statistics*—data pertaining to human life, the conditions affecting it, and the maintenance of the population during a specified time period—by governmental and other organizations during the late 19th century.

Like Quetelet, Gustav Fechner was a physical scientist who became interested in human behavior. But unlike Quetelet, Fechner devoted his attention to the small rather than the large. Fechner was the founder of *psychophysics,* which was concerned with the mathematical relationships between mental events and the physical stimuli that give rise to them. His principal contributions consisted of methods for studying sensation and the formulation of the first psychological law. Known as *Fechner's law,* this formulation describes the relationship between the subjective magnitude of a sensation and the intensity of the physical stimulus that causes it in terms of a logarithmic function. Fechner's law holds fairly well in the intermediate range of stimulus intensities, but other formulations, such as a power function, apply better outside this range (Guilford, 1954). In any event, Fechner's ideas were subsequently extended to include perception, feeling, action, attention, and other psychological processes related to stimulus events.

Another versatile 19th-century scientist who demonstrated that the study of human behavior could be placed on a solid, scientific footing was Sir Francis Galton. Inspired by the statistical research of Quetelet and the observations and experiments of Charles Darwin (Galton's cousin) on the origins of species differences, Galton made numerous methodological contributions to the study of individual differences in abilities and other psychological phenomena. He is particularly noted for his sensorimotor tests and his collaboration with Karl Pearson in devising various statistical methods (correlation, standard scores, median, etc.). In the context of the present volume, Galton's pioneering uses of the ranking (*order-of-merit*) procedure, *rating scales*, and *questionnaires* are particularly noteworthy.

Some psychological and educational measurements were in use before Galton's time. For example, the examination procedure of formally administering a series of orally presented questions had been employed by the Chinese since the second millennium B.C. to determine whether government officials were fit to perform their duties. In Europe and America, until the middle of the 19th century, school and university examinations consisted almost exclusively of oral examinations. Prompted by the need for more efficient evaluation of students, written examinations were instituted in many American schools during the latter part of the century.

Questionnaires (from the French "question(er)") were also used prior to Galton's time to study sociological and political events, but he is credited as the first scientist to construct and administer questionnaires to study psychological phenomena. Galton's first questionnaire, a lengthy instrument covering a wide range of environmental factors presumed to be related to mental giftedness, was completed by many eminent scientists of the day. A similar approach was taken in a questionnaire administered to 94 sets of twins. Galton's interest in the nature of mental imagery led him to design a third questionnaire (see Figure 1.1).

As with other studies that he conducted on mental abilities, Galton found extensive individual differences in the intensity and characteristics of mental images (Forrest, 1974).

Statistics

Statistics, derived from the Latin word for "state," was traditionally concerned with precisely that—matters of state. Even the government in ancient Rome needed to know how many legions and soldiers it had,

Questions on Visualizing, etc.

E—QUESTIONS ON VISUALIZING AND OTHER ALLIED FACULTIES.

The object of these Questions is to elicit the degree in which different persons possess the power of seeing images in their mind's eye, and of reviving past sensations.

From inquiries I have already made, it appears that remarkable variations exist both in the strength and in the quality of these faculties, and it is highly probable that a statistical inquiry into them will throw light upon more than one psychological problem.

Before addressing yourself to any of the Questions on the opposite page, think of some definite object—and consider carefully the picture that rises before your mind's eye.

1. *Illumination.*—Is the image dim or fairly clear? Is its brightness comparable to that of the actual scene?

2. *Definition.*—Are all the objects pretty well defined at the same time, or is the place of sharpest definition at any one moment more contracted than it is in the real scene?

3. *Colouring.*—Are the colours of the china, of the toast, bread crust, mustard, meat, parsley, or whatever may have been on the table, quite distinct and natural?

4. *Extent of field of view.*—Call up the image of some panoramic view (the walls of your room might suffice), can you force yourself to see mentally a wider range of it than could be taken in by any single glance of the eyes? Can you mentally see more than three faces of a die, or more than one hemisphere of a globe at the same instant of time?

5. *Distance of images.*—Where do mental images appear to be situated? within the head, within the eye-ball, just in front of the eyes, or at a distance corresponding to reality? Can you project an image upon a piece of paper?

6. *Command over images.*—Can you retain a mental picture steadily before the eyes? When you do so, does it grow brighter or dimmer? When the act of retaining it becomes wearisome, in what part of the head or eye-ball is the fatigue felt?

7. *Persons.*—Can you recall with distinctness the features of all near relations and many other people? Can you at will cause your mental image of any or most of them to sit, stand, or turn slowly round? Can you deliberately seat the image of a well-known person in a chair and see it with enough distinctness to enable you to sketch it leisurely (supposing yourself able to draw)?

8. *Scenery.*—Do you preserve the recollection of scenery with much precision of detail, and do you find pleasure in dwelling on it? Can you easily form mental pictures from the descriptions of scenery that are so frequently met with in novels and books of travel?

9. *Comparison with reality.*—What difference do you perceive between a very vivid mental picture called up in the dark, and a real scene? Have you ever mistaken a mental image for a reality when in health and wide awake?

Figure 1.1. Galton's Breakfast Table Questionnaire. (From Galton, 1883, pp. 255–256)

10. *Numerals and dates.*—Are these invariably associated in your mind with any peculiar mental imagery, whether of written or printed figures, diagrams, or colours? If so, explain fully, and say if you can account for the associations?

11. *Specialties.*—If you happen to have special aptitudes for mechanics, mathematics (either geometry of three dimensions or pure analysis), mental arithmetic, or chess-playing blindfold, please explain fully how far your processes depend on the use of visual images, and how far otherwise?

12. Call up before your imagination the objects specified in the six following paragraphs, numbered A to F, and consider carefully whether your mental representation of them generally, is in each group very faint, faint, fair, good, or vivid and comparable to the actual sensation:—

    A. *Light and colour.*—An evenly clouded sky (omitting all landscape), first bright, then gloomy. A thick surrounding haze, first white, then successively blue, yellow, green, and red.

    B. *Sound.*—The beat of rain against the window panes, the crack of a whip, a church bell, the hum of bees, the whistle of a railway, the clinking of tea-spoons and saucers, the slam of a door.

    C. *Smells.*—Tar, roses, an oil-lamp blown out, hay, violets, a fur coat, gas, tobacco.

    D. *Tastes.*—Salt, sugar, lemon juice, raisins, chocolate, currant jelly.

    E. *Touch.*—Velvet, silk, soap, gum, sand, dough, a crisp dead leaf, the prick of a pin.

    F. *Other sensations.*—Heat, hunger, cold, thirst, fatigue, fever, drowsiness, a bad cold.

13. *Music.*—Have you any aptitude for mentally recalling music, or for imagining it?

14. *At different ages.*—Do you recollect what your powers of visualizing, etc., were in childhood? Have they varied much within your recollection?

General remarks.—Supplementary information written here, or on a separate piece of paper, will be acceptable.

Figure 1.1. *(Continued)*

how many taxpaying Roman citizens there were, how many of each kind of foodstuffs had been harvested, and how much money was in the state treasury each year. The vital statistics (births, marriages, divorces, deaths, etc.) collected by Quetelet and his successors, the preferences and purchases of consumers, the numbers of votes received by political candidates, the crime statistics reported annually by the FBI, all are examples of this use of statistics. These kinds of data summaries, referred to as *descriptive statistics*, involve determining the frequency distributions, measures of central tendency, variability, and other quantifiable characteristics of people, products, and events. In addition, measures of relationships and differences between two or more such variables may be determined.

Descriptive statistical information is extremely useful in the economic and social planning engaged in by governmental organizations, as well as in the product-making, service, and marketing activities of business organizations. All large organizations in modern society collect masses of data, compute various statistics to describe the results in an efficient way, and report and use those statistics in decision-making and planning.

Planning involves prediction, but unless the planner is fortunate enough to have measured the entire population to which the plans pertain, the predictions are likely to contain considerable error. For this reason, the advent of *inferential statistics,* which permits one to make predictions, or estimates, about populations on the basis of sample data, was a breakthrough for scientific decision-making. Whereas statistical description is limited to making statements about samples, the procedures of statistical inference enable an investigator to infer, within a certain range of error and according to a specified probability, the characteristics of populations from measures computed on samples selected from those populations. As with most scientific theorizing, the accuracy with which population characteristics *(parameters)* are predicted from sample characteristics *(statistics)* depends on the prediction model that is employed and the assumptions underlying it.

Many famous mathematicians and scientists, notably Jakob and Johann Bernoulli, Abraham De Moivre, Pierre-Simon Laplace, Blaise Pascal, Karl Gauss, Karl Pearson, and Sir Ronald Fisher, made contributions to the theory and methods of inferential statistics. Prior to the 20th century, statistical theory was based on the assumption of a normal distribution of measures in populations of interest and on selecting large samples at random from such populations. Following this theory of probability, population parameters could be estimated and tests of hypotheses concerning population characteristics could be made only on the basis of large samples.

The first half of the 20th century saw the development of small-sample statistics, more complex parametric statistical procedures, and nonparametric procedures that make no assumptions regarding the nature of the parent population distribution. In addition, multivariate statistical procedures, which involve not only several independent variables but several dependent variables as well, have been devised that increase the efficiency and utility of statistics in decision-making.

In addition to more powerful and versatile statistical procedures, refinements in sampling methods have increased the accuracy of generalizations made from samples to populations. Furthermore, improvements in the design of questionnaires, inventories, rating scales, and other paper-and-pencil measures have increased the value of these instruments for forecasting population characteristics from samples. Finally, the ever-increasing speed and versatility of digital computers have combined with advances in statistical theory and questionnaire design to make the decision-making processes of agencies and organizations easier and more accurate than ever before.

Psychological and Sociological Questionnaires and Inventories

Strictly speaking, a questionnaire should consist of a set of questions; but whether facts, opinions, attitudes, or other personal and social characteristics are being studied, a questionnaire may be composed of various kinds of objective or semiobjective items, including short-answer, completion, true-false, multiple-choice, rating scale, matching, ranking, checklist, or even essay. In addition, rather than being called a questionnaire, the resulting instrument may be labeled an inventory, an opinionnaire, a test, a scale, a survey, a schedule, a study, a profile, an index or indicator, or even a sheet or blank.

By the first quarter of the 20th century, questionnaires and surveys—by whatever name—were becoming fairly common methodology in all sorts of theoretical and applied studies. Not only demographers and psychologists, but educational researchers, market researchers, political scientists, and other investigators of human behavior and its correlates were conducting and administering questionnaires. During the late 1930s and afterward, survey research was developed as a part of the scientific mission of American universities by the Bureau of Applied Social Research at Columbia University (The Bureau), the National Opinion Research Center (NORC) at Denver and the University of Chicago, and the Survey Research Center/Institute for Social Research (SRC/ISR) at the University of Michigan.

In the early years of this century, the fledgling science of psychology was approximately equally divided between those who preferred a more objective, experimental approach and those who felt that psychologists should follow a more subjective, clinical path in research and practice. The objective appeal of direct questioning is illustrated by an anecdote concerning the administration of the Rorschach Inkblot Test, which consists of a series of ten inkblot-display cards. The cards are shown one at a time to a person, who is asked to tell what he or she sees in the blot; that is, what it might represent. According to the anecdote, one examinee gave repeated sexually-related responses to each card: pelvis, penis, vagina, sexual intercourse, and so on. After a while, the examiner sighed and said, "You certainly seem preoccupied with sex." The unruffled examinee quickly replied, "Yes, that's all I think about. But you didn't have to go to the trouble of giving me this test to find that out. You could have just asked me. I would have told you." This little tale illustrates that it is not always necessary to be indirect or devious to elicit information from a person: Ask him or her; he or she may tell you.

All personality tests are not subjective. In 1918, a 116-item questionnaire—the Woodworth Personal Data Sheet—was constructed for the purpose of determining which American soldiers were most likely to be unable to adjust to the stress of military life. The questions on this first *personality inventory* were concerned with neurotic symptoms of the sort that might be detected in a psychiatric screening interview. As illustrated by the following items, the questions dealt with physical symptoms, abnormal fears and worries, social and environmental adjustment, unhappiness, obsessions, compulsions, tics, nightmares, fantasies, and other feelings and behaviors.

> Do you feel sad and low-spirited most of the time?
> Are you often frightened in the middle of the night?
> Do you think you have hurt yourself by going too much with women?
> Have you ever lost your memory for a time?
> Do you usually feel well and strong?
> Do you ever walk in your sleep?
> Do you ever feel an awful pressure in or about your head?
> Are you troubled with the idea that people are watching you on the street?
> Do you make friends easily?
> Are you troubled by shyness?
> Did you have a happy childhood?
> Are you ever bothered by feeling that things are not real?
> (Hollingworth, 1920, pp. 120–126)

This inventory was prepared too late to be used for the selection of military personnel in World War I, but it provided a basis for the development of other paper-and-pencil inventories of personality after the war.

Following on the heels of early personality inventories were the various attitude inventories constructed by L. L. Thurstone and his colleagues, and the Strong Vocational Interest Blank for Men developed by E. K. Strong, Jr. Questionnaires designed to assess personality traits, interests, attitudes, values, and other affective characteristics were an outgrowth of the *mental testing movement*. This movement, which began with Galton and his American colleague J. M. Cattell, was concerned primarily with the measurement of mental abilities (intelligence, special aptitudes, achievement). It became clear fairly soon that behavior could not be predicted or explained solely by differences in abilities, but that measures of motivation, emotion, interests, and other affective characteristics could contribute to forecasting individual performance and attitude.

Social Surveys

Extensive use of social surveys and questionnaires was made by sociologists in community studies encouraged by the *reform movement* of the late 19th and early 20th centuries. Stimulated by Charles Booth's *Life and Labour of the People in London*, American reformers such as Jane Addams at Hull House in Chicago undertook surveys of their own communities with the objective of reforming them. The six-volume Pittsburgh surveys of 1907–1909, which provided a description of industrial life in that city, is considered to have been the culmination of the American social survey. Low wages, poor housing, inadequate public health facilities, and unsafe working conditions for the laboring classes were among the problems emphasized by these surveys (Hoover, 1993).

Some Continuing Problems

Psychological and social assessment has traveled a somewhat rocky road during the 20th century. To some extent, the mental testing movement found itself unable to deliver on all of its promises or to meet all expectations. Politics and social factors became interwoven with science, and mental testers were often unable to extricate themselves from the confusion. Objective measures of achievement and aptitudes made important contributions to educational and employment selection and counseling, in addition to the diagnosis and treatment of mental disorders, but the results were not uniformly beneficial.

The instruments devised by psychologists and other social scientists were, and continue to be, sharply criticized for their questionable validity and the personal and social consequences of using them. In the realm of public-opinion polling, the *Literary Digest* straw poll of 1936—in which Alfred M. Landon was predicted to be the winner in the presidential sweepstakes that Franklin D. Roosevelt actually won—prompted a closer examination of survey methodology. George Gallup, who employed a quota-sampling procedure to predict the results of the 1936 election, had more success, but even the Gallup poll was off the mark in the 1948 election. Like all the other major pollsters, Gallup incorrectly predicted that Thomas E. Dewey would defeat Harry S. Truman for the presidency. Consequently, after 1948, professional pollsters switched to probability sampling. The success of this strategy was demonstrated in the 1976 *New York Times*/CBS poll, which correctly predicted 51.1% of the votes for Jimmy Carter and 49.9% for Gerald Ford.

Surveys based on straw polls, such as the one in Shere Hite's study of *Women in Love* (Wallis, 1987), still make the headlines. In that study, an analysis of the data from 3,000 returned questionnaires out of 100,000 that were distributed indicated that 70% of women who had been married more than five years were having extramarital affairs, 84% were not satisfied emotionally with their marital relationships, and 78% were treated only sporadically as equals by their husbands. A subsequent, more carefully conducted ABC/*Washington Post* survey yielded rather different results. Only 6% of the women respondents said they were having an extramarital affair, 93% expressed satisfaction with their marriages, and 81% said that most of the time they were treated as equals by their husbands (Haney, 1995).

Rather than being limited to the questionnaires, tests, and other instruments that are administered in social science research, public concern and suspicion are also often directed toward research on human behavior in general and to the suggestion of manipulation or "big brotherism," which such research connotes. Adherence to the ethical codes of research and practice in psychology and other social sciences can improve public acceptance of research on human behavior (see Box 1.2). Nevertheless, constant attention must be directed toward ensuring that behavioral research methods are properly implemented and that the findings are applied with a sensitivity to human needs and values.

Box 1.2
Preamble to the APA Ethical Principles of Psychologists and Code of Conduct

Psychologists work to develop a valid and reliable body of scientific knowledge based on research. They may apply that knowledge to human behavior in a variety of contexts. In doing so, they perform many roles, such as researcher, educator, diagnostician, therapist, supervisor, consultant, administrator, social interventionist, and expert witness. Their goal is to broaden knowledge of behavior and, where appropriate, to apply it pragmatically to improve the condition of both the individual and society. Psychologists respect the central importance of freedom of inquiry and expression in research, teaching, and publication. They also strive to help the public in developing informed judgments and choices concerning human behavior. This Ethics Code provides a common set of values upon which psychologists build their professional and scientific work.

This code is intended to provide both the general principles and the decision rules to cover most situations encountered by psychologists. It has as its primary goal the welfare and protection of the individuals and groups with whom psychologists work. It is the individual responsibility of each psychologist to aspire to the highest possible standards of conduct. Psychologists respect and protect human and civil rights, and do not knowingly participate in or condone unfair discriminatory practices.

The development of a dynamic set of ethical standards for a psychologist's work-related conduct requires a personal commitment to a lifelong effort to act ethically; to encourage ethical behavior by students, supervisors, employees, and colleagues, as appropriate; and to consult with others, as needed, concerning ethical problems. Each psychologist supplements, but does not violate, the Ethics Code's values and rules on the basis of guidance drawn from personal values, culture, and experience.

RESEARCH METHODS

Research, which means literally "to look again," consists of a search for information that can be used to answer questions and help solve practical and theoretical problems. A research investigation may be totally *exploratory,* in which case the investigator essentially has few if any preconceptions or ideas about what might turn up, but merely hopes that something interesting will be discovered—some new fact or phenomenon that may be useful for some purpose. In contrast, research of the *hypothesis-testing* sort has a narrower, more deliberate aim: to test the truth or falsity of a hypothesis concerning some event or situation.

Description and Explanation

In addition to classifying it as either exploratory or hypothesis-testing, research may be dichotomized as descriptive versus explanatory. Many investigations involving the administration of questionnaires and inventories are of the *descriptive* type: The investigator wishes to obtain data that describe the characteristics of certain people, objects, or events. The aims of *explanatory research* go beyond description: The investigator is interested in finding an explanation, a reason or cause, for the particular condition or situation. Explanatory research may be of either the exploratory or hypothesis-testing type, depending on the extent to which the results are predicted beforehand and competing explanations can be eliminated.

Variables, Correlation, and Causation

All science is concerned with *variables*—independent and dependent, controlled and uncontrolled, causal and concomitant. In purely descriptive research, distinctions between the various kinds of variables are of less concern than in explanatory research. The relationships between variables and the extent to which one variable can be predicted from another may be of interest in descriptive research. For example, if we find that variables A and B are significantly correlated, then we can predict—at least better than chance—the state or value of variable A from that of variable B, or vice versa. We may not be able to explain one variable on the basis of the other, but at least we can predict it.

In actuality, most behavioral science research is correlational in nature. Whether a correlation coefficient or some other statistic is computed, an investigation is basically correlational when the independent variable is not manipulated by the researcher and no effort is made, either by randomization or matching, to control extraneous variables. Manipulation alone will not suffice; control over extraneous variables must be exercised if cause-and-effect conclusions are to be drawn.

Functional relationships between variables—*independent* and *dependent*—are the hallmark of explanatory research. The functional relationship between the independent variable X and the dependent variable Y may not, however, be a causal one or even the true one; extraneous, or confounded, variables may affect the observed relationship between X and Y. For this reason, explanatory research, and particularly hypothesis-testing research, requires that some sort of control—statistical or experimental—be imposed over extraneous variables.

In research on human subjects, it is usually impossible to move subjects around like chess pieces, to do whatever one likes to them. Although admittedly second-best approaches to controlling for extraneous variables, special correlational procedures, analysis of covariance, and path analysis are often helpful in obtaining some assurance that changes in specified variables are the results of changes in other designated variables rather than extraneous, perhaps unknown, variables.

Internal and External Validity

The most effective procedure of controlling for extraneous variables is to conduct an *experiment.* Experimentation requires initial matching of subjects on selected extraneous variables that might influence the results, and/or randomly assigning the available subjects to separate experimental and control groups. Random assignment of subjects to different states of the independent variable(s) improves the *internal validity* of an experiment—that is, its relative freedom from errors of measurement produced by extraneous variables—but it has no effect on the external validity of the investigation. *External validity* is concerned with the generalizability of the results of a scientific investigation to the population of interest, and requires random or representative selection of subjects from that population.

To some extent, there is a trade-off between research conducted in the laboratory and research conducted in a field ("real-life") setting. Laboratory research studies presumably permit greater control over extraneous variables and thereby greater internal validity, whereas field research is supposed to be more realistic and hence more externally valid. Despite its prearranged and seemingly artificial setting, laboratory-based research may be quite realistic as long as the number of variables being manipulated and studied is not overwhelming, and care is taken not to overgeneralize the interpretations of results. On the other hand, investigations conducted in field settings may be rather tightly controlled, and consequently relatively free from the disruptive effects of extraneous variables. Thus, location (laboratory or field) alone does not determine the degree of internal or external validity of an investigation; the nature of the problem, the research design, and the skills and perceptiveness of the researchers are just as important.

Observational Studies

Although an experiment—either laboratory- or field-based—is required to answer cause-effect questions, many of the facts and theories of the social sciences have been generated in nonexperimental contexts. Most of what social scientists understand about people and events was obtained not from the results of controlled laboratory experiments but by careful observations made in clinics, classrooms, and uncontrived, naturally occurring situations. Such *clinical* or *naturalistic* observation is usually uncontrolled, although the observers may exert some control by attempting to make themselves unobtrusive and even being accepted as participants in the human drama they are observing. Sometimes, however, as in developmental studies of children or in certain assessment and interrogation situations, the investigator devises a controlled, semistructured situation in which the observations take place. For example, a child may be placed in a room with his or her mother or some other adult, and their interactions are observed by means of an unobtrusive television monitor while they are subjected to a series of preplanned stimulus events.

Developmental Research Methods

Observations and studies of children are of particular interest to developmental psychologists. But developmental investigations, in which time is the independent variable and some physical or behavioral measure is the dependent variable, are not limited to children; they can be conducted with individuals ranging in age from infancy through later adulthood. In a *longitudinal study,* the same group of individuals is followed over a period of months and years, and physical or behavioral measurements are obtained at the end of each of several time intervals. In a *cross-sectional study,* groups of people of different ages are all measured at the same point in time.

The cross-sectional approach, which was first applied by Adolphe Quetelet in 1838, is more efficient than the longitudinal approach. But even when different age groups are matched initially on physical characteristics, education, socioeconomic status, or other relevant but extraneous variables, one still cannot be certain whether the observed differences found between various age groups in a cross-sectional study are due to the developmental process itself, to generational or cultural differences *(cohort differences)*, or to other time-related variables.

Like cross-sectional investigations, longitudinal investigations have shortcomings. In addition to being less efficient than cross-sectional designs, longitudinal designs tend to confound the ages of the subjects with the times at which their physical and behavioral characteristics are measured. And when the same questionnaire or inventory is readministered to the same individuals at different times, practice effects can influence the results of a longitudinal investigation.

The shortcomings of longitudinal and cross-sectional developmental research designs have led to the construction of more complex designs. The following are illustrative:

- In a *time-lag design,* several cohorts are measured at different time periods. The subjects in a study employing this type of design are all of the same age when they are measured, but they were born at different times and are measured or examined at different times.

- A *cohort-sequential design* involves making comparisons of successive cohorts over the same age ranges. For example, changes in attitudes and cognitive abilities from ages 20 to 40 in a group of people born in 1950 are compared with changes in the same variables from ages 20 to 40 in a group born in 1960.

- A *most efficient design* consists of a complex combination of the longitudinal and cross-sectional strategies. The researcher begins with a cross-sectional study of two or more age groups measured at the same point in time, retests these groups after several years to provide longitudinal data on several cohorts, tests two or more new age groups to form a second cross-sectional study, and repeats the entire process every 5 to 10 years. Previously tested age groups are retested to add to the longitudinal data, and new age groups are tested to add to the cross-sectional data. (Schaie, 1977)

Retrospective and Prospective Studies

Also related to developmental research is the distinction between prospective and retrospective studies. Longitudinal studies are often conducted by medical researchers to determine what *risk factors* are associated with particular diseases. These investigations, which are designated as *epidemiological studies,* can be either prospective (looking forward) or retrospective (looking backward). A *prospective study* entails identifying a disease-free group of people and following them over time to determine which members of the group develop the disease and what characteristics and behaviors are associated with its occurrence. A *retrospective study,* on the other hand, entails a careful study of the life histories of a group of people who already have a certain disease, the intent being to identify causal or contingency factors. Comparisons of these *index cases* with a comparable group of people who are presently free of the disease are also made in a retrospective study.

The variables assessed by questionnaires and inventories may form a part of a research investigation involving any of the methods discussed. Although measurements of variables assessed by questionnaires and other psychometric or sociometric instruments usually are not as precise as those made with physical instruments, the scale on which such measurements are made is of less concern in deciding which research method to use than it is in analyzing the resulting data. Particular statistical procedures assume that the measurements being analyzed are on a particular scale or level of measurement. Still, when designing a research investigation it is wise to consider the statistical procedures that might be applied in analyzing the data. Statistics is not just the tail that wags the research dog; it is an integral part of the research process and should be considered from the beginning of a scientific investigation. Further details concerning these matters are presented in Chapter 5.

In addition to their widespread use in research, questionnaires are administered and surveys are conducted in innumerable practical settings to provide information for decisions and planning involving political strategy, employee and student selection, education and training, treatment and other interventions, product and service marketing, economic forecasting, land and facilities use, governmental expenditures, and many other matters. Data on behaviors, demographic characteristics, and other objective facts, as well as opinions, attitudes, interests, values, abilities, and related personal and social variables, may be collected (see Figure 1.2). Analysis of such data ideally provides a sounder

Directions: This is an anonymous questionnaire, so the results will not influence your grades or college career in any way. Indicate your answer to each item by writing the corresponding letter in the marginal dash.

_____ 1. What is your sex?   a. female   b. male

_____ 2. How tall are you (in inches)?

a. Under 60 inches	g. 70–71 inches
b. 60–61 inches	h. 72–73 inches
c. 62–63 inches	i. 74–75 inches
d. 64–65 inches	j. 76–77 inches
e. 66–67 inches	k. 78 inches or over
f. 68–69 inches	

_____ 3. What is your current weight (in pounds)?

a. Under 90 pounds	j. 170–179 pounds
b. 90–99 pounds	k. 180–189 pounds
c. 100–109 pounds	l. 190–199 pounds
d. 110–119 pounds	m. 200–219 pounds
e. 120–129 pounds	n. 220–239 pounds
f. 130–139 pounds	o. 240–259 pounds
g. 140–149 pounds	p. 260–279 pounds
h. 150–159 pounds	q. 280 pounds or over
i. 160–169 pounds	

_____ 4. How much did you weigh when you were born?

a. Under 4 pounds	f. 8–8.9 pounds
b. 4–4.9 pounds	g. 9–9.9 pounds
c. 5–5.9 pounds	h. 10–10.9 pounds
d. 6–6.9 pounds	i. 11–11.9 pounds
e. 7–7.9 pounds	j. 12 pounds or over

_____ 5. How old was your mother when you were born?

a. Under 18	f. 26–27
b. 18–19	g. 28–29
c. 20–21	h. 30–31
d. 22–23	i. 32–33
e. 24–25	j. 34 or older

_____ 6. How old was your father when you were born?

a. Under 18	f. 30–32
b. 18–20	g. 33–35
c. 21–23	h. 36–38
d. 24–26	i. 39 or older
e. 27–29	

Figure 1.2.   Survey of student characteristics.

(Continued)

_____   7. In what order were you born compared with your brothers and
             sisters?

     a. first-born   d. fourth-born or later
     b. second-born   e. only child
     c. third-born

_____   8. How many brothers do you have?

     a. 1   d. 4
     b. 2   e. 5
     c. 3   f. 6 or more

_____   9. How many sisters do you have?

     a. 1   d. 4
     b. 2   e. 5
     c. 3   f. 6 or more

_____   10. What is the approximate annual income of your family?

     a. Under $20,000   e. $80,000–$99,999
     b. $20,000–$39,999   f. $100,000–$149,999
     c. $40,000–$59,999   g. $150,000–$199,999
     d. $60,000–$79,999   h. $200,000 or above

_____   11. In which of the following ranges did your high-school grade-point
             average fall?

     a. Below 2.00   d. 3.00–3.49
     b. 2.00–2.49   e. 3.50–4.00
     c. 2.50–2.99

_____   12. In which of the following ranges does your total score on the SAT
             fall?

     a. 400–499   h. 1100–1199
     b. 500–599   i. 1200–1299
     c. 600–699   j. 1300–1399
     d. 700–799   k. 1400–1499
     e. 800–899   l. 1500–1599
     f. 900–999   m. I didn't take the SAT
     g. 1000–1099

_____   13. In which of the following ranges does your total score on the ACT
             fall?

     a. 1–4   f. 21–24
     b. 5–8   g. 25–28
     c. 9–12   h. 29–32
     d. 13–16   i. 33–36
     e. 17–20   j. I didn't take the ACT

Figure 1.2.   *(Continued)*

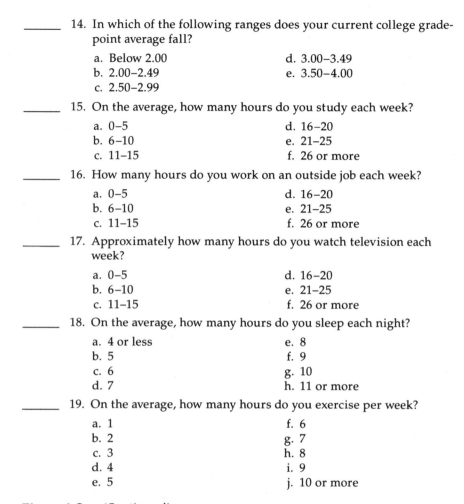

_____ 14. In which of the following ranges does your current college grade-point average fall?

a. Below 2.00   d. 3.00–3.49
b. 2.00–2.49   e. 3.50–4.00
c. 2.50–2.99

_____ 15. On the average, how many hours do you study each week?

a. 0–5   d. 16–20
b. 6–10   e. 21–25
c. 11–15   f. 26 or more

_____ 16. How many hours do you work on an outside job each week?

a. 0–5   d. 16–20
b. 6–10   e. 21–25
c. 11–15   f. 26 or more

_____ 17. Approximately how many hours do you watch television each week?

a. 0–5   d. 16–20
b. 6–10   e. 21–25
c. 11–15   f. 26 or more

_____ 18. On the average, how many hours do you sleep each night?

a. 4 or less   e. 8
b. 5   f. 9
c. 6   g. 10
d. 7   h. 11 or more

_____ 19. On the average, how many hours do you exercise per week?

a. 1   f. 6
b. 2   g. 7
c. 3   h. 8
d. 4   i. 9
e. 5   j. 10 or more

Figure 1.2.   *(Continued)*

basis for organizational and individual decision-making than total reliance on supposition or conjecture.

ORGANIZATIONS AND SOURCES

Most questionnaires are ad hoc devices constructed to obtain information in educational, clinical, business/industrial, governmental, military, and other organizational settings. Many of these questionnaires are constructed by graduate students in education, business, and the social sciences for use in their thesis or dissertation research.[1] Although appreciable effort may go into the preparation of such instruments, the preparers typically have little experience in the construction and evaluation of psychometric instruments. After serving their purposes, the questionnaires are usually filed, and no effort is made to standardize them or to determine their psychometric characteristics (reliability, validity, etc.).

Polling Organizations and Survey Research Centers

Questionnaire design and administration are not limited to nonprofessionals. Many organizations, associations, and institutions, such as the survey/polling organizations listed in Table 1.1 and the university survey research centers listed in Appendix F, are devoted to constructing questionnaires and conducting surveys in a professional, scientific manner. Several of the organizations in Table 1.1 provide a forum for individuals and companies in the United States that are concerned with survey research to interact with each other and disseminate applied and theoretical information pertaining to surveys and polling. An annually updated list of survey research consulting organizations in countries throughout the world and representative survey findings are provided by an organization of Survey Research Consultants International, Inc. in the *Index to International Public Opinion* (Hastings & Hastings, 1995).

Of the various university-based survey research centers, the largest is the Survey Research Center (SRC), a division of the Institute for Social Research at the University of Michigan. SRC conducts multidisciplinary studies of large populations, organizations, and special segments of society. Among the ongoing studies of SRC are those concerned with economic attitudes and behavior, health and stress in organizational settings, the transition from school to work and from youth to adulthood in young people, social indicators and quality of life, the way that environments—especially urban environments—influence behavior, how organizations utilize knowledge to achieve organizational goals, and family structure and demography. Surveys concerned with these matters are conducted primarily by means of face-to-face or telephone interviews of national, state, regional, and local populations. A computer-assisted telephone interviewing and direct-data-entry (CATI-DDE) system is used by SRC to make its large-sample surveys and interviews more cost-effective (Institute for Social Research, n.d.).

TABLE 1.1.   Representative Survey and Polling Associations/Organizations

American Association for Public Opinion Research (AAPOR)
P.O. Box 1248
Ann Arbor, MI 48106
(313) 764–1555

Council of American Survey Research Organizations (CASRO)
3 Upper Devon Belle Terre
Port Jefferson, NY 11777
(516) 928–6954

Gallup Organization, Inc.
47 Hulfish St., Suite 200
Princeton, NJ 98542
(609) 924–9600

Institute for Social Research
University of Michigan
P.O. Box 1248
Ann Arbor, MI 48106–1248
(313) 764–1817

Interuniversity Consortium for Political and Social Research (ICPSR)
P.O. Box 1248
Ann Arbor, MI 48106
(313) 763–5010

Louis Harris and Associates
630 Fifth Avenue, 11th Floor
New York, NY 10111
(212) 698–9600

National Council of Public Opinion Polls (NCPP)
205 E. 42nd Street, Room 1708
New York, NY 10017
(213) 986–8262

National Opinion Research Center
University of Chicago
1155 East 60th Street
Chicago, IL 60637
(312) 753–7500

The Roper Center for Public Opinion Research
P.O. Box 440
Storrs, CT 06268
(203) 486–4440

World Association for Public Opinion Research (WAPOR)
c/o Prof. Valarie Lauder
School of Journalism and Mass Communication
University of North Carolina
CB-3365, Howell Hall
Chapel Hill, NC 27599–3365

Yankelovich Partners, Inc.
101 Merritt Corporate Pkwy
Norwalk, CT 06851
(203) 227–2700

As indicated by the preceding description of the activities of SRC, surveys have been conducted on numerous social and political issues. Among these are abortion and birth control, consumer affairs, crime, economic matters, education, employment, environmental pollution, health and health care, housing, marriage and divorce, mortality, natural resources, nutrition, politics, poverty, prejudice, retirement, senior citizens, technology, and sex and violence on television and in the other media. Some surveys, in Maryland and Minnesota for example, are conducted on a regional or statewide basis to assess the problems, possibilities, and business climate of the area.

Professional Organizations

Professional organizations such as the American Psychological Association, the American Sociological Association, the American Political Science Association, and the American Business Association are also involved in the design and application of questionnaires and inventories. One role of these organizations is to ensure that such instruments and the ways in which they are used are technically sophisticated and socially sensitive.

Descriptions of both published and unpublished questionnaires and inventories, and studies in which they have been used, may be found in numerous professional journals in business, the social sciences, the health sciences, and education. The following is a representative list of relevant journals:

American Journal of Public Health

American Sociological Review

American Statistician

Archives of Sexual Behavior

Journal of Applied Psychology

Journal of Gerontology

Journal of Marriage and the Family

Journal of Personality and Social Psychology

Journal of Research in Crime and Delinquency

Journal of Sexual Behavior

Journal of Social Psychology

Monthly Labor Review

Psychology of Women Quarterly

The Public Opinion Quarterly

Rural Sociology

Social Casework

Social Science Quarterly

The Sociological Quarterly

Survey

The Gallup Poll Monthly

The Gerontologist

The Sociological Quarterly

Trial

In addition, listings and reviews of various psychometric and sociometric instruments are given in volumes such as the *Mental Measurements Yearbooks* (Buros, 1978 and earlier editions; Conoley & Kramer, 1989; Conoley & Impara, 1995; Kramer & Conoley, 1992; Mitchell, 1985), *Tests in Print* (Mitchell, 1983; Murphy, Conoley, & Impara, 1994), *Tests* (Sweetland & Keyser, 1991), *Test Critiques* (Keyser & Sweetland, 1984–1994), *A Consumer's Guide to Tests in Print* (Hammill, Brown, & Bryant, 1992). Many other printed and computer database sources of information on published and unpublished questionnaires and inventories are listed on pages 25–27 of Aiken (1996b).

SUMMARY

The formal use of paper-and-pencil questionnaires and related methods to obtain scientific information about people, products, and events began in the 19th century. Many natural and social scientists contributed to these beginnings, foremost among them Adolphe Quetelet and Francis Galton. Both of these men devised a number of methodological and statistical procedures, Quetelet for his studies of vital statistics and Galton for his studies of mental abilities. Galton also devised several questionnaires to study the backgrounds and characteristics of eminent, and/or mentally gifted individuals. Questionnaires were constructed and surveys conducted by social scientists in their studies of the demographic characteristics of communities and other large-scale investigations during the late 19th and early 20th centuries.

Statistical methods have been used for descriptive purposes for hundreds of years, but developments in the mathematics of probability and inferential statistical procedures during the 19th and 20th centuries made it possible to logically infer the characteristics of populations from an analysis of sample data. Inferential procedures based on large samples made their appearance in the late 19th century, followed by small-sample inferential procedures in the early part of the 20th century.

The first formal personality inventory—the Woodworth Personal Data Sheet—appeared in 1918, although a number of paper-and-pencil measures of achievement and intelligence preceded it. In sociology, the reform movement of the late 19th century was accompanied by studies of communities that involved surveys and questionnaires. Subsequently, conducting surveys for practical purposes by means of self-report questionnaires and telephone and face-to-face interviewing became popular. Due to improper sampling procedures, as well as misinterpretation and overgeneralization, the reported results of many of these surveys were inaccurate.

Research may be characterized as exploratory versus hypothesis-testing, descriptive versus explanatory, and correlation versus experimental. Although correlational procedures can facilitate the prediction of one event from another and suggest possible causes, a controlled experiment must be conducted in order to draw definitive conclusions regarding the causation of events. Experiments may be conducted in the laboratory or in field settings. In general, laboratory-based experiments involve tighter controls—and hence greater internal validity than field studies. On the other hand, the results of field studies are typically more realistic—and hence more externally valid or generalizable—than most studies conducted in the laboratory.

Because it is not always possible to assign people or other sampling units at random to experimental conditions, social scientists must rely on the results of careful observations and on correlational and developmental studies for information. Traditional developmental research, which is concerned with determining how behavior and physical condition vary across time, has been either longitudinal or cross-sectional. Since both approaches involve confounding time, testing procedure, and cohort differences, more complex developmental research designs (time-lag design, cohort-sequential design, most efficient design) have been devised. Related to developmental research methodology are retrospective and prospective epidemiological studies. Retrospective studies involve scrutinizing the life histories of patients who have a certain disease to ascertain any significant differences between their backgrounds and those of comparable groups of people who are free of the disease. Prospective studies involve tracking individuals who are presently free of the disease to determine which ones acquire it and with what factors it is associated.

Numerous professional and commercial organizations are interested in the design of questionnaires and inventories and in applied and theoretical studies involving the use of these instruments. Many universities, governmental organizations, and private foundations have research centers that conduct surveys on social, political, economic, health, crime, and other issues or concerns of people. Organizations of professionals in sociology, psychology, political science, economics, education, and other sciences also support research involving questionnaires, inventories, and related procedures. The results of many of these studies are published in hundreds of professional journals throughout the world.

QUESTIONS AND ACTIVITIES

1. Define each of the following terms used in this chapter in a sentence or two. Consult the Glossary at the back of the book and a dictionary if you need help.

clinical method	explanatory research
clinical observation	exploratory research
cohort differences	external validity
cohort-sequential design	Fechner's law
cross-sectional study	Gaussian distribution
dependent variable	hypothesis-testing research
descriptive research	independent variable
descriptive statistics	index case
developmental research	inferential statistics
epidemiological studies	internal validity
experiment	l'homme moyen

longitudinal study
mental testing movement
most efficient design
naturalistic observation
observational study
order-of-merit
parameters
personality inventory
prospective study
psychophysics
questionnaire

rating scales
reform movement
research
retrospective study
risk factor
social survey
statistics
time-lag design
validity
variables
vital statistics

2. List several of the most important questions that you have ever been asked. Then list several of the most important questions that you have asked someone else.

3. In what ways is a survey research study different from a correlational study, a developmental study, and an experiment?

4. In what kinds of surveys—mailed questionnaire, telephone, or in-person—have you participated? What were your impressions of the survey questionnaire or the interviewer, and what did you learn from the survey?

5. Look under the topics of "questionnaires" and "inventories" in PsycLit, ERIC, SSCI, or other computer-based sources. Describe the kinds of books and articles that you find.

6. Run several of the programs in category I on the diskette of computer programs accompanying this book. Summarize your results and compare them with those obtained by several of your friends or associates.

7. Make several copies of the questionnaire in Figure 1.2, and administer it to several people. Summarize the results, and compare the answers to the various questions.

SUGGESTED READING

Aiken, L. R. (1994). Some observations and recommendations concerning research methodology in the behavioral science. *Educational and Psychological Measurement, 54,* 848–859.

Aiken, L. R. (1996). *Rating scales and checklists: Evaluating behavior, personality, and attitudes* (pp. 1–23). New York: Wiley.

Converse, J. M. (1987). *Survey research in the United States: Roots and emergence 1890–1960.* Berkeley: University of California Press.

Diamond, S. (1988). Francis Galton and American psychology. In L. T. Benjamin, Jr. (Ed.), *A history of psychology: Original sources and contemporary research* (pp. 261–269). New York: McGraw-Hill.

Forrest, D. W. (1974). Scientists and twins. In *Francis Galton: The life and work of a Victorian genius* (pp. 122–132). New York: Taplinger Publishing Co.

Smith, T. W., Presser, S., Schuman, H., et al. (1989). The questionnaire. In E. Singer & S. Presser (Eds.), *Survey research methods* (pp. 99–185). Chicago: University of Chicago Press.

NOTE

1. Unfortunately, it has become so commonplace for graduate students to conduct some sort of survey by administering a questionnaire to a small, unrepresentative sample of individuals to fulfill a thesis or dissertation requirement that almost any research project in the behavioral or social sciences may be assumed to have involved a survey.

2

Constructing, Administering, and Scoring Questionnaires

Questionnaires are designed to serve a variety of purposes: as aids in screening or selecting employees, students, trainees, and recruits; as providers of patient information in health-related settings that contribute to diagnostic and treatment decisions; and as survey instruments for obtaining data on populations of interest in applied or theory-based research. The first two purposes focus on the background and characteristics of individuals, whereas the group data collected by procedures directed by the third purpose are of greatest interest in research contexts.

The content and format of a questionnaire vary not only with the purposes for which it was designed but also with the method by which it is administered. Like other paper-and-pencil psychometric instruments, questionnaires may be administered on an individual or a group basis. Individual, or one-to-one, administration involves one administrator or questioner and one subject or respondent. The questioner either asks the questions orally or/and presents them in printed form to the respondent, who, in turn, provides oral or written answers. This procedure is followed in a typical face-to-face or telephone interview. Questionnaires can also be administered by a computer on either an individual or a group basis. The computer is programmed not only to present the questions and record the respondent's answers, but also to evaluate the answers and print the results. A typical *mail survey* entails sending a questionnaire by mail to a large group of people. However, group administration does not necessitate mailing the questionnaire if the selected individuals can be scheduled to complete it as a group at a designated time and place.

Face-to-face, telephone, mail, and computer-based administration of questionnaires all have advantages and disadvantages. As with personal interviewing, face-to-face administration provides an opportunity for clarification of both the questions that are asked and the answers that are given. In addition, more detailed information can be obtained regarding not only the content of the responses to specific questions but also the feelings, attitudes, and other affective reactions of the respondents to the questions that are presented. A major disadvantage of face-to-face administration is that it is more expensive and time-consuming than other procedures. In addition, the physical presence and behavior of the questioner can influence the respondent's interpretation of the questions and how they are answered. For example, the comments and body language of the person who is asking a series of questions may indicate approval or disapproval of certain subjects and influence the respondent's answers.

Interviewing by telephone is typically only about half as costly as face-to-face interviewing and is more likely to elicit thoughtful, complete answers than mailed questionnaires. As with face-to-face administration, the social connection that is established by personal, vocal interaction over the telephone can create an obligation to listen to the caller and provide answers to his or her questions. Furthermore, additional details can be elicited through follow-up questions. Unlike the biased samples obtained in some telephone surveys of yesteryear (e.g., the 1936 *Literary Digest* poll), people of all socioeconomic levels are now accessible by telephone, and calls are much less expensive. Random-digit dialing and computer-assisted telephone interviewing have also increased the validity and popularity of surveys conducted by telephone. *Random-digit dialing* involves dialing the last four digits of a seven-digit telephone number at random, thereby including nonlisted numbers in the sample. In *computer-assisted telephone interviewing (CATI)*, the interviewer reads the questions aloud from a computer monitor and the interviewee's responses are recorded and analyzed by the computer. This procedure is also adaptable to individual differences, in that items that are not applicable to particular respondents can be skipped. Among the disadvantages of telephone surveys are that groups of people without immediate access to a telephone may be underrepresented, it is more difficult to keep the respondent's attention and to ask sensitive questions, and visual stimuli cannot be used.

Although most opinion-polling organizations conduct surveys over the telephone, mailed questionnaires remain the least costly and most popular of all survey techniques. Computer-generated questionnaires for use in mail surveys can be designed cheaply and attractively, complete with various fonts and interesting graphics. Unfortunately, a person who attempts to fill out a mailed questionnaire cannot ask for clarification of the directions or explanations of particular questions. Other disadvantages are that a respondent may fill out the questionnaire incorrectly or only in part; or someone other than the person to whom the cover letter was addressed may complete the questionnaire; or the answers may represent a group effort. For whatever reason, the sample of persons who attempt and return a mailed questionnaire may not be truly representative of the population for which it was intended. This is most likely when the return rate is low, a common result when questionnaires are mailed.

DESIGNING AND CONSTRUCTING QUESTIONNAIRES

Questionnaires are designed for a wide range of purposes and for populations of varying composition and magnitude. Research questionnaires are designed to survey the attitudes, opinions, beliefs, and information possessed by a group of people regarding a social, political, educational, or economic issue, or some other matter, and their attributes (age, sex, race, etc.) and behaviors. The data obtained from questionnaires administered in such surveys provide information on which many different decisions are based. At the local level, an educational researcher may be interested in determining parents' knowledge and attitudes concerning various school programs. At the state level, an official may wish to obtain more information about the business climate and ways of attracting more industry to the particular geographical area. This is one of the purposes of large-scale surveys such as the Maryland Poll and the Minnesota State Survey. At the national level, common questions are those concerning how well the president and members of Congress are doing their jobs and other matters of concern to the nation (see Figure 2.1 on pages 34–35). These kinds of questions have been asked by the Gallup and Roper polls for many years.

Purposes and Objectives

The construction of a questionnaire should begin with a clear statement of its purposes or objectives. *Focus groups* of interested, informed people can help generate ideas for a survey questionnaire as well as suggest solutions to problems identified by the survey. Prior published research on the topic of interest should also be examined carefully before beginning the process of constructing the questionnaire. Not only will this provide the researcher with more information about what is already known and how it has been discovered, but it may reveal that a questionnaire suitable for the specific purposes under consideration is already available. Whether a previously designed questionnaire or a newly constructed one is used, the items on it should be directly related to the stated purposes of the study.

The main purpose for which a questionnaire is constructed is often stated in the form of a question, such as:

What should be the role of organized religion in politics?

What should be the role of the government regarding the right of women to have abortions?

How satisfied are the people in this locality with their lives, and what are their major sources of satisfaction and dissatisfaction?

Does the American public believe that affirmative action programs should be broadened, narrowed, or eliminated altogether, and why?

What kinds of sanctions should be imposed on foreign countries that violate the trade laws and treaties of the United States?

Unlike the multitude of questions included in omnibus questionnaires of the sort administered in the General Social Surveys of the National Opinion Research Center (Davis & Smith, 1994), the Current Population Survey of the Bureau of Labor Statistics, or the Survey of Program Participation conducted by the Census Bureau, most of the preceding questions deal with a fairly narrow range of issues.

After the specific purposes or objectives of a questionnaire have been defined, a detailed outline of the contents of the proposed instrument, including the topics and the types and number of questions with which it will deal, should be prepared. A flowchart such as the one in Figure 2.2 is a good way to begin the task of preparing the questions.

REPUBLICAN NATIONAL SURVEY

1996 STATE OF THE NATION
Public Opinion Research Survey

REPUBLICAN NATIONAL COMMITTEE
310 First Street, SE
Washington, DC 20003

DEFICIT

To lower the deficit should we:

	STRONGLY AGREE	MODERATELY AGREE	MODERATELY DISAGREE	STRONGLY DISAGREE	UNDECIDED
1. Raise taxes?	☐	☐	☐	☐	☐
2. Cut taxes to spur economic growth?	☐	☐	☐	☐	☐
3. Cut spending?	☐	☐	☐	☐	☐
4. Cut government waste?	☐	☐	☐	☐	☐
5. Other _____	☐	☐	☐	☐	☐

JOBS

To create more jobs should we:

	STRONGLY AGREE	MODERATELY AGREE	MODERATELY DISAGREE	STRONGLY DISAGREE	UNDECIDED
6. Create new Federal jobs programs?	☐	☐	☐	☐	☐
7. Foster economic growth by lowering taxes and cutting red tape?	☐	☐	☐	☐	☐

IMMIGRATION

	STRONGLY AGREE	MODERATELY AGREE	MODERATELY DISAGREE	STRONGLY DISAGREE	UNDECIDED
8. Do you support making English the official language of the United States?	☐	☐	☐	☐	☐

MEDICARE

	STRONGLY AGREE	MODERATELY AGREE	MODERATELY DISAGREE	STRONGLY DISAGREE	UNDECIDED
18. Are you concerned about the projections that show Medicare going bankrupt within 5 years?	☐	☐	☐	☐	☐
19. Under the Medicare plan the Republican Congress passed but Clinton vetoed, did Medicare spending increase?	☐	☐	☐	☐	☐
20. Do you believe AARP has called for Medicare spending to be reduced?	☐	☐	☐	☐	☐
21. Do you believe Medicare spending is higher because there is a lot of waste, fraud and abuse in the system?	☐	☐	☐	☐	☐
22. Do you think it would improve Medicare if senior citizens were given more choices in their health care program?	☐	☐	☐	☐	☐
23. Do you believe the Republicans would have forced senior citizens to enter HMO's or other managed care plans?	☐	☐	☐	☐	☐

CRIME

9. Generally, do you believe our legal system is more concerned with criminals' rights than victim's rights? ☐ ☐ ☐

10. Do you believe Congress should close legal loopholes that allow convicted murderers to delay their execution for years through repeated appeals? ☐ ☐ ☐

DRUGS

11. Do you believe drug abuse is seriously damaging our country? ☐ ☐ ☐

12. Should there be mandatory drug testing for jobs involving public safety? ☐ ☐ ☐

TAXES

13. Generally, do you support replacing our current tax code with some version of a "Flat Tax" – where everyone pays the same low tax rate? ☐ ☐ ☐

14. Should cutting taxes be a top priority in a balanced budget? ☐ ☐ ☐

15. Should Republicans give up on a tax cut for now and pursue only the spending cuts needed for a balanced budget? ☐ ☐ ☐

BALANCED BUDGET AMENDMENT

16. Are you in favor of a Constitutional Amendment that requires Congress to balance the federal budget? ☐ ☐ ☐

LINE ITEM VETO

17. Should the President have a line item veto to cut spending out of budget proposals "line-by-line"? ☐ ☐ ☐

EDUCATION

Which do you feel are some of the most important problems facing our schools:

24. Not enough discipline ☐ ☐ ☐

25. Not enough "basics" taught ☐ ☐ ☐

26. Not enough money spent ☐ ☐ ☐

27. Education "bureaucracy" too large ☐ ☐ ☐

28. Unions in control ☐ ☐ ☐

GUN CONTROL

29. Should more attention be paid to controlling criminals who use guns rather than controlling guns themselves? ☐ ☐ ☐

FOREIGN TRADE

30. Generally, do you support the United States' open trade policy? ☐ ☐ ☐

OPTIONAL SECTION

Your Personal Top Five Issues of Greatest Concern

Please list, in order of importance, the five issues you consider the most critical:

31. _____

32. _____

33. _____

34. _____

35. _____

Figure 2.1. Republican National Survey. (Reprinted by permission of the Republican National Committee)

35

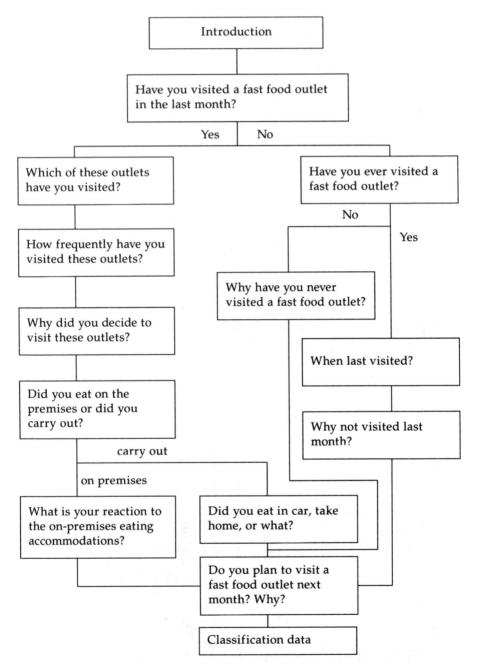

Figure 2.2. Illustrative flowchart for constructing a questionnaire on fast food outlets. (Reprinted with permission of McGraw-Hill Book Company from Kinnear & Taylor, 1991.)

Note the logical flow of this outline, including the branching or skip format in which not all respondents answer the same questions.

The phrasing and format of the items on a questionnaire depends to some extent on whether it will be administered in a face-to-face interview, over the telephone, or by mail. But long questions with complex wording are not recommended for any questionnaire, and especially not one that will be read aloud to the respondents. Furthermore, certain types of tasks, such as ranking 10 or more items in order of merit, are more difficult to accomplish when they are presented orally rather than in printed form.

The following are general recommendations regarding the format of questionnaires, regardless of how they are to be administered:

- Questions of the same type or that deal with the same topic should be grouped together. Grouping according to form and content may not be strictly obtainable, but it should be approximated as closely as possible.

- The general directions for a questionnaire should be clear and brief, including, in relatively simple language, a statement of the purpose(s) of the questionnaire, how responses should be indicated, approximately how long it should take to complete, and what the respondent should do with it when finished.

- Short questions are preferable to long ones, but enough information should be included to make the form and nature of the requested response clear.

- The most important questions should not be placed at the end of the questionnaire. Boredom, fatigue, and time pressure increase the likelihood that questions near the end will not be answered as conscientiously as those at the beginning of the questionnaire.

- The terms used should not be overly technical, too general, unclear, or ambiguous. As a rule, always choose the simplest way to say something.

- Emotionally loaded words, loaded questions, leading questions, double questions, and hypothetical questions should be avoided. Because of prior associations, *emotionally loaded words* elicit an emotional reaction in the respondent and thus bias the answer. *Loaded questions,* including *leading questions* such as "Isn't it reasonable to suppose that . . . ," or "Don't you believe that . . . ," are phrased in such a way that the respondent is more likely to give a desired answer. **Double questions** (or doubled-barreled questions) are those that contain more than one query (e.g., "Do you go to the movies every week, and do you enjoy it?") **Hypothetical** (what-if?) **questions,** such as "What if you lost your job . . . ," are typically too speculative to provide useful information.

- *Nonspecific adjectives or adverbs* (e.g., many or sometimes), words having more than one meaning, double negatives, and slang and colloquialisms should be avoided. These kinds of terms tend to make questions ambiguous and unclear.

- Multiple questions should be used to assess attitudes, beliefs, opinions, interests, aspirations, expectations, and other affective variables. A sum of scored responses on several nonfactual items dealing with the same matter is usually necessary to obtain a reliable measure.

- A logical, conversational sequence should be followed in presenting questions. Neither the content nor the style of the questionnaire should "jump around." It should begin with a few simple, interesting, and nonthreatening questions and proceed in a logical order to more complex questions and to more specific topics. Progression from topic to topic should be smooth and facilitated by linking sentences such as, "Now I'd like to ask you about . . . ," or "Let's move on now to the matter of . . ." When uninteresting and difficult questions are included, they should be placed near the end of the questionnaire.

- The questions should be sensitive to the feelings and values of the particular individuals to whom the questionnaire is administered. Otherwise, strong emotions and defensiveness, rather than accurate answers, will be likely reactions.

- Questions concerning socioeconomic and other demographic data should be placed near the end of the questionnaire. When such questions are asked near the beginning of a questionnaire, they may appear to be inconsistent with the stated purpose of the questionnaire expressed in the title and the general directions.

- A mailed questionnaire should require no more than 30 minutes to finish, and a telephone interview only half that. A statement concerning how long it will take to complete the questionnaire should be included in the general directions. It may also be helpful to have respondents indicate their starting and stopping times on the questionnaire.

- The respondent should be thanked for his or her cooperation, either personally or in printed form, at the end of the questionnaire.

Some specific recommendations for administering questionnaires in face-to-face or telephone interviews are:

- Different fonts or various type attributes such as underlining should be used to distinguish between what the questioner says out loud and what he or she reads silently.

- Skip patterns, indicating which questions can be skipped by respondents who answer a previous question in a certain way, should be clearly marked. The inclusion of skip or filter questions makes for more efficient administration, in that it permits questions that do not pertain to the respondent to be omitted.

- Sufficient space should be left for the interviewer (questioner) to record additional observations and information.

- The number of response options for an item should be sufficiently small so that the respondent can keep all of them in mind.

- The interviewer should be careful not to overreact to the respondent's answers so the latter will be more concerned with giving accurate answers to questions rather than with pleasing the interviewer.

- The interviewer should avoid asking intimidating questions that lead to under- or over-reporting of certain behaviors.

Some specific recommendations for mailed questionnaires or those otherwise sent to respondents are:

- An identification number should be placed on the questionnaire, except in the case of anonymous administration.

- The questionnaire should be attractive, interesting, and arranged in booklet form.

- The title should be placed at the beginning of the questionnaire, but words such as "questionnaire" and "opinionnaire" should be avoided.
- Instructions, both general and for each part, should be underlined or printed in boldface type.
- The pages of the questionnaire should not be overcrowded and should be numbered or otherwise identified.
- Each question should be typed in its entirety on one side of a page and not be overly long (more than 20 words or so).
- Important questions should not be placed at the end of the questionnaire.
- The questions should be directly related to the variables and hypotheses that the questionnaire has been designed to investigate. Questions of peripheral interest that are not directly related to the purposes and hypotheses of the study should not be included.
- "Over," "continued on back," or a similar word or phrase should appear at the bottom of the first side of a page that is printed on both sides.
- Responses should be marked close to the questions to which they refer. If a separate response sheet is used, it should be coordinated with the questionnaire and easy to follow.
- The questionnaire should be printed in an attractive format and on good-quality paper.
- Even when a return envelope is included with a mailed questionnaire, the name and address of the person to whom the completed questionnaire is to be returned should be listed at the bottom or top of the form.

Open-Ended Questions

Many of the recommendations for constructing effective questionnaires are the same as those for constructing items for objective tests that are found in textbooks on psychological and educational testing (e.g., Aiken, 1997). Most of these recommendations apply to all types of questions; for example: clarity, brevity, simplicity, and unbiased wording. However, some recommendations concerning item format and style vary with the type of question.

Two general types of questions—open-ended and closed-ended—may be found on questionnaires. *Open-ended questions* are those in which response options do not form part of the questions and the respondent is free to provide any answer he or she wishes. Examples are completion, short-answer, and essay questions. Open-ended questions are particularly valuable in exploratory research when a more detailed picture of the respondents' attitudes, beliefs, and thoughts is needed, and when the variables of concern are not defined clearly enough to be assessed by closed-ended questions. The items in Part V of the questionnaire in Figure 2.3 are illustrative of open-ended questions. The first seven items in Part V require a short answer, whereas a longer response is expected in question 8. In constructing short-answer or completion items, questions are preferable to incomplete statements, and blanks should come at the ends of incomplete statements. Multiple blanks in the same statement are to be avoided, since they often make the respondent's task unclear.

Responses to short-answer, completion, and essay questions must be categorized in some way for purposes of tabulation and scoring. This can be especially cumbersome on essay questions, which may produce unclear, rambling responses. To reduce the difficulty in interpreting responses to essay items, the items should be short, clear, and deal with only one concept or idea. If completion and short-answer questions are phrased clearly, respondents should have no problem understanding what kind of information is being requested. Even so, before including open-ended items on a questionnaire, they should be carefully examined by other experts in questionnaire design and the content area. The questions should also be pretested by administering them to a small sample of persons to obtain representative responses and comments.

It is preferable to place open-ended questions at the end rather than at the beginning of the questionnaire. Because it usually takes longer to answer open-ended questions, respondents may get bogged down if they are located near the beginning of the instrument and consequently be unable to answer them in a reasonable period of time.

Closed-Ended Questions

Construction of closed-ended questions often is preceded by the administration of open-ended questions to a small sample of individuals for the purpose of obtaining a list of possible response options. Questions having a *closed-ended format* are referred to by specialists

College Experiences and Attitudes

General Directions: The purpose of this questionnaire is to obtain information from students concerning their experiences at this institution and their attitudes toward those experiences. We hope that this information will help us to make improvements that will increase the benefits students obtain from this institution and make their future experiences here more positive. Please answer each of the questions as thoughtfully and completely as possible. Follow the directions for each part. It should take you about 15 minutes to finish. Give the completed questionnaire to your instructor when you are through.

Part I. Plans and Perceptions.   Write the letter corresponding to your response to the question in the marginal dash.

_____   1. Did you begin your freshman year at this college (university)?
  a. Yes
  b. No

_____   2. Do you plan to graduate from this college (university)?
  a. Yes
  b. No
  c. Not sure

_____   3. Have you found your experiences at this institution to be different from what you expected them to be?
  a. Yes
  b. No

  If you answered "Yes" to question 3, in what way have your experiences at this institution been different from what you expected? ___
  _____
  _____

_____   4. How satisfied are you with your decision to enroll in this college (university)?
  a. Very satisfied   d. Dissatisfied
  b. Satisfied   e. Very dissatisfied
  c. Uncertain

_____   5. Was this college (university) your
  a. First choice?   d. Fourth choice?
  b. Second choice?   e. Other _____
  c. Third choice?

_____   6. If you had it to do over again, would you choose to attend this college (university) rather than another college or university?
  a. Yes   c. Not sure
  b. No

_____   7. What do you think of the social and political attitudes of the students at this college (university)?
  a. Too conservative c. Neither too conservative
  b. Too liberal   nor too liberal

Figure 2.3.   Questionnaire for surveying students' experiences and attitudes toward college attendance.

Part II. Ranking. What factors influenced you to enroll at this college (university) rather than at another college (university)? Rank-order the following reasons from 1 = most important to 15 = least important.

_____ a. academic reputation
_____ b. affordable tuition and fees
_____ c. athletics (sports) programs
_____ d. emphasis on values
_____ e. influence of family and friends
_____ f. location
_____ g. nonathletic extracurricular activities
_____ h. personableness or friendliness
_____ i. received scholarship or other financial aid
_____ j. size of the campus
_____ k. social life
_____ l. specific program or major
_____ m. teachers/professors
_____ n. tuition and fees
_____ o. other (describe) _____

Part III. Checklist. Check each of the following problems or sources of frustration that you have experienced at this college (university).

_____ a. administrative or bureaucratic hassles
_____ b. courses too difficult
_____ c. high tuition and other expenses
_____ d. inadequate social life
_____ e. poor academics
_____ f. poor athletic teams
_____ g. poor housing
_____ h. poor meals
_____ i. poor selection of courses
_____ j. poor teachers
_____ k. too far from home
_____ l. too many rules
_____ m. unfriendly people
_____ n. uninteresting courses or curricula

Part IV. Demographic Data. Write the letter corresponding to your response in the marginal dash.

_____ 1. What is your sex?
         a. Male
         b. Female
_____ 2. Are you married?
         a. Yes
         b. No

Figure 2.3. *(Continued)*

_____ 3. What is your classification?
   a. Freshman   d. Senior
   b. Sophomore   e. Graduate student
   c. Junior   f. Other (specify) _____

_____ 4. In which of the following ranges did your overall grade-point average in high school fall?
   a. Below 2.00   d. 3.00–3.49
   b. 2.00–2.49   e. 3.50–5.00
   c. 2.50–2.99

_____ 5. In which of the following ranges does your overall grade-point average in college fall?
   a. Below 2.00   d. 3.00–3.49
   b. 2.00–2.49   e. 3.50–5.00
   c. 2.50–2.99

Part V. Additional Information.   Write your answer in the blank.

   1. How old are you (nearest year)?   _____   years

   2. What is your major?   _____

   3. On the average, how many hours do you study each week?
      _____ hours

   4. On the average, how many hours do you work on a job each week?
      _____ hours

   5. Approximately how many hours do you watch television each week?
      _____ hours

   6. On the average, how many hours do you sleep each night?
      _____ hours

   7. On the average, how many hours do you exercise per week?
      _____ hours

   8. What do you plan to do after graduating from college?
      _____

Figure 2.3.   *(Continued)*

in educational and psychological measurement as *objective items.* Included among these are true-false, multiple-choice, matching, ranking, checklists, and rating scales. Responses to closed-ended questions are certainly easier to tabulate than responses to open-ended questions, but they may not provide as much detailed information as the latter. Conversely, many more closed-ended than open-ended questions can be answered in a fixed period of time.

   Multiple-choice items, such as those in Parts I and IV of Figure 2.3, are popular on psychometric instruments of various types. The stem of a multiple-choice item may be either an incomplete statement or a question, but the latter is preferred. As with other types of items, the wording of multiple-choice items must be appropriate for the reading level of the respondents. As much of the item as possible should be included in the stem and not repeated in the response options. Options having a natural order, such as dates, should be placed in sequence; otherwise, the options should be arranged in random or alphabetical order. All options must be grammatically correct with respect to the stem, homogeneous in style, approximately equal in length, and mutually exclusive (selection of one option excludes selection of another). The use of negative expressions, such as "not," should be avoided in both the stem and the response options.

The options on a multiple-choice item should contain all conceivable responses to the stem. If, on a factual question, it is possible that respondents do not know the answer, a "Don't know" option should be included. However, "all of the above," "none of the above" and "more than one of the above" should be employed sparingly. Uncommon abbreviations and *specific determiners,* such as always, sometimes, and never, should also be avoided.

A stacked or vertical arrangement of the response options, as on the items in Parts I and IV of Figure 2.3, is preferable to a tandem or vertical (side-by-side) arrangement. When the response options to a multiple-choice item form a scale, such as the *Likert scale* format of "Strongly Disagree, Disagree, Undecided, Agree, and Strongly Agree," the scale should be balanced. That is, the number and labels of categories above the middle category should balance with those below the middle category. Another illustration of this *balanced scale* format is given in item 4 in Part I of Figure 2.3.

There is no restriction on the number of response options that may be included on a multiple-choice item. Dichotomous (two-choice) items, such as items 1 and 3 in Part I and items 1 and 2 in Part IV of Figure 2.3, are common; in fact, true-false items contain two response options. Rather than limiting the number of choices to two, it is often wise to include a third, middle-category option, as in items 2 and 6 in Part I of Figure 2.3. The downside is that respondents' answers may not really fit in the neutral category, but they select it in order to avoid embarrassment. In such cases, it may be better to limit the number of response options to two, thereby forcing the respondent to select one answer or the other.

True-false items are much less common than multiple-choice items on questionnaires, but many of the same rules apply to them. True-false statements should be short, not doubled-barreled, and deal primarily with a single proposition stated in a straightforward, unambiguous manner. Negatively stated items, especially those containing double negatives, are no-nos, as are statements containing specific determiners (always, never, sometimes, etc.) that slant the response in a positive or negative direction. The *acquiescence response set*—that is, the tendency to respond in the affirmative direction when in doubt—may also be a problem on true-false items.

Rating, ranking, and checklist items are also common on questionnaires, but they impose a more difficult task on the respondent than single-response items. Long lists of things to be placed in rank-order are particularly difficult in face-to-face and telephone interviews. The item in Part II of Figure 2.3 is a ranking item, and the item in Part III is a checklist item. Item 5 in Part I requires the respondent to make a mental rating or ranking of institutions to which he or she applied for admission, but only the ranking (rating) of the institution the respondent is actually attending is recorded. The construction of checklists and rating scales is considered in depth in Chapter 2 of *Rating Scales and Checklists* (Aiken, 1996), and questionnaire designers who plan to use these kinds of items would do well to examine it.

Other Factors Affecting Responses to Questionnaires

Questionnaires offer a number of advantages as methods of data collection and research: They are economical to construct, administer, and evaluate, and they can yield a great deal of data on numerous variables in a wide range of situations. But like all self-report instruments, questionnaires have disadvantages as well. Because of reading difficulties or other verbal comprehension problems, respondents may not understand the questions; and even when they do understand the task, their answers may be superficial or insincere. Second, respondents are affected by the context, not only of the surrounding questions, but the nature of the situation and the time in which they are administered. Finally, respondents who agree when in doubt *(acquiescence)*, give what is perceived as the more socially desirable response, or over- and underreport, can also impact the results of a questionnaire or an inventory.

The need to control for, or at least take into account, factors that have an influence on responses to questionnaires has led to a number of research designs and statistical procedures. From a design perspective, demographic variables such as sex and ethnicity and task variables such as instructions, question specificity, size and color of the questionnaire (Jansen, 1985; Weller & Livingston, 1988), order of presentation of items (Evans & Scott, 1984), and in face-to-face or telephone questioning, the appearance and behavior of the questioner, may serve as either independent variables or covariates in research studies involving the administration of questionnaires. Manipulating and/or evaluating the effects of these kinds of variables on responses to questionnaires can become expensive and time-consuming. Consequently, efforts are often made to control for the effects of extraneous variables by designing questionnaires so that such variables have less effect; or an attempt is made to treat the variables as sources of error to be controlled by randomization. For example, modern word-processing and printing equipment facilitate the preparation of different forms of the same questionnaire in which the questions are arranged randomly or in different orders to reduce context effects. Administering the same, highly similar, or contradictory items to determine whether the respondent answers consistently is one technique for detecting uninformed or dishonest reporting. In addition, questions that a majority of people answer in a particular way but may induce the unwary or incautious responder to answer in a different way, can be helpful. Another technique is to inspect completed questionnaires for random or unusual response patterns.

Bogus Pipeline and Randomized Response Techniques

Most adults will probably give the same answers to questionnaire items whether or not their responses are anonymous. In general, however, sensitive or threatening questions, such as those dealing with illegal or otherwise personally or socially unacceptable behavior (e.g., sexual behavior and attitudes, accident frequency, alcohol and drug usage), are more likely than nonsensitive questions to be answered untruthfully. Answers may be more honest and less self-protective when respondents believe they are answering anonymously, but anonymity may not serve the purposes of the investigation. For example, a researcher may wish to compare the responses of the same individuals at different points in time, but the inability to link responses to respondents would make this impossible.[1]

A number of techniques have been proposed for dealing with the reluctance to give truthful answers to sensitive questions, such as those dealing with sexual behavior and alcohol use. For example, wording a sensitive question in such a way as to suggest that the behavior is rather common or that the response refers to "other people" can encourage truthful responses. Or, as Sudman and Bradburn (1982) maintain, threatening or sensitive questions are more likely to be answered truthfully if they are open-ended, fairly long, and contain familiar words. The perceived importance of sensitive questions also will be reduced if they are embedded among other questions dealing with both sensitive and nonsensitive topics.

Two other procedures that have been suggested as ways of obtaining valid answers to sensitive questions are the bogus pipeline and the randomized response technique. In the *bogus pipeline,* efforts are made to deceive respondents into believing that their answers to sensitive questions will be verified by an independent scientific procedure. For example, before answering a questionnaire concerning smoking, the preadolescents under investigation viewed a videotape concerning the use of a new test for detecting the presence of nicotine in saliva (Evans, Hanson, & Mittelmark, 1977). They were then asked for a saliva specimen and told that it would be analyzed by the test described in the video. The result was that significantly more youngsters who had seen the video admitted to smoking than those who had not. Other procedures, such as a polygraph test (Sigall & Page, 1971), have also been employed in bogus pipeline studies. The bogus pipeline procedure is not, however, feasible with large samples of subjects. Furthermore, its purpose is defeated if subjects realize they are being deceived.

In the *randomized response technique* (Warner, 1965; Greenberg et al., 1969), the respondent is presented with two questions—one sensitive and one innocuous (nonsensitive). A probability procedure, such as having the respondent reach into an urn and randomly select a ball from a mixture of red and white balls, or toss a coin, is used to determine which of the two questions is presented. Because only the respondent knows which question is presented, his or her response is anonymous and therefore more likely to be honest. Although this procedure does not permit the investigator to determine which respondents received the sensitive question, or of those who did which answered it in a particular direction, by applying a conditional probability formula, an estimate of the number and percentage of respondents who answered the sensitive question in the affirmative may be determined. To illustrate the procedure, assume that the sensitive question is "Have you shoplifted in the last month?" and the innocuous question is "Were you born in January?" The respondent selects one ball from an urn containing equal numbers of red and white balls. If a red ball is selected, a card containing the sensitive question is presented; if a white ball is selected, a card containing the innocuous question is presented. In either case, the interviewer does not know which question is on the card. The conditional probability, $p(y/s)$, of giving an affirmative response to the sensitive question is computed as:

$$p(y/s) = \{p(y) - p(y/i)[1 - p(s)]\}/p(s), \qquad (2.1)$$

where $p(y)$ is the proportion of respondents answering yes to both questions, $p(s)$ is the proportion of respondents receiving the sensitive question, and $p(y/i)$ is the proportion of respondents receiving the innocuous question who answered yes to it.

If $p(y) = .10$, $p(y/i) = .08$, and $p(s) = .5$, then

$$p(y/s) = [.10 - .08(1 - .5)]/.5 = .06/.5 = .12.$$

Note that the value of $p(y/i)$, the proportion of people born in January, was obtained from census data. Thus, in this example it is estimated that 12% of the respondents who received the shoplifting question answered yes (Kinnear & Taylor, 1991).

In a simplified version of the randomized response technique, only the sensitive question is presented. The respondent flips a coin, and regardless of the correct answer to the question, answers yes if the coin comes up heads. If the coin comes up tails, the respondent answers the question truthfully (yes or no). In this case, formula 2.1 for estimating the proportion of respondents who answered yes to the sensitive question reduces to:

$$p(y/s) = 2p(y) - 1 \qquad (2.2)$$

where $p(y)$ is the total proportion of yes responses.

Program A8 in the set of computer programs accompanying this book can also be used to make the appropriate calculations required by the randomized response technique. But like an anonymous questionnaire, the technique provides response data on groups, not individuals; and even then, only an estimate is provided of the actual proportion of the sample answering yes to the sensitive question.

Computer Programs for Constructing Questionnaires

A number of professionally designed computer programs for constructing questions, such as the Ci2 system of Sawtooth Software, have become available during the past two decades. Some of these programs are quite versatile, allowing for custom-tailored formats in the questions, response options, instructions, and other design features. The computer programs on the diskette accompanying this book are rather simple by comparison with some of the commercially available software, but they are straightforward, economical, and instructive to use.

Program A1 may be used to construct single- and multipart questionnaires containing both open- and closed-ended questions. The six options available on program A1 are:

1. Construct a questionnaire or inventory.
2. Edit a constructed questionnaire or inventory.
3. Print and store a questionnaire or inventory.
4. Change the password(s).
5. Enter respondent identification numbers.
6. Quit.

The password for program A1 is *question*, but, like the password for program A2 *(answer)*, it can be changed by selecting option 4 on the A1 menu. In addition, identification numbers for up to 100 respondents may be entered by using option 5.

By selecting option 5 from the A1 menu, a questionnaire generated by this program can be output on a line printer and simultaneously stored in the file named *results* for later retrieval. Subsequently, it can be reedited on a word processor, then printed by invoking the DOS COPY command or the word processor's print option, or by running the Print program on the diskette.

Program A3 is designed to store any previously constructed single- or multipart questionnaire or inventory in a designated ASCII file. Program A4 administers any questionnaire stored in a designated file by program A3.

Program A6 generates a questionnaire for the specific task of assessing interpersonal attraction or cohesiveness in a group of people (Aiken, 1992). An example of a questionnaire produced by this program is shown in Figure 2.4. The number of possible response categories on

Preferences for Social Interactions

Directions: For each of the names listed below, indicate how much you like or dislike interacting socially with that person. Mark your responses according to the following key:

1 = Dislike extremely
2 = Dislike moderately
3 = Dislike mildly
4 = Neither like nor dislike
5 = Like mildly
6 = Like moderately
7 = Like extremely

If you feel that you don't know a person well enough to rate him or her, circle a number toward the middle of the scale. Circle 'Me' if the person is you.

	Dislike						Like	
George Brown	1	2	3	4	5	6	7	Me
Arlene Fitzpatrick	1	2	3	4	5	6	7	Me
Paula Francis	1	2	3	4	5	6	7	Me
Eugene Johnson	1	2	3	4	5	6	7	Me
Bill Kingston	1	2	3	4	5	6	7	Me
Frances Mayfield	1	2	3	4	5	6	7	Me
Dorothy Samuels	1	2	3	4	5	6	7	Me
Audrey Tucker	1	2	3	4	5	6	7	Me
Lewis White	1	2	3	4	5	6	7	Me
John Williams	1	2	3	4	5	6	7	Me

Figure 2.4.   Questionnaire for assessing interpersonal attraction and group cohesiveness.

questionnaires generated by program A6 ranges from two to seven; seven were used in constructing the instrument in Figure 2.4. In addition to the number of response categories, the title and directions are specified by the user, permitting a great deal of flexibility in the purposes for which this program may be used.

The construction of rating scales and checklists can be facilitated by the use of programs A1 and A2 on the diskette of computer programs accompanying *Rating Scales and Checklists*. Program A2, in particular, enables users to construct many different types of rating scales with a minimum of effort.

ADMINISTERING QUESTIONNAIRES

Before administering a questionnaire to a large, representative sample of the population for which it was designed, it is important to have the questionnaire examined closely by one or more unbiased experts, then pretested on a group of people. The pretest group need not be large, perhaps 5% of the sample. But the respondents should be motivated, conscientious, and similar to the actual sample to which the questionnaire will ultimately be administered. Methods of selecting samples are described in Chapter 4. Only after the responses and comments of the pretest group are examined and taken into consideration in revising the questionnaire should the final version be administered to a representative sample of the target population.

Administration by Mail

The *cover letter*, or letter of transmittal, accompanying a mailed questionnaire should be brief but fully communicate the essential information to the recipient. As shown in Figure 2.5, the letter should introduce the writer, indicate the purposes for which the questionnaire is being administered and why it is being sent to the recipient in particular, and what person or organization is conducting the study or survey. It should be clear to the recipient that the study is important and that his or her responses are needed and valuable; he or she should also be assured that all responses will be kept confidential. The date by which the completed questionnaire should be returned in the enclosed stamped envelope is also indicated in the cover letter. Finally, the letter should be signed, preferably by a person of recognized stature.

Assuming that the cover letter and instructions are clear and complete, that the questionnaire is understandable and not too long,[2] and that the sample of people to whom it is sent are willing to complete and return it in the enclosed addressed and stamped envelope, the questionnaire should pose few problems of administration. Of course, high respondent motivation cannot be taken for granted, even when the cover letter is interesting and a small monetary or other incentive is enclosed. The return rate can be improved by follow-up mailings of the questionnaire and accompanying materials to the nonrespondents in successive 10-day to 2-week periods after the initial mailing. Unfortunately, return rates higher than 80% are rarely obtained even with one or more follow-up mailings. Administering the questionnaire over the telephone or in

John R. Franks, Ph.D.
School of Business Management
Crosscreek University
Bonaventure, CA 93567
Phone (805) 523-8165

January 1, 1997

Mr. Paul Adams
12449 Hillmount Avenue
Lessington, CA 90756

Dear Mr. Adams:

   I am conducting a survey of the practices and opinions of a selected sample of Southern California residents regarding fast food outlets. The results of this survey will be of interest and value to both the proprietors of these outlets and the individuals who patronize them. After the results have been analyzed, they will be made available, free of charge, to all interested parties.

   The enclosed questionnaire has been carefully designed to provide information concerning the extent to which people such as yourself frequent fast food outlets, which outlets are most popular, what features of these outlets are most appealing, and other opinions concerning them. You have been selected as part of a representative sample of the residents in this area to complete the questionnaire. I shall be very grateful if you will fill it out at your earliest convenience. Please return the completed questionnaire in the enclosed self-addressed, stamped envelope by February 1, 1997.

   If you desire, I shall be pleased to send you a copy of the results of the survey when they have been analyzed. Thank you for your assistance.

Sincerely,

John R. Franks, Ph.D.
Professor of Business Management

Encl. Survey questionnaire

Figure 2.5. Illustrative cover letter.

person to nonrespondents can also increase the response rate, but telephone or face-to-face interviewing does not necessarily produce the same results as mailed questionnaires. Furthermore, it is possible that the nonrespondents who complete the questionnaire over the phone are significantly different from the total group of nonrespondents.

Face-to-Face and Telephone Administration

The procedure for administering a questionnaire in a face-to-face situation or over the telephone is similar to that employed in any structured interview. The interviewer begins by introducing himself or herself in a friendly manner and briefly describing the reasons for the interview. The interviewee is told how and why he or she was selected and how long it will take to answer the questions (see Box 2.1). If other people are present, the interviewee is asked if there is somewhere that the interview can be conducted privately. Following this exchange, the interviewer waits for the interviewee to agree and then begins the interview. If it is not convenient for the interview to be conducted immediately, the interviewer attempts to schedule an appointment for a mutually convenient time.

Once the interview has begun, the interviewer is neutral but interested, showing neither approval nor disapproval at the interviewee's answers. A questionnaire administered in a person-to-person situation usually contains a number of routing questions and, depending on the respondent's answers to previous questions, several questions that can be skipped. The responses are recorded in writing or electronically in an unobtrusive manner and with the respondent's permission (preferably in writing). The interviewer records the responses accurately, being careful not to let the recorded responses deviate from the actual responses made by the interviewee. After all the questions have been presented, the interviewee is asked if he or she wants to ask anything. Any questions asked by the interviewee are either answered immediately or

---

Box 2.1
Introduction for a Face-to-Face Questionnaire Interview

Good morning/afternoon/evening. I am George Jones from Southernmost University. The university is conducting a survey for the Housing Department of the Cartersville City Government to find out what the residents of Cartersville think about their housing and various aspects of the services provided by the city government. A representative sample of residents has been selected to interview about their opinions concerning the matter of housing. I shall appreciate it if you will take part in this survey so that we can obtain an accurate picture of the views of Cartersville residents.

Your answers to the questions that I am going to ask will be kept confidential. Please answer all questions as accurately as you can. The Housing Department will not be able to identify you or any other resident from the answers or comments that you make.

The interview will take approximately 30 minutes. If it is convenient for you, I'd like to start right now .... If you would prefer that I come back at a later time, when would it be most convenient for you?

the interviewer promises to obtain the answers as soon as possible. The interviewee is then thanked for his or her participation.

Computer Programs for Administering Questionnaires

Questionnaires and inventories constructed and stored by programs A1 and A3 on the diskette of computer programs accompanying this book can be administered by programs A2 and A4, respectively. To run program A2, first enter the password *answer,* the respondent's identification number, and the identification number of the questionnaire to be administered. As noted previously in the chapter, the password and the identification numbers are recorded by running program A1. After program A2 has been loaded, the title and general directions for the questionnaire are presented, followed by the specific directions for each part. The items in that part are presented individually and answered by the respondent. The respondent can change his or her response to a question as many times as desired, but only the first and last responses and their associated times (in seconds) are recorded. After all questions have been answered, the results are printed in a six-column table, each row of which lists the part and item numbers, the first response given by the respondent, the time for the first response, the respondent's last (changed) response to the item, and the time for the last response. In addition to printing this table of results at runtime, it can be saved in a file designated by the user.

Program A4 administers any questionnaire or inventory that has been stored in an ASCII file by program A3. The respondent enters his or her name and the numerical code of the questionnaire. The answers given by the respondent to all items, in addition to the part and total scores, are recorded in the file named *results* and may be printed at runtime or later.

SCORING QUESTIONNAIRES

The items on a typical questionnaire have no right or wrong answers in the same sense as items on a test. Responses to open- and closed-ended questions are usually coded in some manner; for example, by using letters or numbers to indicate that a particular response should be categorized in a certain way. Such a *coding frame,* indicating what and how items are to be coded, is usually prepared when the questionnaire is being constructed. When numerical codes or labels are used, it should be understood that they are not ordinal or cardinal numbers corresponding to a value on a measurement scale. The "scoring" of responses to most questionnaire items is a matter of simple coding or categorization rather than true measurement. Consequently, it makes no sense to perform mathematical operations (addition, subtraction, multiplication, division, etc.) on these numbers. Although the coded responses can be grouped in a frequency distribution to determine how many people gave each response, little else of a statistical nature can be done with them.

The evaluation of attitudes, opinions, beliefs, and other affective variables takes place on a somewhat higher level of measurement than the categorical, or nominal, level. These variables are often assessed by means of rating scales and scored according to procedures described in Chapters 2 and 8 of *Rating Scales and Checklists* (Aiken, 1996). The response to each item on a rating scale is assigned an ordinal number, say from 1 to 10, depending on the quality or quantity of the rated attribute. Furthermore, the ratings or rankings assigned to each of several items may be combined to yield a more stable, and preferably more meaningful, composite measure of the variable that is being measured. Sometimes, the composite measures obtained by combining the scores from a large number of questionnaire items of this sort are viewed as being on an equal-interval scale (see Chapter 5) and treated accordingly.

Computer programs A5 and A7 on the diskette accompanying this book can be used to store and score responses to questionnaires. Program A5 stores questionnaire responses that are entered from a computer keyboard into a designated output file; it also determines the scores on specific items or groups of items as well as total scores. Various scoring weights may be assigned to the responses to different kinds of items.

Program A7 scores responses obtained by administering an interpersonal attraction or cohesiveness questionnaire constructed by program A6. Three kinds of cohesiveness coefficients are computed: a coefficient for each respondent, indicating how he or she feels toward the other members of the group; a coefficient for each evaluated person, indicating how the rest of the group feels toward him or her; and a coefficient reflecting how the group as a whole feels about itself. The statistical significance of each coefficient is evaluated by an exact probability test when the sample is small and a normal approximation test when the sample is large (Aiken, 1992).

The last program in category A on the computer diskette, program A9, is designed to evaluate the responses to a special type of questionnaire—a voting ballot. From an n by c matrix of the ranks assigned by n voters to c candidates, this program package determines:

- The frequency distributions, means, medians, and Borda counts for the candidates.
- The Condorcet candidate.
- The elected candidates, by using the Hare system of single transferable vote (STV).
- Agreement indexes across voters for each candidate, an overall (mean) agreement index, and a z value for testing the statistical significance of the mean agreement index.
- The number of votes distributed among the c candidates by the n voters, as determined by the cumulative or approval voting procedures.

The ranked data should first be stored in an n by c matrix format in a data file. Brams and Fishburn (1991) provide details concerning the various voting systems incorporated in this program.

SUMMARY

The process of constructing a questionnaire begins with a purpose, which leads to a plan. Depending on the complexity of the purpose(s) for which a questionnaire is being designed, the plan may be fairly straightforward or highly complex. In particular, when the plan calls for constructing an omnibus questionnaire that solicits information on a wide variety of matters, a detailed outline, a table of specifications, or a flowchart is a useful preliminary to preparing the actual directions and questions. The format of the questions and the directions that precede them vary with the purposes of the questionnaire and whether it will be administered in a face-to-face situation, over the telephone, or by mail. For example, lengthy questions or long lists of items to be considered by the respondent are less appropriate in face-to-face or telephone administration than on a mailed questionnaire.

The overall purpose of any questionnaire is to motivate the sample of people selected from the target population to give truthful and thoughtful answers to all relevant items on the questionnaire.

Achieving this goal can be facilitated by making the questionnaire clear, attractive, brief, meaningful, and interesting. From the administrator's or interviewer's point of view, it also helps if the responses given to the questions are understandable, codifiable, and reliable.

Lists of suggestions for constructing questionnaires in general, and specifically for mailed, face-to-face, and telephone administration, were presented. Designers of questionnaires do a better job when they possess the technical skills needed to construct such instruments, coupled with a clear understanding of its purposes, its topic(s), the conditions of administration, and the characteristics of the people to whom it will be administered.

Both open-ended and closed-ended questions may be included on a questionnaire. The latter are easier to administer and score or code, but the former may provide more information. The rules for writing good test items also apply to the construction of items to be included on questionnaires. Recommendations for constructing closed-ended, or objective, items, in particular, were considered in some detail in the chapter.

Questionnaires can be designed to minimize, but not eliminate, dishonest and careless reporting. Anonymous administration and the randomized response technique can reduce the frequency of lying on certain threatening items, but both procedures make it difficult, if not impossible, to evaluate intra-individual consistencies and changes over time.

Administration of a questionnaire in a face-to-face situation or over the telephone is facilitated by establishing rapport with the respondent, being brief but attentive, and encouraging cooperation. Effective administration of a questionnaire requires a well-designed cover letter that introduces the correspondent, describes the purposes of the questionnaire, explains why the recipient was selected and why he or she should complete the questionnaire, and to whom, when, and how the completed questionnaire should be returned.

Responses to the items on questionnaires are not generally scored in the same way as test item responses, although certain groups of items or "scales" concerning attitudes, opinions, and beliefs, can be scored on an ordinal or rank scale. In general, responses are simply tabulated and frequency distributions prepared for further analysis.

Several programs in category A of the computer programs on the diskette accompanying this book were described. These programs can facilitate the process of constructing and administering questionnaires, and tabulating and scoring responses to them.

QUESTIONS AND ACTIVITIES

1. Define each of the following terms used in this chapter in a sentence or two. Consult the Glossary at the back of the book and a dictionary if you need help.

   acquiescence
   acquiescence response set
   balanced scale
   bogus pipeline
   closed-ended question
   coding frame
   computer-assisted telephone
     interviewing (CATI)
   cover letter
   double (double-barreled)
     question
   emotionally loaded word
   focus group
   hypothetical question

   leading question
   Likert scale
   loaded question
   mail survey
   multiple-choice item
   nonspecific adjectives
     (adverbs)
   objective items
   open-ended question
   random-digit dialing
   randomized response
     technique
   specific determiner

2. Construct and print a questionnaire using program A1. Administer the questionnaire using program A2.

3. Take the file that you constructed in question 2, enter and store it using program A3, and administer it using program A4.

4. From a list of 10 of your friends or classmates, construct a cohesiveness questionnaire using program A6. Print the questionnaire, make 10 copies, and administer it to the same 10 individuals. Use program A7 to enter the data and compute the three types of cohesiveness coefficients.

5. Describe the relative advantages and disadvantages of administering a questionnaire by mail, face to face, and over the phone.

6. Using the randomized response technique, an interviewer presented one of these two questions to each of 100 persons:
   A. During the past 12 months, have you been charged by a police officer for driving under the influence of liquor?
   B. Is your birthday in the month of September?

   A box containing 35 red and 15 blue beads was shaken, after which the interviewee selected a bead at random. If the bead was red, the interviewee was told to answer question A; if it was blue, he or she was told to answer question B. Assume that one-twelfth of the interviewees were born in September and that 15 of the

50 persons answered yes to both questions. What is your best estimate of the percentage and number of individuals in this sample who had been charged with drunk driving during the past 12 months? Use program A8 or formula 2.1 to find the answer.

7. In what ways does administering and scoring a mailed questionnaire differ from administering and scoring a questionnaire administered in a face-to-face situation or over the telephone?

SUGGESTED READING

Bauman, L. J., & Adair, E. G. (1992). The use of ethnographic interviewing to inform questionnaire construction. *Health Education Quarterly, 19*(1), 9–23.

Bradburn, N. M., & Sudman, S. (1992). The current status of questionnaire design. In P. N. Biemer, R. M. Grovers, L. E. Lyberg, N. A. Mathiowetz, & S. Sudman (Eds.), *Measurement errors in surveys.* New York: Wiley.

Ellard, J. H., & Rogers, T. B. (1993). Teaching questionnaire construction effectively: The Ten Commandments of question writing. *Contemporary Social Psychology, 17*(1), 17–20.

Fink, A. (1995). *How to ask survey questions.* Newbury Park, CA: Sage.

Foddy, W. H. (1993). *Constructing questions for interviews and questionnaire: Theory and practice in social research.* New York: Cambridge University Press.

Fowler, F. J., Jr. (1995). *Improving survey questions: Design and evaluation.* Thousand Oaks, CA: Sage.

Fowler, F. J., Jr., & Mangione, T. W. (1990). *Standardized survey interviewing: Minimizing interviewer-related error.* Newbury Park, CA: Sage.

Newell, R. (1993). Questionnaires. In N. Gilbert (Ed.), *Researching social life* (pp. 94–115). Newbury Park, CA: Sage.

Roberson, M. T., & Sundstrom, E. (1990). Questionnaire design, return rate, and response favorableness in an employee attitude questionnaire. *Journal of Applied Psychology, 75,* 354–357.

Rosier, M. J. (1994). Survey research methods. In T. Husén & T. N. Postlethwaite (Eds.), *The international encyclopedia of education* (2nd ed., pp. 5854–5862). New York: Elsevier.

Sanchez, M. E. (1992). Effects of questionnaire design on the quality of survey data. *The Public Opinion Quarterly, 6,* 206–217.

NOTES

1. A self-generated identification coding procedure has been employed with some success to preserve anonymity while permitting linkability across time in questionnaire administration (Kearney, Hopkins, Mauss & Weisheit, 1984).
2. As a rule of thumb, the time limits for a questionnaire should be set so that approximately 90% of the respondents are able to complete it in the allotted time.

3

Constructing, Administering, and Scoring Psychological Inventories

Like any other inventory, a psychological inventory is a procedure for identifying and listing possessions, but the possessions counted and recorded are psychological attributes such as personality traits, interests, attitudes, values, and personal orientations. Conducting inventories of such variables may be facilitated by commercially available paper-and-pencil instruments, the most popular of which are referred to as *personality inventories* and *interest inventories*. Psychometric instruments for inventorying other personal events and circumstances also have wide application.

This chapter focuses on two types of paper-and-pencil instruments for assessing personality traits and interests, but some attention is also given to measures of attitudes, values, personal orientations, and life history (biography). Not all of these instruments are designated explicitly as *inventories*; they may be labeled as *questionnaires, opinionnaires, scales, tests, studies, surveys, indexes, indicators,* or by other terms. Whatever the term, the common goal of these devices is to count or otherwise measure the presence of certain psychological variables or constructs that are important in motivating and directing the behavior of individuals. Most of these are self-report measures on which a person describes and evaluates himself or herself; but, like scales for rating other people, some inventories are designed to be completed by a parent, another relative, or a close associate to describe a child or adult.

The first personality inventory, the Personal Data Sheet, was constructed by Robert Woodworth in 1918, and a revision of it—the Woodworth Psychoneurotic Inventory—provided a model for the construction of other personality inventories. Like its predecessor, the Woodworth Psychoneurotic Inventory provided a single-score, as did pioneering inventories such as the X-O Test (Pressey & Pressey, 1919) and the A-S Reaction Study (Allport & Allport, 1928). The first multiscore personality inventory, the Bernreuter Personality Inventory, appeared in 1931 and could be scored for six variables: Neurotic Tendency, Self-Sufficiency, Introversion-Extroversion, Dominance-Submission, Sociability, and Confidence. Another multiscore inventory, the Bell Adjustment Inventory, made its appearance during the same period and also yielded six scores: Home, Health, Submissiveness, Emotionality, Hostility, Masculinity. Like the Woodworth Psychoneurotic Inventory, the Bernreuter, Bell, and other early paper-and-pencil measures of personality were designed primarily to identify emotional or adjustment problems. Subsequent personality inventories were designed not only for research and applications concerned with emotional problems but also to measure a wide range of "normal" personality characteristics that were considered predictive of behavior and development.

CONSTRUCTING PERSONALITY INVENTORIES

As with the construction of a test, the process of constructing a personality inventory begins with certain assumptions about what is to be measured and what purposes the instrument is supposed to serve. Unlike the cognitive abilities that are measured by standardized and nonstandardized tests, the constructs that personality inventories are designed to measure refer to dispositional, temperamental, stylistic, or other affective variables.

Item Construction

As illustrated in Figure 3.1, a variety of item formats may be employed in designing a personality inventory. The most popular of these are the true-false and multiple-choice formats, although checklists and rating scales are also common (Aiken, 1996b). Whatever the item type, it

True-False:

_____ T or F? I am a very sociable person who likes to be around other people a lot.

Multiple-Choice:

_____ Write the letter in the marginal dash corresponding to the adjective that is most descriptive of your personality.

    a. calm
    b. imaginative
    c. organized
    d. sociable
    e. soft-hearted

Forced-Choice: Write "M" on the line segment corresponding to the adjective that is most descriptive of you and "L" on the line segment corresponding to the adjective that is least descriptive of you.

_____ independent
_____ disorganized
_____ retiring
_____ trusting

Rating Scale: Circle the number that best indicates your standing on the characteristic.

| retiring | 1 | 2 | 3 | 4 | 5 | 6 | 7 | sociable |
| trusting | 1 | 2 | 3 | 4 | 5 | 6 | 7 | suspicious |

Checklist: Put a check mark on each line corresponding to an adjective that is descriptive of you.

_____ agreeable
_____ calm
_____ conforming
_____ conscientious
_____ disorganized
_____ imaginative
_____ insecure
_____ reserved
_____ sociable
_____ suspicious

Completion: Fill in the blanks with the most appropriate word(s):

I would describe myself as a very _____ person and a very _____ person.

Listing: List five adjectives that are most descriptive of your personality.

_____
_____
_____
_____

Essay: Write a one-page description of your personality.

Figure 3.1. Examples of personality test items.

should be short, and simple enough to be understood on the first reading. Wolfe (1993) also recommends that the items be stated in the first person, the active voice, the indicative mood, and (except for biographical facts) in the present tense. Either statements or questions may be used, but negatives, commas, connectives, and subjunctives should be avoided. The number of items designed to measure particular variables (a *scale*) should be short and highly related to each other.

Frequency versus Intensity of Response

Traditionally, the different response categories on many items on personality inventories have been designed to reflect varying frequencies of experiences or behaviors, the assumption being that the frequency of a response is an indicator of the intensity of the underlying drive or experience. Items in this format that might appear on an inventory designed to measure the construct of *anxiety* include:

1. I am under a mental strain:
   a. always
   b. frequently
   c. occasionally
   d. rarely
   e. never

2. I feel nervous:
   a. all of the time
   b. most of the time
   c. much of the time
   d. some of the time
   e. none of the time

The items on such a *frequency inventory* need not be in multiple-choice format; many true-false inventories, such as the Taylor Manifest Anxiety Scale (Taylor, 1953) are actually frequency inventories based on the assumption that the total scores are indicative of the magnitude or intensity of the construct. In contrast, the items on an *intensity inventory* might take the following form:

1. When I am under a mental strain, my feeling is:
   a. mild
   b. moderate

    c. intense

    d. severe

  2. When I feel nervous, my feeling is:

    a. mild

    b. moderate

    c. intense

    d. severe

That the two formats—frequency and intensity—produce somewhat different results is seen in the moderate correlation between scores on inventories with frequency and intensity formats (Aiken, 1962). In addition, varying the number of response categories from 2 to 3, 4, 5, 7, or even more can affect the results (Aiken, 1983).

Trait Theories and the Rational-Theoretical Strategy

Everyone who possesses at least a modicum of intelligence has some ideas or common sense theories as to why people behave as they do. Most of these "theories" are not very well formulated, but they are gleaned from observation and experience and assist the individual in coping with personal and social problems. Many of these conceptions are derived and sustained by language. Everyday language is replete with descriptive and explanatory terminology related to personality. Innumerable adjectives and nouns refer to personality traits, tendencies, types, and behaviors associated with them.

    Beginning with a list of 17,953 words in the English language referring to characteristics of personality, Allport and Odbert (1936) were able to reduce them to a relatively small number of traits. Lists of trait names were also derived by Henry Murray (1938), Raymond Cattell (1965), and Hans Eysenck (1981).

    The most common approach or strategy applied to the design of a personality inventory begins with a list of traits, not necessarily an exhaustive list of the sort proposed by Allport and Cattell. Given a fairly short list, one can then prepare a set of descriptive, self-report statements or questions to assess the degree to which respondents possess each trait. Content-based, intuitive, judgmental, logical, and theoretical are among the terms used to describe this approach to inventory construction. The term *rational-theoretical* (Lanyon & Goodstein, 1982) will be used to designate the combination of logic and theory applied in this strategy. The conception of personality inherent in the rational-theoretical strategy is derived from common sense, professional judgment, research findings, and theory.

Henry Murray's conceptualization of personality in terms of needs and press has been particularly influential in the construction of personality assessment instruments by means of the rational-theoretical strategy. According to Murray, people are motivated to reduce the tensions created by forces within them *(needs)* and forces outside them *(press)*. Needs may be either *physiogenic* (biologically based) or *psychogenic* (psychologically based). There are also two kinds of press: alpha and beta. *Alpha press* is actual—from the environment—while *beta press* is perceived but not necessarily real. A list of Murray's psychogenic needs is given in Table 3.1. Several of these needs are included among the variables assessed by a number of personality inventories and checklists, including the Edwards Personal Preference Schedule, the Personality Research Form, and the Adjective Check List.

Trait conceptions of personality have had the greatest impact of all theories on the development of personality inventories, but other theories (psychodynamic, phenomenological (self), type, social learning) have also been influential. For example, Carl Jung's analytic/type theory served as a basis for the development of the Myers-Briggs Type Indicator and the Singer-Loomis Inventory of Personality. The self theories of Carl Rogers and Abraham Maslow influenced the development of many self-concept inventories; and Julian Rotter's social learning theory provided the stimulus for the construction of measures of generalized expectancies and locus of control. Theories of single concepts, such as Arnold Beck's conceptions of anxiety, depression, and suicide ideation, and Donald Byrne's concept of repression-sensitization, have also played a role in the development of various personality inventories.

Factor-Analytic Strategy

Also known as the inductive, internal consistency, clustering, and itemetric strategy, this approach to the construction of personality inventories is directed toward the development of internally consistent sets of highly intercorrelated items. In addition, the items comprising such a subtest or *scale* should have low correlations with other scales on the inventory. The name *factor-analytic* derives from the fact that the statistical methods of factor analysis are applied to determine the

TABLE 3.1. Murray's Psychogenic Needs

Abasement
Achievement
Acquisition
Affiliation
Aggression
Autonomy
Blame avoidance
Change
Cognizance
Construction
Counteraction
Deference
Dominance
Excitance
Exposition
Harm avoidance
Nurturance
Passivity
Playmirth
Recognition
Rejection
Retention
Sentience
Sex
Succorance
Understanding

minimum number of factors needed to account for most of the variability among scores on the various scales, and the percentage of scale score variability accounted for by those factors. The results of successive factor analyses lead to refinements in the items and progress toward achieving the goal of constructing a multiscore inventory of internally consistent, independent measures of personality traits.

The Guilford-Zimmerman Temperament Survey, the 16 Personality Factor Questionnaire, and the Eysenck Personality Inventory are prominent examples of personality inventories constructed by the factor-analytic strategy. Also based on this strategy and the notion that personality can be fairly well explained in terms of five factors are the NEO Personality Inventory—Revised (NEO PI-R) and the NEO Five-Factor Inventory (NEO—FFI). The five factors measured by these inventories are neuroticism, extraversion, openness to experience, agreeableness, and conscientiousness. The inventory in Figure 3.2 is an example of the kinds of items that may be devised to measure the factors in the "Big Five" model. Neuroticism is assessed by items 2, 9, and 14, extraversion by items 1, 7, and 11, openness to experience by items 4, 6, and 10, agreeableness by items 8, 12, and 15 agreeableness, and conscientiousness by items 3, 5, and 13.

Criterion-Keying Strategy

The rational-theoretical and the factor-analytic strategies were the first strategies for constructing personality inventories to be employed, and are still the most prevalent. With the construction of the Minnesota Multiphasic Personality Inventory (MMPI) in the early 1940s, the *criterion-keying strategy* made its debut. It had been used earlier in designing the Strong Vocational Interest Blanks (SVIB) and, to some extent, the A-S Reaction Study, but the first multivariable inventory of personality to be constructed by the criterion-keying approach was the MMPI.

The criterion-keying strategy, which is also referred to as the external, empirical, group-contrast, criterion-group, or criterion-validated strategy, consists of selecting items according to their effectiveness in distinguishing between certain criterion groups. The criterion groups may consist of patients having different psychiatric diagnoses, employers in different occupational groups, or groups classified from their behavior as having different amounts of a psychological variable. Examples are schizophrenic versus nonschizophrenic, delinquent versus nondelinquent, teachers versus nonteachers, and anxious versus nonanxious. Constructing a scale to differentiate between schizophrenics and nonschizophrenics, for example, entails administering a large number of personality test items to both groups, and retaining for the scale those items that schizophrenics answered differently from nonschizophrenics. The items on a scale formed in this manner would then be expected to distinguish between other schizophrenics and nonschizophrenics.

Personality Inventory

Directions: For each of the following paired items, circle the adjective that is most descriptive of your personality.

1. A. affectionate
   B. reserved
2. A. calm
   B. worrying
3. A. careful
   B. careless
4. A. conforming
   B. independent
5. A. disorganized
   B. well-organized
6. A. down-to-earth
   B. imaginative
7. A. fun-loving
   B. sober
8. A. helpful
   B. uncooperative
9. A. insecure
   B. secure
10. A. prefer routine
    B. prefer variety
11. A. retiring
    B. sociable
12. A. ruthless
    B. soft-hearted
13. A. self-disciplined
    B. weak-willed
14. A. self-pitying
    B. self-satisfied
15. A. suspicious
    B. trusting

The following key may be used to compute scores on the five factors:

$$\text{Agreeableness} = 8(A) + 12(B) + 15(B)$$
$$\text{Conscientiousness} = 3(A) + \ 5(B) + 13(A)$$
$$\text{Extraversion} = 1(A) + \ 7(A) + 11(B)$$
$$\text{Neuroticism} = 2(B) + \ 9(A) + 14(A)$$
$$\text{Openness to Experience} = 4(B) + \ 6(B) + 10(B)$$

The item number is outside the parentheses and the answer option to be given 1 point is inside the parentheses.

Figure 3.2.   Five-factor personality inventory.

The various clinical scales on the MMPI were all constructed in this way, according to which scores on them differentiate between particular psychiatric groups and other groups of individuals. Likewise, in constructing the Strong Vocational Interest Blank for Men (SVIB), items were keyed on particular occupational scales (engineer, physician, psychologist, etc.) only if they differentiated significantly between men in a designated occupation and men in general. On the MMPI, the SVIB, and other criterion-keyed inventories, items were assigned a numerical scoring weight (i.e., "keyed") for a specific group if the responses given by that group were significantly different from those given by an appropriate control group.

The items selected initially for tryout to determine whether they are answered differently by the contrast group and the control group in the criterion-keying strategy do not come "out of the blue." Reason, experience, and even theory play a role in constructing or selecting the initial item pool. Still, the items on an inventory devised in this way are typically less homogeneous than the items on scales devised by the rational-theoretical and factor-analytic strategies. In fact, certain items on the MMPI and SVIB scales would, according to logic or common sense, seem not to belong to the particular scales on which they are included. An example is the item "My parents and family find more fault with me than they should." on the Psychopathic Deviate scale of the MMPI and the item "I like men with gold teeth." on the Banker scale of the SVIB. These kinds of items, which appear to be misfits on those particular scales, have been the objects of derision by social satirists, and, according to Jackson (1971), do not hold up well on cross-validation.

Combination Construction Strategy

Each of the inventory-construction strategies described has its merits. The rational-theoretical approach involves less work and yields inventories having greater face validity than the criterion-keying strategy. Both Burisch (1984) and Wolfe (1993) argued that transparent scales consisting of a few items are usually just as effective as scales composed of a large number of highly polished, convoluted items with low-face validity. In any case, Goldberg (1972) found that inventories devised by each of the strategies were equally effective in predicting external criteria. Inventories produced by the rational-theoretical strategy, however, are more easily faked than those constructed by the criterion-keying approach (Burisch, 1984).

Today, designers of personality inventories do not limit themselves to a single strategy, but rather employ a combination of various approaches. The inventory-construction process usually begins by carefully defining the variables or constructs to be measured. Next, a large set ("pool") of items is prepared or selected to measure each construct, and the item pool is administered to a large sample of people, preferably 200 or more, who are representative of the target population. The item responses of this sample group are then analyzed to determine which items should be discarded or edited.

Constructing a frequency distribution of responses for each item is a recommended first step in item analysis. Items for which a particular response category is selected much more often than other response categories will be less effective than those answered in one way by half the sample and in another way by the remaining half. Furthermore, items that have low correlations with total scores on a scale cause the scale to be more heterogeneous and consequently less reliable than it would otherwise be, and thus should probably be eliminated. Other statistical procedures applied at this stage include internal consistency analysis by means of coefficient alpha and related statistics and factor analyses of item and scale scores. Following these procedures will not guarantee that the items, and hence the scale or inventory on which they appear, will be valid measures of the constructs of interest. Nevertheless, the validity of items and scales will be greater if these procedures are followed.

After the initial analyses have been completed and poorly functioning items have been edited or discarded, the remaining items are administered to a new representative sample and the responses analyzed. In addition to further item analyses and reliability checks, statistical analyses of the criterion-related and construct validities of scores on the various scales are made (see Chapter 6). Determination of the construct validity of each scale is particularly important. The *construct validity* of a psychometric instrument is concerned with the extent to which the scores of a group of people who, on the basis of independent evidence, are known to have a high amount of whatever psychological construct the instrument was designed to measure are significantly different from the scores of a group known to have a low amount of the construct. Of course, validation of the scales on a personality inventory does not end here; it is a continuing process of research and application of the inventory in a variety of contexts and with other groups of patients, employees, or students.

Exploratory and Diagnosticity Approaches

The three strategies just described have been used for decades in designing personality inventories and rating scales, and they appear to yield acceptable measures of a variety of psychological constructs. Tellengen and Waller (1993) have argued, however, that these strategies are not very useful in the initial stage of attempting to formulate and understand a construct. They suggest that the conceptualization of measurable constructs is better served by a philosophy of scale construction that promotes theoretical development. To this end, they advocate beginning with a general idea about the personality construct and preparing a large pool of items that would seem to measure it. These items are then administered to a large sample of people, after which statistical analyses are conducted to refine the psychometric properties of the scale and to generate new theories concerning the nature of the construct. Based on the results of these analyses, a new set of items is prepared. These items are, in turn, administered to another sample and the responses analyzed. In this way, the theory proposed during the earlier stages of the item-construction process is reevaluated. The process is repeated until the theoretical nature of the construct has become delineated in the final item set. This *exploratory approach,* which aims to make the elaboration of the construct to be measured an integral part of the process of scale construction, was used by Tellengen and Waller (1993) in the development of the Multidimensional Personality Questionnaire.

Just as the exploratory approach of Tellengen and Waller (1993) may be viewed as an extension and enhancement of the rational-theoretical and factor-analytic strategies of scale construction, Lippa and Connelly's (1990) notion of diagnosticity can be viewed as an extension of the criterion-keying strategy. Like the exploratory approach, the *diagnosticity approach* appears to be most useful when the constructs to be measured are not well understood. As noted previously, in the criterion-keying strategy items are retained for a particular scale if they differentiate between a specified target (criterion or contrast) group and a complementary (control) group. For example, the statement "I like adventure films better than romantic films" may be endorsed significantly more often by executives than by nonexecutives. If so, then it may be included on the Executive scale of the inventory. The sum of a person's scores on a set of such items constituting a scale will be his or her raw score on that scale.

The diagnosticity approach is similar to the criterion-keying approach in that two or more criterion groups are established initially. Then responses to items *(indicator variables)* that appear to differentiate between the groups are analyzed by means of discriminant function analysis. Under this strategy, a person's score is the probability, as determined by Bayes' formula, that he or she is a member of a certain criterion group. According to Lippa and Connelly (1990, p. 1013), the scores reflect "the degree to which individuals are prototypic of indexing groups given a set of diagnostic indicators of group membership." The concern shown in the diagnosticity approach for the careful and extensive sampling of attributes that differentiate between the criterion groups sets it apart from earlier criterion-keying approaches to inventory construction (Ozer & Reise, 1994). This concern is particularly evident in Lippa's (1991) research on gender.

ADMINISTERING AND SCORING PERSONALITY INVENTORIES

Personality inventories are administered in a variety of clinical, educational, medical, and legal settings. In clinical, or mental health, settings, they serve as aids in diagnosis, treatment, and residential placement. In educational settings, they contribute to the formulation of remedial procedures. In legal settings, they provide information for determining sanity, competency, and other court evaluations, as well as helping judicial authorities plan rehabilitation measures. And in medical settings, they contribute to the evaluation of psychological aspects of physical illnesses (Petzelt & Craddick, 1978).

Administration

Although certain inventories, such as the Personality Inventory for Children, are completed by a parent or other person who is familiar with the examinee, most psychological inventories are answered by the person being evaluated. These self-report instruments may be administered on either an individual or a group basis.

Written instructions to be read by the respondents are usually printed on the front cover of a personality inventory. These instructions tell the respondents how and where the questions or items are to be answered. The instructions should contain fairly brief statements concerning the importance of responding thoughtfully and sincerely; how to mark responses; that there are no right or wrong answers; not to spend too much time on any one item; and what to do when finished. They should also provide respondents with an explanation of why they are taking the inventory, what it purports to measure, and how the results will be used. For legal reasons, it is wise to have the examinee sign an informed consent form such as the one in Figure 3.3 before administering an inventory.

The time period in which the respondent should focus—right now, last week, sometime in the past or future, and so on—should be made clear in the instructions or in the phrasing of the items. *Trait inventories* focus on continuing, pervasive characteristics, such as trait anxiety, whereas *state inventories* focus on a transitory feeling or experience,

Informed Consent for a Personality Assessment

I, _____ , voluntarily give my consent to serve as a participant in a personality assessment conducted by _____ . I have received a clear and complete explanation of the general nature and purposes(s) of the assessment and the specific reason(s) why I am being examined. I have also been informed of the kinds of tests or/and other procedures to be administered and how the results will be used.

I realize that it may not be possible for the examiner to explain all aspects of the assessment to me until it has been completed. It is also my understanding that I may terminate my participation at any time without penalty. I further understand that I will be informed of the results and that they will be reported to no one else without my permission. At this time, I request that a copy of the results of this examination be sent to:

_____

_____

_____	_____
Examinee's Name	Signature of Examinee
_____	_____
Date	Signature of Examiner

Figure 3.3. Form for obtaining informed consent for a psychological examination.

such as state anxiety. Illustrative of the state/trait distinction are the State-Trait Anxiety Inventory and the State-Trait Anger Expression Inventory. Each of these instruments consists of two inventories—one for measuring state anxiety or anger and a second for measuring trait anxiety or anger. Another example of a state inventory is the Profile of Mood States, on which the respondent is instructed to focus on the past week, including the current day.

Administering a self-report inventory does not require as much training and experience as administering a projective technique or other individual psychological test. Teachers, psychological assistants, and other individuals with limited training in testing can administer self-report inventories, but they should do so under the guidance of a licensed or certified psychologist.

Scoring

Most inventories can be scored objectively from an answer key, and therefore scoring may be done by a competent clerk. Converting the raw scores to norms is also a routine process, but interpreting the scores usually requires fairly extensive training and experience.

Responses to true-false items on personality inventories are typically scored according to the key, as 0 or 1. Other numerical weights may be applied, particularly on criterion-keyed instruments, but 0 to 1 scoring is common. The scores on the subset of items constituting a particular variable or scale are then summed to yield a total raw score on that scale. Finally, the raw scores may be transformed to percentile ranks, standard scores, or other converted scores or norms.

Scoring responses to multiple-choice items on personality inventories is also fairly straightforward when the response options are on a continuum and can be converted to successive numerical values. For example, the five options on Likert scale items (Strongly disagree, Disagree, Undecided, Agree, Strongly agree) may be designated with the successive integers from 1 to 5 or 0 to 4. Scoring is more difficult when the response options do not fall on a continuum, as on the following item:

Which of the following is most descriptive of you?

a. I am a calm and secure person.

b. I am an affectionate and sociable person.

    c. I am an imaginative and independent person.

    d. I am a trusting and cooperative person.

    e. I am a well-organized and cautious person.

Each of these statements represents a different factor in the "Big Five" model of personality, and hence the five options are discrete. One solution to the problem of scoring this item might be to score it as 1 if a designated option was selected and 0 if any other option was selected. Other approaches to scoring such items are possible, but 0-1 scoring is the simplest.

    Forced-choice items containing three or four response options also present special scoring problems. Like the preceding multiple-choice item, forced-choice items are ipsative in nature: The selection of one response category eliminates the possibility of selecting a response in another category. Consider the following forced-choice item on which the respondent must indicate which adjective is most descriptive and which is least descriptive of him or her:

1. Calm	M	L
2. Careless	M	L
3. Conforming	M	L
4. Cooperative	M	L

Each of the four adjectives refers to a different factor in the "Big Five" model, but two of the adjectives are at the negative poll and two are at the positive poll of the corresponding factor. If a respondent indicates that cooperative (agreeableness factor) is most descriptive and careless (conscientiousness factor) is least descriptive of him or her, his or her scores on both the Agreeableness and Conscientiousness factors are raised. However, his or her total scores on the Neuroticism and Openness factors are lower or higher than they would have been if other choices had been made.

    The analysis of ipsative scores requires different statistical procedures than those used with normative scores. When the scores are *normative,* scores on the different traits or variables do not affect each other. Consequently, a person may score high on all scales, low on all scales, or a mixture of the two. But *ipsative* scores cannot all be high, nor can they all be low. Either all the scores are of average magnitude, or, a more likely result, some are high and some are low.

As discussed in Chapter 6, for purposes of interpretation, raw scores on personality inventories and scales are usually converted to norms—percentile ranks, T scores, stanines, and other special transformed scores based on a sample of people who are similar to the respondent in certain important ways (chronological age, gender, ethnic group, socioeconomic status, etc.).

Response Sets and Faking

Response sets, or tendencies to respond to test items on the basis of their form rather than their content, have been the subject of extensive research and discussion for many years. Among the response sets that have received particular attention are:

> *acquiescence:* the tendency to agree when in doubt
>
> *social desirability:* the tendency to answer in a socially desirable direction
>
> *overcautiousness:* the tendency to be excessively careful in responding
>
> *extremeness:* the tendency to give more extreme responses than mentally disturbed people actually do
>
> *oppositionalism:* the tendency to respond in a direction opposite to that in which one actually believes

The first two of these response sets have stimulated the greatest amount of research, but any of them may detract from the valid assessment of personality.

Special scales designed to detect response sets and special item formats (e.g., forced-choice) to control for them have been devised. Some authorities, however, have criticized test-makers' preoccupation with response sets as unwarranted and counterproductive (Rorer, 1990).

Related to the matter of response sets, in that it can also detract from a candid appraisal of individual personality, is dissimulation or faking. An accurate description of test-takers should be more subtle than the classification "liars, damn liars, and statisticians," but lying is a common practice in all walks of life and test-taking is no exception. Test administrators can exhort respondents to answer truthfully and accurately, and this may have some effect unless the respondent does not know the truth.

Depending on the perceived repercussions of their responses, examinees may "fake bad," that is, say that they are worse than they really are, or "fake good" by saying that they are better than they are. Special *validation scales* and keys designed to detect faking, malingering, dissimulation, or downright lying have been incorporated into most contemporary inventories of personality. Scores on these scales, such as the ? (Cannot say) scale, L (Lie) scale, the F (Frequency or infrequency) scale, and the K (Correction) scale of the MMPI are inspected before proceeding with the process of interpreting and applying the scores on this inventory (see Chapter 8).

Traits versus Situations and Clinical versus Statistical Prediction

Response sets and faking clearly pose problems in scoring and score interpretation. Two other issues pertaining to the use of personality inventories are the traits versus situations and clinical versus statistical prediction controversies. Traditionally, most personality assessment has been oriented around the conception that personality is best understood and assessed in terms of a finite number of traits or factors. These traits are conceived of as states within the individual that are expressed in behavior across a wide range of situations. Trait theorists do not deny the influence of situational variables on behavior; They just believe that situations are less important than traits in determining behavior. Mischel (1968) and other social learning theorists have taken the opposite position; that is, that situations are more important than traits. And therein lies the debate, which has continued for several decades but has diminished in intensity during recent years. Still, it remains a cause célèbre for certain personality theorists and researchers.

Another time-honored issue in personality assessment is concerned with the relative effectiveness of the clinical and statistical approaches (seer versus sign) in the assessment and prediction of behavior. Advocates of the traditional clinical, or impressionistic, approach maintain that a professionally trained clinician is a more sensitive and valid diagnostician and predictor than a statistical formula, an actuarial cookbook, or a digital computer. Summaries of research by Meehl (1954, 1965), however, attest to the superiority of the statistical approach to behavior prediction, if not clinical diagnosis. During recent years, the clinical versus statistical debate has continued but with much less energy and with signs of compromise in both camps (Holt, 1970; Sines, 1970; Meehl, 1973; Korchin & Schuldberg, 1981).

Computer-Based Administration, Scoring, and Interpretation

The advent of microcomputers not only has increased the efficiency of processing and analyzing psychometric information, it has also facilitated the administration, scoring, and even the construction and interpretation of psychological tests and inventories. The spread of computer-assisted testing has, however, led to a number of ethical and technical problems in psychological and educational assessment. The American Psychological Association (1986, 1992) and certain other professional organizations (American Educational Research Association et al., 1985) concerned with testing have recognized the importance of subscribing to a set of ethical standards for psychological assessment in general and computer-based testing in particular. Both psychological practitioners and commercial organizations that market assessment materials are urged to adhere to these standards.

A continuing question with respect to computer-based test administration is whether equivalent results are obtained as with face-to-face and/or paper-and-pencil administration of the same instruments. The jury is still out on the matter, but research on the power of situational factors in determining behavior would seem to point to a need for treating the two administration contexts as nonidentical, therefore necessitating the determination of different norms for paper-and-pencil and computer administration.

OTHER PSYCHOLOGICAL INVENTORIES

The primary purpose of personality inventories such as the Woodworth Personal Data Sheet and the Minnesota Multiphasic Personality Inventory has been to identify and diagnose emotional problems and psychopathological conditions. Because they can be administered on a group basis, inventories are more efficient in screening large numbers of people in employment, military, educational, and other contexts in which individuals are selected for and assigned to certain treatments, jobs, programs, and courses. In a sense, personality inventories and other psychometric measures of affective (nonintellective) variables latched on to the coattails of measures of cognitive abilities, which were developed somewhat earlier and administered more extensively. Today, more measures of personality are commercially available than measures of general intelligence and special aptitudes.

Although the mass administration of tests of cognitive and psychomotor abilities occurred somewhat earlier than that of personality assessment instruments, the appearance of various cognitive and affective measures did not follow a clear-cut historical sequence. Standardized measures of achievement and aptitude have not invariably preceded measures of personality, interests, and other affective variables; rather, there has been an extensive interweaving and simultaneity in the production and distribution of these two types of psychometric instruments.

The first standardized measures of interests—the Strong Vocational Interest Blank for Men and the Kuder Vocational Preference Test—were published during the 1930s, a bit later than the first personality inventories but at the same time as many others. These interest inventories were designed for use principally in vocational and academic counseling, and for the most part they have retained this orientation.

Interest Inventories

The construction procedures, item formats, and scoring of interest inventories are similar to those described for personality inventories. Some inventories, such as those devised by E. K. Strong, Jr. and his successors, employed a multiple-choice, normative format and criterion-keyed scoring. Scoring of the Strong Interest Inventory is proprietary, in that it can be scored only by computer, and that the item weights and scoring procedure are a trade secret. On the other hand, G. F. Kuder employed a rational-theoretical strategy, a forced-choice (triad) item format, and ipsative scoring in devising his interest inventories. It is noteworthy that more recent editions of the Strong Interest Inventory have employed both criterion-keyed scoring and a cluster scoring procedure like that of the Kuder Vocational Preference Inventory.

Responses to the Kuder Vocational Preference Inventory are scored according to rationally determined interest clusters (outdoor, mechanical, clerical, artistic, etc.). In constructing this inventory, items were grouped into interest clusters according to their content. And, as seen in the criterion-keying procedure for scoring the Kuder Occupational Interest Survey (KOIS), Kuder paid tribute to Strong in adopting this method. Responses to the KOIS are scored by comparing them with the responses of employees who persisted in and expressed satisfaction with their occupational choices and with the responses of college students who were majoring in particular subjects. A person's score on an occupational or college-major scale of the KOIS is expressed as a special kind of correlation coefficient, a *lambda coefficient,* between the person's responses to the items and the proportion of people in the particular occupational or college major group who endorsed the item. The score report for the KOIS lists these lambda coefficients, by occupation and college major, separately by sex of the norm group. The occupations or majors corresponding to the highest lambda coefficients are interpreted as those in which the respondent has the greatest interest. The changes in scoring procedures of the Strong and Kuder inventories are another example of the willingness of developers of psychological inventories to apply a variety of construction and scoring strategies.

Attitudes, Values, and Personal Orientations

Unlike personality inventories, which were designed initially to serve clinical purposes, and unlike interest inventories, which were designed for vocational and academic counseling purposes, inventories of attitudes, values, and personal orientations were designed principally for research in social psychology. The construction, scoring, and administration of attitude inventories or scales is discussed at length in Chapter 8 of *Rating Scales and Checklists* (Aiken, 1996b). Rather than being highly polished, standardized, and commercially distributed instruments, most attitude scales are ad hoc devices designed for a particular purpose in a particular situation.

A number of standardized inventories of *values*—the worth or esteem associated with certain things—are commercially available. Examples are the Work Values Inventory (D. E. Super, Riverside Publishing Company) and the Temperament and Values Inventory (C. B. Johansson & P. L. Webber, NCS Assessments). However, these and other standardized measures of values are not administered nearly as widely as the multitude of published inventories of personality and interests.

Clearly related to interests, attitudes, and values are *personal orientations*—generalized personality dispositions, such as gender role, self-actualization, or religious orientation that influence behavior in a variety of situations. *Gender role* refers to the pattern of appearance and behavior that is associated by a society or culture with being male or female. *Self-actualization* refers to a state in which the individual has developed his or her abilities to the fullest, thereby becoming the kind of person he or she would ideally like to be. Several inventories, prominent among which are the Bem Sex-Role Inventory (S. L. Bem, 1974) and the Personal Orientation Inventory (E. L. Shostrum, EdITS) have been designed to assess these two constructs.

Biographical Inventories

One of the most common procedures in applying for a job or for admission to a school or program is filling out an application form. Similar to, but usually more comprehensive than an application form, is a biographical inventory consisting of a variety of items pertaining to the applicant's life history and current situation. The multiple-choice items on these inventories deal with the applicant's personal, medical, educational and employment history, family relationships, friendships, activities, interests, and the like. Responses may be keyed to performance in particular occupations, majors, or other categories of behavior.

An extensive amount of research has been conducted on longer biographical inventories, or biodata blanks, in blue-collar, white-collar, and executive positions of all kinds (see Stokes, Mumford, & Owens, 1994). These inventories have been found to have fairly good validity for predicting performance in a variety of occupational fields and good generalizability from one context to another. For a number of reasons, however, including legal problems associated with asking applicants for certain kinds of personal information (age, sex, religion, marital status, etc.), biographical inventories are not widely used in selection contexts. Applicants may also object to items dealing with such matters as personal finances and family background as being too personal or otherwise offensive.

COMPUTER PROGRAMS FOR CHAPTER 3

Programs 1 through 5 in Category A on the accompanying computer diskette can be used to construct and score psychological inventories as well as questionnaires. If a specific inventory has been planned but not yet prepared, the user should begin with program A1. The constructed inventory can then be printed, duplicated, and administered in paper-and-pencil format or by computer via program A2. If the inventory has already been constructed and one wants to store it for further editing and administration by computer, it can be stored by using program A3 and then administered with program A4. Regardless of how it was constructed and administered, the responses to a completed inventory can be checked for errors using program D1.

In constructing, administering, and scoring rating scales, checklists, and attitude scales, it is recommended that users refer to programs A1 through A7 on the computer diskette accompanying *Rating Scales and Checklists* (Aiken, 1996b). These programs are quite versatile and will facilitate the construction and administration of a wide variety of scales.

A number of illustrative inventories are stored under category I (Illustrative Questionnaires and Inventories) of the program diskette accompanying the present volume. Inventories for measuring the personality constructs of sensation-seeking, altruism, sociability, activity level, emotionality, and personal identity may be administered and scored by programs I5, I6, I7, and I9. Program I8 administers a measure of vocational interests and personality, and indicates their relationships to career choices. Users are cautioned, however, that these programs are illustrative only: The norms and interpretations are very tentative and should be taken with a large grain of salt.

SUMMARY

Three strategies—rational-theoretical, factor-analytic, and criterion-keying—have traditionally been applied to the construction of psychological inventories and rating scales. The rational-theoretical strategy is based on reason or logic and theory. The factor-analytic strategy relies on the statistical procedures of factor analysis, and the criterion-keying approach selects items on the basis of their ability to distinguish between specified criterion groups.

The majority of personality inventories have been developed from a trait-factor orientation, although the construction of certain instruments has relied on phenomenological (self), psychodynamic, and social learning theories. Henry Murray's need/press conception of personality has been particularly influential in guiding the development of personality inventories. Measures of many other psychological constructs (achievement, affiliation, anxiety, depression, hostility, identity, self-concept, etc.) have also been based on theory. The foremost example of a personality inventory designed by a criterion-keying strategy is the Minnesota Multiphasic Personality Inventory.

A combination of rational-theoretical, factor-analytic, and criterion-keying strategies is often employed in devising a personality inventory. In addition, the exploratory approach of Tellengen and Waller and the diagnosticity approach of Lippa and Connelly have recently been applied to the process of inventory development. These two approaches are, respectively, extensions of the rational-theoretical and criterion-keying strategies to inventory development.

In administering a psychological inventory, it is important to have clear, short, but complete instructions concerning the purpose of the inventory; how the items should be answered; and what will be done with the results. Dichotomous (0-1) scoring of items on personality inventories is most common, but other numerical weights may also be applied in combining scores on items and scales. For interpretive purposes, raw scores on the variables or constructs assessed by a personality inventory are converted to norms and other types of transformed scores.

Scores on the majority of psychological inventories are normative, in that a person's score on one variable or trait is unaffected by his or her scores on other variables. However, forced-choice inventories are scored ipsatively, in that variables are played off one another. Consequently, scores on such ipsatively scored inventories cannot be all high or all low.

Response sets and faking detract from the valid assessment of a person's standing on the content variables that an inventory was designed to measure. Special item formats and validation scales can reduce the influence of response sets and faking, but cannot eliminate them entirely.

With regard to the applications of scores on personality assessment instruments, the longstanding issues concerning the relative importance of traits versus situations in determining behavior and the relative accuracy of clinical versus statistical procedures in diagnosis and prediction should be considered. Another important issue is concerned with the comparative effectiveness of traditional and computer-based methods of administering, scoring, and interpreting test results.

Second only to personality inventories in the frequency with which they are administered are vocational interest inventories of the sort devised by E. K. Strong, Jr. and G. F. Kuder. Inventories of attitudes, values, and personality orientations are also widely administered for research and, to some extent, selection purposes, but fewer standardized instruments of these kinds exist than standardized inventories of personality and interests. A final type of psychological inventory on which a great deal of research has been conducted and that has sometimes been used in personnel selection contexts is the biographical inventory.

This chapter ends with a consideration of several programs in categories A and I of the computer-program package accompanying this book. The programs in category A can facilitate the construction, administration, and scoring of psychological inventories of all kinds. The inventories of personality, interests, and values in category I can serve as examples of these kinds of instruments and the variables they are designed to assess.

QUESTIONS AND ACTIVITIES

1. Define each of the following terms used in this chapter in a sentence or two. Consult the Glossary at the back of the book and a dictionary if you need help.

acquiescence	frequency inventory
alpha press	gender role
anxiety	indicator variables
attitude	intensity inventory
attitude inventory	interest inventory
beta press	ipsative scores
biographical (biodata) inventory	lambda coefficient
	need
construct validity	normative scores
content scales	oppositionalism
criterion group	overcautiousness
criterion-keying strategy	personal orientation
diagnosticity approach	personality inventory
exploratory approach	physiogenic needs
extremeness	press
factor-analytic strategy	psychogenic needs

rational-theoretical   social desirability
   strategy   state inventory
response set (style)   trait inventory
scale   validation scales
self-actualization   values

2. Compare and contrast the rational-theoretical, factor-analytic, and criterion-keying approaches to inventory construction.

3. Describe at least three purposes that personality inventories are designed to serve.

4. Distinguish between the stylistic and the conceptual components of a personality inventory.

5. In what sense are inventories of interests, attitudes, values, and personal orientations actually measures of personality?

6. Why is it necessary to include validation scales on personality inventories, and how effective are they in achieving the purposes for which they are designed?

7. Take and score the Sensation Seeking Scale by running program I5, and interpret the T scores corresponding to your raw scores on this inventory.

8. Run programs I6, I7, and I9 and summarize your results.

9. Use program A1 to construct a 10-item true-false inventory of self-concept. Five of the items should be worded in such a way that a true (T) response indicates a positive self-concept and a false (F) response indicates a negative self-concept. The remaining five items should be worded in the reverse direction. An example of a statement of the first kind is: "I believe that I can accomplish almost anything that I try to do." An example of a statement of the second kind is: "At times I have serious doubts about my ability to do what I want to do."

SUGGESTED READING

Burisch, M. (1984). Approaches to personality inventory construction. *American Psychologist, 39,* 214–227.

Burisch, M. (1986). Methods of personality inventory development—a comparative analysis. In A. Angleitner & J. S. Wiggins (Eds.), *Personality assessment via questionnaires* (pp. 109–123). New York: Springer-Verlag.

Finn, S. E., & Butcher, J. N. (1991). Clinical objective personality assessment. In M. Hersen, A. E. Kasdin, & A. S. Bellack (Eds.), *The clinical psychological handbook* (2nd ed., pp. 362–373). New York: Pergamon.

Golden, C. J., Sawicki, R. F., & Franzen, M. D. (1990). Test construction. In G. Goldstein & M. Hersen (Eds.), *Handbook of psychological assessment* (2nd ed., pp. 21–40). New York: Pergamon.

Hansen, J. C. (1990). Interest inventories. In G. Goldstein & M. Hersen (Eds.), *Handbook of psychological assessment* (2nd ed., pp. 173–196). New York: Pergamon.

Keller, L. S., Butcher, J. N., & Slutske, W. S. (1990). Objective personality assessment. In G. Goldstein & M. Hersen (Eds.), *Handbook of psychological assessment* (2nd ed., pp. 345–386). New York: Pergamon.

Ozer, D. J., & Reise, S. P. (1994). Personality assessment. *Annual Review of Psychology, 45,* 357–388.

Wolfe, R. N. (1993). A commonsense approach to personality measurement. In K. H. Craik, R. Hogan, & R. N. Wolfe (Eds.), *Fifty years of personality psychology* (pp. 269–290). New York: Plenum.

4

Samples and Populations

I nformation obtained from administering a questionnaire or a psychological inventory to a particular individual is frequently of interest in itself, that is, without referring to the responses made by other people. Thus, it may be of interest to know that a respondent is married, has three children, graduated from college, has no home mortgage, and runs his own business. It may also be worthwhile to know that he marked the following statements true on a personality inventory:

"I am under a severe mental strain much of the time."

"I have trouble sleeping at night."

Such information is potentially valuable in that it permits the formation of expectations and predictions concerning the person's behavior.

In many instances, however, a person's responses to a questionnaire or inventory become meaningful only when they are compared with those of other people. Interpreting the responses of a single person to most items on a questionnaire or inventory is not an absolute process, but a relative matter of comparing those responses with population averages. Whether a response to a question is interpreted as higher or lower, better or worse than the average depends on how the questions were answered by a sample of people similar to the respondent in significant ways.

In addition to serving as a framework for interpreting the responses of an individual, group data obtained on a large sample of people are useful in describing the group itself and in making predictions concerning the behavior of its members in the aggregate. When a *census* of a population is taken, an attempt is made to count and question every member of that population. A population, however, may be very large, and it is costly to administer a questionnaire or an inventory to everyone in the population. In addition, having to question every member of a specified population severely limits the number of questions that can be asked. For this reason, a population census may yield less information than that obtained by questioning a representative sample of individuals in greater depth. Questioning, or otherwise examining, every person in the population may also destroy or contaminate the elements or persons in that population for any future investigation. Consequently, rather than examining the entire population to which the results will apply, a sample is selected from that population and only the individuals in the sample are examined.

Sample selection is not always a painstaking, highly scientific process. In many exploratory or preliminary scientific investigations, as when conducting a pilot study to provide suggestions, ideas, and guidelines for a more thorough study later on, a relatively small, convenient sample of available persons may do just as well as a more carefully selected sample. This is also true when pretesting a questionnaire or inventory, in which highly accurate estimates of population values are not needed but the researcher seeks only to detect problems of procedure and content that require attention before beginning the main administration.

The method of selecting a sample from a particular target population is also of less concern in theory-based laboratory or field investigations dealing with processes that are presumably common to all individuals. For example, examining or testing certain propositions derived from a behavior theory may not require a sample of subjects identical to a particular population. Because the principles of the theory are presumed to apply to all people, regardless of sex, ethnicity, or social class, almost any group of individuals will do.

In many scientific investigations, the responses of a sample of people who are questioned or otherwise studied can vary appreciably with demographic characteristics such as gender, ethnicity, and social class, and with other individual and group differences. If the results of these investigations are to be generalized to a larger target population, it is essential to obtain a sample that is truly *representative* of that population: The sample must be very similar to the population with respect to variables that are known to be significantly related to responses to the types of items included on the questionnaire or inventory. Selecting a sample that matches the target population on these significant *concomitant variables* is, understandably, difficult, expensive, and not always possible. For this reason, a sample may be selected that matches the population on only a few salient variables. But matching is not the only way; and seldom is it the best way of selecting a sample from a specified target population. Rather, a special random sampling process may be employed to minimize the effects of extraneous variables that might affect the outcome of the survey or study.

PROBABILITY AND NONPROBABILITY SAMPLING

In general, there are two types of sampling procedures—probability and nonprobability sampling. Nonprobability sampling is more convenient, but probability sampling is more accurate in providing estimates of population values *(parameters)*. *Probability sampling* is a procedure in which the probability of any population element or unit being included in the sample is specified. This probability is determined from the *sampling frame*—a list of elements in the population. As the term implies, *nonprobability sampling* consists of selecting a sample by other than probabilistic procedures.

Nonprobability Sampling

The most common type of nonprobability sample is a *convenience sample,* where the criterion of sample selection is the convenience of the researcher; thus the sample is limited to those individuals who are easiest to contact. Convenience samples may be *random,* in the sense that anyone who shows up or is otherwise available may be selected. It may also be *purposive* or based on judgment, in that the available subjects are not selected at random but must possess certain characteristics.

The elements in a purposive sample are selected according to the researcher's interest or judgment with respect to the purpose of the investigation. For example, if the research questions or hypotheses are limited to students, then only students will be included in the sample. If they are limited to corporation presidents, then only men or women in those positions will be selected. Purposive samples are particularly appropriate for descriptive or explanatory purposes in exploratory, pilot, and theory-development studies, and in the pretesting of questionnaires, interviewing procedures, or other instruments and procedures. Purposive sampling can be combined with probability sampling in multistage sampling: The first-stage units (blocks, schools, or other groups) are selected by purposive sampling, and probability sampling is employed in selecting units at the second and subsequent stages.

Whether random or purposive, convenience samples are likely to be biased, that is, not representative of the target population. An error in judgment on the part of the researcher concerning what a particular group of individuals can contribute in supplying answers to the research questions can produce grossly misleading results. Two extreme examples are the *haphazard samples* questioned in the *Literary Digest* poll of 1936 and Shere Hite's *Women in Love* report (Hite, 1976).[1]

Convenience also plays an important role in selecting a sample by the *snowball* procedure, in which the population of interest is either unknown or a list of population members is difficult to obtain. For example, a researcher may be interested in determining the attitudes toward the American judicial system of African-Americans who believe O. J. Simpson is guilty of murder. After identifying and questioning one such person, that person is asked to name another African-American who believes O. J. Simpson is guilty. Then this second person is contacted, questioned, and asked to name another African-American who believes O. J. Simpson is guilty, and so forth, in a kind of snowballing process.

Somewhat more systematic than convenience or snowball sampling is *quota sampling*. A sample is selected that reflects the numerical composition of various subgroups in the population. A quota sample is actually a type of purposive sample in which various population characteristics thought to be related to responses to a questionnaire or to other behaviors of interest are controlled. Control over these extraneous variables is achieved by selecting sample groups in the same proportions, or quotas, as they exist in the population to which the findings are to be generalized.

Depending on the research questions and variables being studied, quota samples are selected on the basis of demographic variables or other relevant characteristics. For example, in a study of attitudes toward capital punishment, it would be important to select proportional or quota samples of males and females, different age groups, different ethnic groups, different socioeconomic groups, individuals living in different geographical areas, and perhaps people of different religions.

Another type of nonprobability sampling consists of *focus groups* of individuals who are questioned and discuss certain products or issues. Rightly or wrongly, the responses of such groups are usually considered typical of the population in which a particular product or service is to be marketed. Focus groups are, of course, not limited to marketing; political,[2] religious, administrative, and even scientific organizations use focus groups to discuss issues, evaluate persons or products, and solve problems. In any event, the bias in the data obtained in a focus group is typically smaller when efforts are made to include individuals who are representative of the various subgroups to which the results of the group's deliberations will be applied.

Probability Sampling

Probability sampling, in which the probability of including any element (member) of a population can be specified, does not guarantee the selection of a random sample but is more likely than nonprobability sampling to yield one. The simplest type of probability sampling is *random sampling,* an equiprobability procedure in which every element in the population has an equal chance of being selected. Samples obtained in this manner are sometimes referred to as *EPSEM* (equal probability of selection method) samples (Kish, 1965).

Simple Random Sampling

In simple random sampling, all elements in the population are first listed and assigned distinct, typically numerical, labels. Then a designated number (n) of elements in the total population (N) is selected by a random procedure, usually by consulting a table of random numbers or running a computer program that generates quasi-random numbers. In theory, the random selection process is "with replacement"; that is, before selecting a new element, the previously selected element is returned to the pool of population elements. Because this process may yield duplicate elements in the sample, in practice sampling is without replacement. This violation of the equiprobability assumption is of little consequence when the sampling fraction (n/N) is fairly small.

Program B1 on the computer diskette accompanying this book generates random samples, with or without replacement. When the number of elements in the sample *(n)* equals the number in the population *(N)*, the result is a random permutation of the *n* numbers. As an illustration, let the population and sample sizes be 100 and 10, respectively. Running program B1 with these values and specifying sampling without replacement produced the following values: 54, 48, 12, 3, 22, 60, 61, 31, 44, 1. These are the numerical labels of the 10 population elements selected for the sample. When the program was run under the "with replacement" condition, the following values were obtained: 72, 95, 70, 29, 45, 88, 75, 88, 74, 11. Note that population element number 88 was selected twice in this case. Duplicate elements do not always occur in random sampling with replacement, but unlike the case in random sampling without replacement, they can occur.

Program B1 provides a set of identification numbers for selecting a random sample, but the data or scores corresponding to these numbers will depend on the particular data file. In contrast, program B2 can be used to select a sequential or random sample of actual scores from a designated data file or bank, print the selected sample, and store it in a second data file. Any number of cases and variables up to the maximum number in the original data file may be selected.

Systematic Sampling

When a list of population elements, such as a telephone or housing directory, is available, a *systematic sampling* of elements from the list provides a convenient form of quasi-random sampling. Assuming that there is no periodicity in the list, that is, no systematic repetition or pattern in the elements with respect to characteristics related to the outcomes of the study, systematic sampling can yield samples similar to those obtained by simple random selection. Selection of a systematic sample by the traditional procedure begins by choosing at random a number between 1 and N/n as the first element, where N is the number in the list as a whole and n the number to be selected. Each of the successive n-1 elements is then obtained by adding n to the previously selected element.

Program B3 on the computer diskette can be used to select a systematic sample by the preceding (traditional) procedure or by an interval procedure devised by the author. The latter procedure consists of grouping the total number of population elements *(N)* into n

intervals and then selecting a value at random within each interval. This method eliminates the effects of any periodicity, in the list. Two samples of size 10 selected from a population of 100 elements by means of program B3 are listed here. The first sample was selected by the traditional systematic procedure and the second sample by the interval procedure:

Traditional Procedure	Interval Procedure
7	6
17	15
27	27
37	40
47	49
57	54
67	67
77	80
87	81
97	96

Note that subsequent runs of program B1 or B3 may yield samples containing quite different elements from those obtained on previous runs.

Random-Digit Dialing

Another combination of purposive and probability sampling is *random-digit dialing.* This method, which is employed in many telephone surveys, consists of dialing random sequences of digits within working telephone exchanges. Typically, only the last four digits from a possible 10,000 four-digit numbers are dialed at random. Both listed and unlisted telephone numbers, the latter being as numerous as 50% of the total, are included. Another problem with random-digit dialing is that both businesses *and* residences are contacted. This can cost a great deal of time and money if the survey is limited to residences. A procedure for increasing the percentage of times that residences are contacted was recommended by Waksberg (1978). It is based on the fact that telephone numbers are assigned in groups, each group being defined by a three-digit area code, an exchange, and two additional numbers. After initially screening the numbers by groups, two-digit numbers (00 to 99) are dialed at random within the groups (e.g., 805–523-81____) within which a residential telephone number has already been found. Once a residence is contacted, some other procedure, depending on the objectives of the survey, must be used to determine whom to question in that household.

Stratified Random Sampling

Combining random sampling with some form of grouping can yield samples that show less variation from each other and from the population than samples selected completely at random. This is more likely to be true when the grouping or stratification variable is related to responses to the questionnaire, inventory, or other criterion instrument. In *stratified random sampling,* the target population is divided into k such groups or strata (e.g., males and females; Asians, blacks, Hispanics, and whites; working class, middle class, and upper class). Then a sample is selected at random from each group, the size of which is proportional to the number of elements in the population falling in that stratum. The population may also be stratified on more than one variable and samples selected at random from the groups defined by the intersections of the several stratified variables. It is recommended that several stratification variables be used, each stratum having two to five categories (Ross & Rust, 1994).

Program B4 on the computer diskette selects stratified random samples. In addition to selecting a proportional sample at random from each stratum, the program randomly assigns the obtained values in each stratum to g groups. If, as in a survey, interest is limited to sample selection,[3] the value of g is set at 1. To illustrate the application of this program, consider the following (finite) population:

	Asian	Black	Hispanic	White
Female	20	30	30	50
Male	10	10	20	40

Each number is the frequency of people in a particular gender/ethnic group *(stratum).* A proportional sample is selected, separately for each sex, at random from the individuals in each ethnic group. Numbering the individuals in each stratum from 1 to n, calculating the total number of individuals in that stratum, and selecting a 10% random sample from the stratum yields the following results:

	Asian	Black	Hispanic	White
Female	8, 9	2, 17, 22	16, 17, 20	2, 15, 23, 33, 37
Male	2	7	15, 18	3, 4, 11, 34

Each of these numbers designates a particular individual in the respective gender/ethnic group. Incidentally, in this case, the four samples in each sex group could also have been selected by running program B1 four times, once for each ethnic group.

Stratified random sampling usually produces samples that are more representative of the population than those selected by other methods, particularly when the variables being investigated are fairly homogeneous within strata. This method of sampling is, however, time-consuming and expensive, especially when there are several stratification variables and each variable has a sizable number of strata. For this reason, stratified random sampling is less common than the following type of sampling in survey research.

Cluster Sampling

More efficient but also more biased than stratified random sampling is *cluster sampling.* In this type of sampling, the population is divided into natural groups, areas, or clusters, and several clusters are selected at random. Then the number of units selected at random from a given cluster is proportional to the total number of units in the cluster. In one type of cluster sampling known as *block* or *area sampling,* a geographical area such as a city is divided into blocks or areas, and a specified number of dwelling units within each block or area is selected at random.

Cluster sampling may occur in several stages: A designated number of clusters is selected at random in stage 1; then subclusters within these clusters are selected at random in stage 2; subclusters within the stage 2 subclusters are selected at random in stage 3; and so on. In order to produce an EPSEM sample, the probability of selecting a particular cluster or subcluster should be proportional to the number of elements or units within that cluster or subcluster.

Program B5 generates multistage cluster samples for one to five stages of sampling. The user specifies the number of clusters (subclusters) to be selected at each stage from each cluster or subcluster selected at the preceding stage. Random samples of the elements in the subclusters selected at the last stage may be selected by using program B1. As a demonstration of program B5, consider the three-stage cluster sampling diagram in Figure 4.1. At stage 1, three out of five school districts are selected. At stage 2, one school is selected from every three schools in each district selected at stage 1. At stage 3, one class is selected from every five classes in each school selected at stage 2. Finally, the survey instrument is administered to a random sample of students in each class proportional in number to the size of that class.

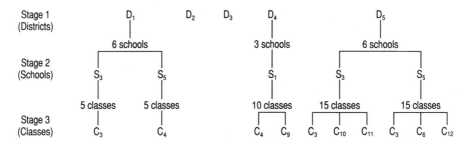

Figure 4.1. Three-stage cluster sampling. See text for explanation.

In the case of a one-stage cluster sample, some adjustment must be made for differences in the number of elements in each cluster. The probability of selecting a cluster should be proportional to the number of elements it contains. A problem also arises when the questionnaire is administered to all individuals in the final subclusters that are selected. Not only does this affect the probability of selecting an individual in a particular cluster, but statistics computed on the responses of people in some clusters will be based on different sample sizes than those in other clusters.

Compensatory Weighting

Depending on the purposes of the research investigation and the method of sample selection, it may be desirable to give more weight to some variables or responses than to other variables or responses. This is the case, for example, when certain groups are oversampled in order to obtain an adequate number of observations from those groups. Before summary statistics are computed, the responses of the individuals in a particular oversampled group should be weighted by a factor obtained by dividing the proportional sample size by the "oversampled" sample size.

It is standard practice to store the numerical responses or scores and the respective values by which they are to be weighted together in a computer data file. Then the scores of individuals in each group can be multiplied by the respective group weight and sample statistics computed. The mean $(\overline{X})$ and variance (s^2) of the total sample may then be computed as $\overline{X} = \Sigma w_j \overline{X}_j / \Sigma w_j$ and $s^2 = \Sigma w_j^2 s_j^2 / \Sigma w_j^2$, respectively, where $\overline{X}_j$ is the mean and s_j^2 is the variance of the jth group.

SAMPLING ERRORS AND CONFIDENCE INTERVALS

Even the most complex sampling design cannot ensure that a sample will be completely representative of the population from which it was selected. Because the elements in the sample do not match the elements in the population with respect to all variables, there is a certain amount of bias or error with which population parameters can be estimated from sample statistics.

Standard Errors

The *standard error* of a statistic is the average amount of deviation of that statistic from the population parameter it is supposed to estimate. Under certain conditions, a numerical value of the standard error of a statistic can be computed. For many statistics computed on large samples ($n > 30$), these conditions are specified by the *central limit theorem*. According to this theorem, if samples of size n are selected at random and independently[4] from an infinite population with a frequency distribution of any shape, as n becomes larger and larger, the shape of the frequency distribution of the means of those samples will approach the normal distribution. In addition, the mean of this *sampling distribution* of means will approach the population mean (μ); and its standard deviation—the *standard error of the mean* ($\sigma_{\bar{x}}$)—will approach the population standard deviation (σ) divided by the square root of the sample size. In symbols:

$$\sigma_{\bar{x}} = \sigma / \sqrt{n}. \tag{4.1}$$

Another measure of average or central tendency in a sample is the median or 50th percentile. The *standard error of the median* is equal to:

$$\sigma_{med} = 1.2533\sigma / \sqrt{n}. \tag{4.2}$$

Because proportions are often computed from the results of administering dichotomous items in questionnaires and psychological inventories, it is useful to have an estimate of how much, on the average, an obtained proportion is in error as an estimate of the corresponding population proportion. When n is large, the *standard error of a proportion* is approximately equal to:

$$\sigma_p = \sqrt{p(1-p)/n}. \tag{4.3}$$

In this formula, p is the population proportion. Because the population proportion is not known in actual practice, it is estimated by the sample proportion.

When sampling is done from a finite population of size N, the standard errors computed from the preceding formulas must be multiplied by $\sqrt{(N-n)/(N-1)}$ Omitting this correction for sampling from a finite population has little effect on the standard error when the sampling fraction (n/N) is small.

The standard errors in formulas 4.1, 4.2, and 4.3 apply only to simple random samples. Standard errors can also be determined for complex sampling plans, but they require more computational labor. For example, the standard error of the overall mean for data obtained from a stratified random sample requires first determining the standard error of the mean of each stratum $(\sigma_{\bar{x}j})$ and then substituting these values and the number of elements in the stratum (n_j) in the formula:

$$\sigma_{\bar{x}} = \sqrt{\Sigma n_j^2 \sigma_{\bar{x}j}^2} / n.$$

(4.4)

where $n = \Sigma n_j$. Formulas and procedures for estimating the standard error of the mean for many other types of sample designs are provided by Cochran (1977) and Binder (1983).

Confidence Intervals for Population Parameters

Knowing the standard error of a statistic such as the arithmetic mean, median, or proportion allows us to determine a range of values within which we can be 90%, 95%, 99%, or any percent certain that the corresponding population parameter falls. For example, given a sample of size n, a mean $\bar{X}$, and assuming that the sample elements were selected at random and independently from a population with a known standard deviation, the following formula can be used to determine the $100p$ confidence interval (C.I.) for the population mean (μ):

$$\text{C.I.} = \bar{X} \pm z\sigma_{\bar{x}}$$

(4.5)

where z is the standard normal deviate below which the proportion $(p+1)/2$ of a normal distribution falls. For example, if the mean of a sample of size 49 is 100, and the estimated standard deviation of the population from which the sample was selected is 10, the 95% confidence interval for the population mean may be computed as $100 \pm$

$1.96(10/\sqrt{49}) = 100 \pm 2.8 = 97.2, 102.8$. Thus, we can be 95% confident that the mean of the population from which this sample was selected falls between 97.2 and 102.8.

Likewise, the following formula can be used to find the confidence interval for a population proportion:[5]

$$p \pm z\sigma_p \qquad (4.6)$$

For example, if 60 out of 100 respondents answer true to a certain question, then we can be 95% certain that the corresponding population proportion falls within $1.96\sqrt{.6(.4)/100} = .096$ units of the value .60, or between .504 and .696.

Program F3 on the computer diskette can be used to compute confidence intervals for population proportions and means. In the case of proportions, however, the program uses the formula in note 1 on page 112 rather than formula 4.6. The user indicates whether the statistics are proportions or means, the desired confidence level, the sample size, whether the population is finite or infinite, and if finite, how large it is. The value of the sample proportion, or the mean and standard deviation, must also be entered. The lower and upper confidence limits for the population proportion or mean are then computed.

SAMPLE SIZE AND NONRESPONSE

As shown in Figures 4.2 and 4.3, the standard errors of a proportion and the arithmetic mean vary inversely with the square root of the sample size. Figure 4.2 also shows that the relationship of the standard error of a proportion to the value of the population proportion is curvilinear: The standard error is a maximum when the population proportion is .5 and decreases on either side of that value. Inspection of Figure 4.3 shows that, although the standard error of the mean varies inversely with both the sample and population sizes, the curves are asymptotic for very large populations. Note that, for a sample size between 10 and 100, whether the population size is 500, 1,000, or 10,000 has little effect on the standard error of the mean. Furthermore, when the population is very large, further increases in the sample size have little effect on the standard error. Although selection of a larger sample improves the accuracy with which the sample mean or proportion estimates the corresponding population

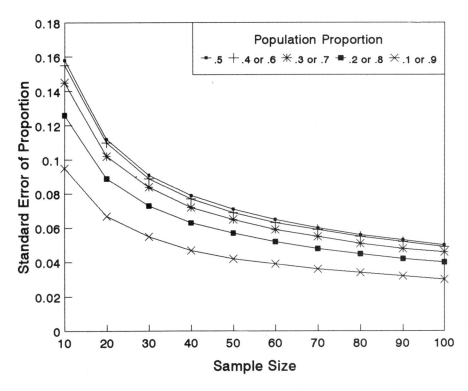

Figure 4.2. Standard error of a proportion as a function of sample size and population proportion.

parameter, the improvement is minimal when the sample is already fairly large.

Required Sample Size

A common question encountered by statistical consultants is "How large should my sample be?" Various percentage figures have been suggested for a reasonable sampling fraction, with 10% perhaps the most common. In national opinion polls, in contrast, 2% and even 1% samples have been found to be adequate when they are carefully selected. Public opinion pollsters are able to draw fairly accurate conclusions regarding the attitudes and actions of the general public from carefully selected samples as small as 1,000 to 2,000 cases.

Rather than permitting a simple straightforward response, the answer to the question of how large a sample should be depends on

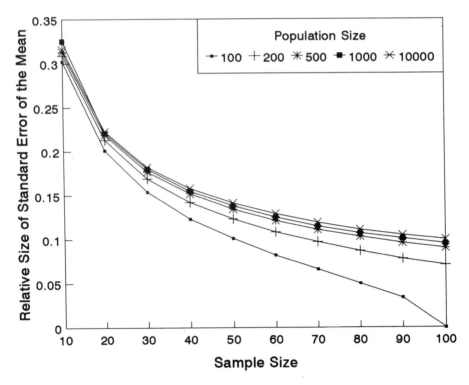

Figure 4.3. Relative magnitude of the standard error of the mean as a function of sample and population sizes.

many factors. In the case of simple random sampling, the required minimum sample size depends on the size of the target population *(N)*; the proportion of the population that would endorse the item *(P)*, or in the case of multipoint items or item composites, the population mean *(μ)* of the variable of interest; the precision or magnitude of the effect to be detected *(d)*; and the z value corresponding to the desired confidence limits with which the population mean is estimated from the sample mean. Because the proportion *(P)* of respondents in the population that would endorse an item is obviously unknown, it is advisable to adopt a conservative strategy of setting *P* equal to .5 in the formula for estimating minimum required sample size *(n)*. Under these conditions, an appropriate formula for *n* is $z^2P(1 - P)/d^2 =$

$$n = (z/2d)^2 \tag{4.7}$$

when sampling from an infinite population, and:

$$n = Nz^2P(1 - P)/[(N - 1)d^2 + z^2P(1 - P)]$$
$$= n = Nz^2/[4d^2(N - 1) + z^2] \tag{4.8}$$

when sampling from a finite population. In these formulas, d is half the difference between the upper and lower limits for the desired percent confidence limits. For example, if a polling organization wants to be 95% sure of predicting the outcome of a political race to within 5%, then, assuming an infinite population, the minimum sample size by formula 4.7 is $n = [1.96/(2(.05)]^2 = 384.16 \approx 385$. If the race is a local one, with an expected voter turnout of 5,000, then formula 4.8 yields:

$$n = 5000(1.96)^2/[4(.05)^2(4999) + 1.96^2] = 356.82 \approx 357.$$

The minimum required sample sizes for the various groups in more complex research designs depend on the nature of the research design, the size of the population, the magnitude of the effect to be detected, and the probability of Type I and Type II errors.[6] It is seldom easy for a researcher to provide anything other than rough approximations to these values, and in any case it is wise to consult an experienced statistician at the sample selection stage of the investigation. Procedures for determining minimum required sample sizes for various types of research designs are described in numerous books and articles (e.g., Wunsch, 1986; Cohen, 1988; Dupont & Plummer, 1990; Hinkle, Oliver, & Hinkle, 1985). Programs C1 through C5 on the computer diskette may be used to compute the minimum required sample sizes for one- and two-sample tests on proportions and means, binomial and sign tests, and randomized groups analysis of variance. Descriptions of these programs are given in Appendix A and on the computer diskette.

Other Sources of Error and Bias

The adequacy of a sample is clearly an important factor in evaluating a research investigation. The sample should be large enough and selected in such a way that the obtained data are representative of the characteristics or behavior of all elements in the target population. Other aspects of a research project are just as important in determining the accuracy of the results, including: (1) the design of the questionnaires, inventories, and other measuring instruments that are administered; (2) the conditions of administration and by whom the measuring instruments are administered and scored; (3) errors made in tabulating and recording the data; (4) the procedures employed in analyzing and interpreting the results. A number of other methodological and substantive factors pertaining to the utility of research investigations are discussed in Chapter 5.

With respect to the selected sample, simply because it is representative of the population of interest is no guarantee that the results of the investigation will apply to that population. For example, there may be significant attrition (or "mortality") in the sample between the time it is selected and when the questionnaires or other instruments are administered. For many reasons, the chosen individuals may respond only in part or decide not to participate. In a study involving a mailed questionnaire, certain people may return the questionnaire with only some of the questions answered, while others may not return it at all. The result is missing data, and consequently, a sample of responses different from what researchers wished to obtain.

Nonresponses and Missing Data

In order to ensure that the sample is representative of the population from which it was selected, a response rate of at least 80% is considered necessary. The recommended rate is usually achievable in the case of interview or telephone surveys. Even with follow-ups, however, the response rate for mailed questionnaires is often substantially lower than 80%. Because the number of nonrespondents may be quite large, the samples are frequently biased in some unknown manner. When a sample is biased, the problem of providing a reasonable estimate of a population proportion or mean is difficult, if not impossible.

A Priori Procedures

Fortunately, the problem of nonresponse is not entirely hopeless. As noted in Chapter 2, certain steps can be taken in planning a survey and designing and administering the questionnaire to improve the response rate. The questions should be fairly short and to the point, and respondents should be given feedback on their answers and other incentives (Powers & Alderman, 1982). Care should be taken in designing the letter of transmittal and in addressing the survey forms to the appropriate persons. Follow-up mailings and reminders, and telephoning or interviewing long-term nonrespondents can also increase the response rate.

A Posteriori Procedures

One a posteriori or post hoc approach to the problem of nonresponse is resampling. *Resampling* consists of obtaining responses from a random sample of the nonrespondents. If the responses of this group are not significantly different from those of the previous responders, then it can be concluded that there is no nonresponse bias (Hartman, Fuqua, & Jenkins, 1985). Thus, we can test the statistical significance of the difference between item endorsement proportions or means in the initially responding and subsequently responding samples. If the difference between the two proportions (or means) is not significant, then we may feel more comfortable in using the data from the initial sample to determine a confidence interval for the proportion of the population that would endorse the item. But if the difference between the endorsement proportions of the initially and subsequently responding samples is statistically significant, we will need to be much more cautious about using the endorsement proportions of the means of either sample to establish confidence limits for the corresponding population parameter. When the sizes of the first and second sample (n_f) and (n_s) are large, the following formula may be used to test the significance of the difference between the proportions of respondents in the first or initial (p_f) and second or resampled (p_s) groups endorsing an item on a questionnaire or inventory:

$$z = (p_f - p_s) / \sqrt{(n_f p_f + n_s p_s) \left[n_f(1-p_f) + n_s(1-p_s) \right] / \left[n_f n_s (n_f + n_s) \right]}. \quad (4.9)$$

A critical value of $z = 1.645$ (.10 level) or 1.96 (.05 level) is recommended when using this formula to test the hypothesis of equal proportions. Option 1 of program C4 on the computer diskette will compute the value of z from formula 4.9 and determine its statistical significance.

It may also be of interest to find the minimum number of nonrespondents in the first wave of a survey who are required to respond on the second wave. Solving formula 4.9 for n_s provides a reasonable estimate of this value. Due to its complexity, however, this formula will not be reproduced here. To compute the minimum size of n_s, select the second option in program C4 on the computer diskette. Then enter the size of the first sample, the proportion in the first sample endorsing the item, the minimum difference to be detected between endorsement proportions in the first and second samples, and the two-tailed probability for a test of the difference between proportions. The two-tailed probability should be set at a fairly liberal value, say .1, and d, the acceptable difference between p_f and p_s, at .05 or .10.

Three other post hoc procedures for dealing with nonrespondents are "hot-decking," reweighting, and modeling the nonresponse mechanism in some manner. *Hot-decking* consists of replacing a missing observation with the value of the last observation having similar known characteristics or with a random selection from all available observations with similar characteristics. Reweighting involves establishing different "weighting classes" and weighting responses according to the relative proportions of responses and nonresponses in those classes.

When an entire record (questionnaire, etc.) is not missing, but only certain scores, statistical procedures such as listwise or pairwise deletion of scores may be employed. In *listwise deletion,* the entire response record of a person who failed to respond to a certain question or for whom there is no score on a certain variable is eliminated from all statistical analyses. In *pairwise deletion,* records containing missing values on certain variables are included in the computation of all statistics except those involving correlations or other measures of relationship on the variables on which the values are missing.

Each of the procedures for dealing with the problem of nonresponding has disadvantages, but some form of imputation—filling in the missing values or "holes" in the data by estimation procedures—is usually preferable. The missing data may be replaced with arithmetic means, estimated values, estimated values plus error, or by hot-decking, multiple imputation, or plausible values imputation (Beaton, 1994). Estimation procedures in which scores on other characteristics or responses of the individual are taken into account in the estimation process provide less biased replacements for the missing values in most cases.

Regardless of whether a sample has been selected at random and whether there are few or many nonrespondents, the minimum and maximum proportions of respondents that would have endorsed the item if the entire population had been sampled, can be computed as:

$$P_{min} = np/N \tag{4.10}$$

and

$$P_{max} = 1 - n(1-p)/N \qquad (4.11)$$

In these formulas, n is the number of respondents, p the proportion of the respondents endorsing the item, and N the population size. Formula 4.10 assumes that none of the nonrespondents would have endorsed the item, and formula 4.11 assumes that all nonrespondents would have endorsed it. Likewise, the minimum and maximum values of the population mean may be computed as $\mu_{min} = X_{min} + n(\overline{X} - X_{min})/N$ and $\mu_{max} = X_{max} + n(\overline{X} - X_{max})/N$, where $\overline{X}$ is the sample mean, and X_{min} and X_{max} are the minimum and maximum values of the variable.

The range of the minimum and maximum values of the population proportion or mean is too wide to be of much practical use, but an approach suggested by Cochran (1977) reduces that range. Applying this approach, it can be shown that lower (P_1') and upper (P_u') bounds for the population proportion (P') endorsing a specific item can be estimated from:

$$P_1' = p_r \{p - z\sqrt{p(1-p)\,(N-n)/[n(Np_r - 1)]}\} \qquad (4.12)$$

and

$$P_u' = p_r \{p + z\sqrt{p(1-p)\,(N-n)/[n(Np_r - 1)]}\} + p_{nr} \qquad (4.13)$$

In these formulas, p_r is the proportion of respondents in the sample, p is the proportion of the respondents who endorse the item, N is the population size, n is the sample size, and p_{nr} is the proportion of nonrespondents in the sample. To illustrate the use of formulas 4.12 and 4.13, let $p_r = .80$, $p = .50$, $n = 200$, $N = 1,000$, and $z = 1.96$; $p_{nr} = 1 - p_r = 1 - .80 = .20$. Then use program F2 on the computer diskette to compute upper and lower confidence limits. Entering the appropriate values and .95 for the confidence level into this program yields $P_1' = .345$ and $P_u' = .655$ as the 95% confidence interval for the proportion in the population who would endorse the item. These are narrower limits than the $P_{min} = .10$ and $P_{max} = .90$ values computed by formulas 4.10 and 4.11 or by program F1, but they are still rather wide.

No statistical procedures for coping with the problem of incomplete or missing data is totally satisfactory. Nevertheless, it is important to extract whatever information one can from the results of administering a questionnaire or inventory that yields less than a 100% return rate or in which many questions are left unanswered. When the response rate to the instrument as a whole is quite low, it is probably best to discard the results, investigate the causes of the low response rate, correct the problem as effectively as possible, and then conduct an entirely new survey.

SUMMARY

The goal of sampling is to obtain a group of individuals or other elements that are representative of the target population. In probability sampling, the probability of selecting an element from the population is determined by constructing a sampling frame. Simple random sampling, systematic sampling, stratified random sampling, and cluster sampling are methods for selecting probability samples. Random-digit dialing is a probabilistic sampling procedure employed in telephone surveys.

Convenience sample, purposive sampling, and quota sampling are methods of selecting nonprobability samples. Nonprobability samples are more likely to be biased or nonrepresentative of the target population than probability samples. However, nonprobability samples are usually satisfactory during the preliminary phases of questionnaire construction and for exploratory research or theory development.

The accuracy with which a sample statistic, such as the arithmetic mean or the proportion endorsing an item, estimates the corresponding population parameter is indicated by the standard error of that statistic. Confidence intervals for population parameters are determined from sample statistics and their standard errors. Although the standard error of a statistic varies inversely with the sample size, further increases in sample size beyond a certain point do not reduce the standard error appreciably.

The minimum required sample size depends on several factors, including the research design, the population size, the magnitude of the effect to be detected, and the probabilities of Type I and Type II errors.

A number of a priori and a posteriori procedures are applicable to the problems of nonresponse and missing data. Careful planning of a survey and the questionnaire, coupled with thorough training of interviewers in telephone and face-to-face surveys, can increase the rate of responding. Follow-up mailings and telephone and house calls also add to the pool of respondents. When missing data cannot be collected, various statistical procedures may be employed to estimate the missing values or to compensate for them.

QUESTIONS AND ACTIVITIES

1. Define each of the following terms used in this chapter in a sentence or two. Consult the Glossary at the back of the book and a dictionary if you need help.

area sampling	parameter
block sampling	probability sample
census	purposive sample
central limit theorem	quota sampling
cluster sample	random sampling
compensatory weighting	random-digit dialing
concomitant variables	representative sample
confidence interval	resampling
convenience sample	sampling distribution
EPSEM sample	sampling error
focus group	sampling frame
haphazard sample	simple random sample
hot-decking	snowball procedure
independent sampling	standard error of a proportion
ipsative approach	standard error of the mean
listwise deletion	standard error of the median
nonprobability sample	stratified random sample
pairwise deletion	systematic sample

2. Use program B1 to select 10 random samples of size 10, with replacement, from a large population consisting of a uniform distribution of the numbers 1 to 10. Construct a frequency distribution of the results (see program D3), and describe its shape. Compute the mean of each of the 10 samples, the mean of the means, and the standard deviation of the means. Compare the mean of the means with the population mean (5.5), and compare the standard deviation of the means with the standard error of the mean (.91). Why aren't the two values identical, as might be expected from the central limit theorem?

3. Use program B2 to select a random sample of 25 observations on three variables (say, variables 1, 12, and 13) from file gss.dat on the computer diskette. There are 33 variables and 300 cases in file gss.dat. Name the output file gss.out. Compare this sample with a sequential sample of 20 cases selected from the same data file.

4. Suppose that you have a list of 5,000 names from which you wish to select a systematic sample with a sampling fraction of 1/100. Use program B3 to select a sample, by both the traditional and the interval procedures.

5. An epidemiologist is interested in mortality as a function of age and gender in the United States. The U.S. Public Health Service supplies her with the following statistical data on the number of deaths in 1995 broken down by age and gender:

Age in Years	Males	Females
Under 1 year	16,465	12,873
1–4	3,614	2,796
5–14	5,217	3,372
15–24	25,494	8,464
25–34	41,686	15,756
35–44	69,961	32,103
45–54	90,419	51,872
55–64	142,373	93,331
65–74	274,685	207,405
75–84	319,726	333,097
85 and over	182,524	378,431
Total	1,172,163	1,139,500

Assume that the investigator can afford to select and study samples of only 100 males and 100 females. Use program B4 to select these two samples, stratified by age.

6. The United States is divided into nine geographical regions, each region consisting of the following numbers of states (including the District of Columbia) listed in parentheses: New England (6), Middle Atlantic (3), East North Central (5), West North Central (7), South Atlantic (9), East South Central (4), West South Central (4), Mountain (8), and Pacific (5). Suppose that a researcher is interested in studying the quality of health

care throughout the United States. Use program B5 to select a two-stage cluster sample with geographical regions as the first stage and states within regions as the second stage. Select five geographical regions at the first stage; for every region selected at the first stage, select one state for every three states in the region. How can you be certain that the result is an EPSEM sample?

7. What is the minimum sample size needed to conduct a z test on a sample selected from a population having 1000 elements and a (hypothesized) proportion of respondents endorsing a specific item of .5? The degree of accuracy of the test should be .05 and the confidence level .90. Use program C1.

8. We need to know the minimum required size of a second sample (second wave) to determine whether the endorsement proportion in the second sample is significantly different from that in the first sample (first wave) of a survey. Assume that there are 200 respondents in the first sample and that 50% of them endorse a specific item. Assume also that we want to detect a difference in endorsement proportions in the first and second samples of no less than .1 at a two-tailed significance level (α) of .05. Use program C4 to determine the minimum required size of the second sample.

9. Use programs F1 and F2 to determine the minimum and maximum values and the lower and upper 95% confidence limits for the proportion of individuals in the population who would endorse a specified dichotomous item. Assume a sample size of 200, a population size of 1,000, a proportion of the sample that responded of .6, and a proportion of the responding sample endorsing the specified item of .5. The proportion of the population that would endorse the item is not known.

SUGGESTED READING

Aiken, L. R. (1988). The problem of nonresponse in survey research. *Journal of Experimental Education, 56,* 116–119.

Fink, A. (1995). *How to sample in surveys.* Thousand Oaks, CA: Sage.

Halt, D. (1994). Missing data and nonresponse in survey research. In T. Husén & T. N. Postlethwaite (Eds.), *The international encyclopedia of education* (2nd ed.) (Vol. 7, pp. 3853–3858). New York: Elsevier.

Henry, G. T. (1990). *Practical sampling*. Newbury Park, CA: Sage.

Kish, L. (1965). *Survey sampling*. New York: Wiley.

Ross, K. N., & Rust, K. (1994). Sampling in survey research. In T. Husén & T. N. Postlethwaite (Eds.), *The international encyclopedia of education* (2nd ed.) (Vol. 9, pp. 5131–5142). New York: Elsevier.

Ross, K, N., & Wilson, M. (1994). Sampling errors in survey research. In T. Husén & T. N. Postlethwaite (Eds.), *The international encyclopedia of education* (2nd ed.) (Vol. 9, pp. 5124–5131. New York: Elsevier.

NOTES

1. Conclusions from the Hite survey, among which were that 70% of women married 5 years or more were having affairs and that 95% of women feel emotionally harassed by the men they love, were based on only a 4.5% response rate from mailings to 100,000 American women. The sample was haphazard and unrepresentative not only because of its size but also because the women who were initially contacted were members of women's organizations. Evidently this didn't matter to Shere Hite, who stated that "It's 4500 people. That's enough for me" or to *Time* magazine, which published a cover story on the findings.

2. Both the Democratic National Committee and the Republican National Committee made extensive use of focus groups in the 1996 election campaigns to obtain information concerning public perceptions of the issues and the candidates.

3. Both random selection and random assignment of the selected individuals to subgroups are used in an analysis of variance randomized blocks design. For example, one may wish to conduct an experiment in which gender is a stratification variable and the subjects in each of the two strata are assigned at random to three treatment conditions. Program B4, with $b = 3$, will accomplish the subject selection and assignment task in this case.

4. In *independent sampling,* the selection of one element has no effect on the selection of any other element in the population. Sampling with replacement is an illustration of independent sampling.

5. More precisely, the confidence interval for a population proportion is computed as:

$$[n/(n+z^2)]\,[p+z^2/2n \pm z\sqrt{p(1-p)/n+z^2/4n^2}\,].$$

6. See Chapter 5 for a discussion of these two types of errors.

5

Statistical Analysis of Questionnaire and Inventory Data

Planning and implementation are critical stages in any research investigation, but they are by no means the only stages. After the questionnaires, inventories, or other instruments have been constructed and administered, one is still faced with the important, and often tedious, task of analyzing the collected data to provide answers or at least information concerning the questions and hypotheses that guided the research.

DECISIONS AND PROBLEMS IN DATA ANALYSIS

It is a poor researcher who waits until the data have been collected to decide how it will be analyzed. Decisions concerning the treatment of research findings and the statistical procedures to be applied should be made, at least in part, during the planning stage of an investigation. This does not mean that these decisions cannot be altered after the results have been obtained and inspected; they can and often are. For example, if the data are terribly skewed, if different groups of subjects have vastly different variances, or if the data have other unexpected features, one may decide to recode or mathematically transform the scores in some way. Other "eleventh-hour" decisions include using a nonparametric instead of a parametric statistical test and combining groups containing small numbers of observations. Whenever possible, however, the research design and the statistical procedures, whether to conduct one- or two-tailed tests, what significance level (α) to use, and the sample size(s) and power associated with the tests should all be considered before the very first datum is collected. Once these decisions have been made, they should not be modified for the sake of convenience alone but only for good and compelling reasons. For example, to change the significance level of a statistical test from .01 to .05 merely because the null hypothesis can be rejected at the latter but not the former level is rather like changing the rules in the middle of a game that one is losing. Not only is it unfair, it also plays havoc with the associated probabilities!

Correlations and Chi Squares

Most research conducted with the types of instruments and procedures discussed in this book is either descriptive or correlational. The researcher is interested in describing the characteristics and behaviors of a group of people and/or in determining the relationships among their responses to the variables that are being assessed by a questionnaire or an inventory. Careful description of the data is interesting and of potential utility in itself. For example, it may be intriguing and valuable to discover that 75% of the U.S. population supports capital punishment under certain conditions or that 70% approve of abortion in specified circumstances.

Correlational analysis may serve exploratory or confirmatory purposes. The fact that two variables are significantly related may confirm or disconfirm a particular hypothesis or suggest another hypothesis or explanation. Relationships between variables may also enable one to make a better than chance prediction of a person's standing on one variable from his or her standing on another variable.

Useful though it may be, correlation is a deceptively simple data analysis procedure. To begin with, variables that are significantly correlated are not necessarily causally related. Knowing that the correlation between variables X and Y is statistically significant may facilitate the prediction of Y from X (or X from Y), but it does not mean that X causes Y or that Y causes X. The X-Y correlation may be due to a spurious third variable that is a cause of both X and Y. To establish cause and effect, it is necessary to conduct an experiment, with X as the independent variable, Y as the dependent variable, and other important extraneous variables controlled.

Another misunderstanding with regard to the method of correlation is that some sort of correlation coefficient must be computed in order for a data analysis procedure to qualify as correlational. Actually, *t* tests, analyses of variance, and many other statistical methods that are often associated with the method of experiment can be used to analyze what is basically correlational data. The use of a particular statistical procedure does not ensure that a research investigation is either correlational or experimental. In order to qualify as an experiment, extraneous and potentially confounding variables must be controlled. Regardless of the statistical procedure that is employed, an investigation is correlational when the independent variable is not manipulated by the researcher and no effort is made—by randomization or matching—to control for extraneous variables. Manipulation of the independent variable(s) is insufficient; control over extraneous variables must be exerted if cause-effect conclusions are to be drawn.

The most popular correlation coefficient, the product-moment coefficient, or **Pearson r,** is derived from the more generalized statistical procedure known as *linear regression analysis.* Therefore, the computation and interpretation of a Pearson *r* is based on the assumption that the predictor (X) and criterion (Y) variables are linearly related. Even when linearity and other assumptions (normality and homoscedasticity of the marginal Y distributions) are met, a second set of data often fails to confirm the significant relationships obtained in the first data set.

Researchers who apply the shotgun approach of computing Pearson r's among dozens or even hundreds of variables merely to see what significant relationships turn up rarely test for linearity (or colinearity) among the variables. But like the well-known principle that all differences are statistically significant when the sample size is large enough, the discovery that 50 out of 1,000 correlation coefficients reached a .05 level of significance is hardly surprising. This is the expected outcome when there are many variables, no specific hypotheses concerning what relationships to expect, a sample size that is not much larger than the number of variables, and a computer that works at the speed of light. Scattergrams are not inspected for nonlinearity, other assumptions are not checked, and the researcher keeps grinding out correlation coefficients or *t* tests until one of them is statistically significant. The result is a messy hodgepodge of uninterpretable statistics that will most likely change substantially on cross-validation or replication of the investigation.

Another statistic that is applied extensively in the analysis of relationships among items or variables in survey research is the *chi square* (χ^2). Researchers often confuse tests of goodness of fit with tests of independence based on the chi-square statistic. They also compute chi squares on small samples, overlook small expected cell frequencies, and violate the principle that scores from the same observational units should not be placed in different cells of a contingency (crosstabs) table.

Scales of Measurement

Considering the multitude of statistical procedures and the ease with which the associated computations are made by high-speed computers, it is no wonder that researchers make mistakes in selecting appropriate data analysis techniques. Not only do many researchers fail to understand the distinction between correlational and experimental research, but they also do not know the difference between independent and dependent groups designs, Type I and Type II errors, or nominal, ordinal, and interval scales of measurement. The discussion in this section is limited to the last distinction—that between scales of measurement; the remaining concepts are considered elsewhere in the chapter.

Although physical scientists may view the counts, checks, and ratings made by behavioral scientists as not being measurement in the true sense of the word, a more liberal interpretation of *measurement* is simply the assignment of numbers to objects or events. According to this interpretation, questionnaires, checklists, rating scales, and psychological inventories are measuring instruments just as, if not as precise as, the meters, scales, and other measuring tools of the physical sciences.

Even in the behavioral sciences, not all instruments yield equally precise measures: Some of them provide more accurate indexes than others of the quantity or quality of behavior and cognition. Checklists or questionnaire items may consist of items on which the simple presence or absence, occurrence or nonoccurrence of something is indicated. Data obtained from checklists and other items on which the possible responses are discrete categories rather than on a continuum represent measurement on a *nominal scale*—the lowest form of measurement. The numbers or other category labels on a nominal scale are simply convenient, frequently arbitrary, designations and cannot be manipulated (added, subtracted, etc.) in the same way as the numbers on other measurement scales. A few statistics—category frequencies, modes, chi squares, and so on—are appropriate with nominal data, but not nearly as many as with data on higher scales of measurement.

As on a nominal scale, data on an *ordinal scale* are not subject to arithmetical operations such as addition, subtraction, multiplication, or division. For example, ordinal numbers indicating order of finishing in a contest of some sort do not indicate how much better the winner was than the person who finished second, third, or fourth. It is correct to say that first was better than second, second was better than third, and third was better than fourth, but not how much better. Rating scales, which are measures of the order of merit or the ranks of objects or events on some attribute are examples of ordinal measurement. A variety of statistics and statistical tests of differences and relationship can be computed on ordinal-scale data. *Nonparametric* procedures, which make no assumptions about the shape of the distribution of measures in the population from which the research sample was drawn, are appropriate with data on an ordinal scale. In fact, some nonparametric techniques are applicable to data on a nominal scale.

Most behavioral science data represent measurement at no higher than an ordinal level, but in some cases the data can be construed as being at an interval level or even a ratio level. The standard scores indicative of performance on various psychological tests and inventories are *interval-level* measures, or perhaps somewhere between an ordinal and an interval level. Like nominal- and ordinal-level measures, the numbers on an interval scale have no true zero. The lowest value on an interval scale is a somewhat arbitrary starting point limited by the "floor" of the measuring instrument. For example, a score of zero on an academic achievement test cannot be interpreted as meaning that the student has no knowledge at all of the subject matter of the test. A more likely interpretation is that the test simply does not have a low enough "floor" to measure the student's ability.[1] If it were possible to construct a test having a true zero, indicating the complete absence of any amount of the attribute of interest, then the test scores would be on a *ratio scale*—the highest level of measurement.

Despite the lack of a true zero, interval-level measures have an advantage over ordinal measures in that equal numerical differences indicate equal differences in the attribute being measured. For example, if the scores on a certain intelligence test are interval-level measures, then the difference in intelligence between a person with a score of 50 and a person with a score of 100 is equal to the difference in intelligence between a person with a score of 100 and a person with a score of 150. Nevertheless, unless these numbers are on a ratio scale, one cannot conclude that a person with a score of 100 is twice as intelligent as a person with a score of 50, or two-thirds as intelligent as a person with a score of 150.

All of the statistical procedures discussed in the remainder of this chapter are appropriate with measures on an interval scale, although many of them can also be used with data on a nominal or ordinal scale. Some of the procedures, namely the parametric ones, are more powerful than others. It is usually wise to apply statistical procedures that are appropriate for the highest level of measurement represented by the data, for these statistics are generally the most powerful in the sense of revealing any significant differences or relationships that exist.

CODING, CHECKING, AND TRANSFORMING DATA

The analysis of responses to questionnaires and inventories begins by reducing the data to some manageable form. Typically, the responses have been precoded in numerical or alphabetical categories to facilitate recording and storing them in a data file or bank. A *coding frame,* or plan for categorizing responses, is often constructed before the data have been collected. Additional codes, however, may be established after the instrument has been administered and the results have been obtained. This is particularly likely when a questionnaire has not been pretested and all possible responses to either open or closed questions have not been anticipated. In addition to designating bona fide responses, codes must be devised for omissions and errors in reporting or recording. Examples of codes for a sample of fixed-alternative items in the General Social Survey are given in Appendix B.

General Social Survey and SPSS/PC+

The General Social Survey (GSS) is conducted yearly by the Roper Foundation for the National Opinion Research Center (NORC) of the University of Chicago. Responses to hundreds of questions concerning the social, psychological, and political attitudes of the respondents, as well as their age, sex, income level, education, ethnicity, marital status, and other demographic characteristics are obtained in the survey. The responses are used extensively by academic researchers, city planners, marketing managers, political campaigns, and in other applied settings.

File gss.dat on the computer diskette accompanying this book contains a random sample of 300 cases from the 2,992 cases in the GSS data bank for 1994. Although responses to 863 variables are stored in the original GSS data bank, only 33 of these variables are included in file gss.dat and described in Appendix B. The data may be accessed via the SPSS/PC+ software package (Norusis, 1992) or by certain programs on the computer diskette for this book.

The SPSS/PC+ data definition statements for file gss.dat are in a system file labeled gss.sys, which is also stored on the computer diskette for this book. Once you are in SPSS/PC+ and you have cleared the menu system by simultaneously pressing the Alt and M keys, type:

```
GET FILE='A:GSS.SYS'.
```

Before pressing the F10 and Enter keys, type any additional data definition or task definition statements that you wish, including the appropriate statistical procedure statement(s). (The procedure statements are described later in this chapter when specific statistical methods are discussed.) The results obtained from running a specific procedure will be recorded in a file named *results* on the diskette (and in file SPSS.LIS on the SPSS directory); the file *results* may be accessed by any text editor. If you wish to print the results at runtime, include the statement:

```
SET PRINTER=ON.
```

as one of the command lines before pressing the F10 and Enter keys.

Data Format

In preparing a data file, some attention must be given to the format in which the data are to be stored. In the case of numeric data, the simplest approach is to leave a blank space between each datum or score.[2] This is what has been done in file gss.dat, each line of which contains the scores of one person on the 33 variables. The data are read, line by line, into a program before proceeding to the next person. File gss.sys reads the data in freefield format, so the user need not be concerned with specifying whether the format is free or fixed. In formatting alphabetic data for storage purposes, the simplest approach is to put each datum on a separate line, followed by a return at the end of each line.

Detecting and Correcting Errors

Because mistakes are common when coding and recording masses of data, it is necessary to conduct several checks on the "cleanliness" of the data before running any statistical procedures. In addition to examining a paper printout of the data, program D1 on the accompanying computer diskette should prove helpful in detecting error in the recorded responses to multipart questionnaires. Program D1 identifies data file errors in two ways: First, the program finds the recorded responses to questions in a particular part that are not among the permissible options for the questions in that part. Second, the entire data bank can be reentered to determine its correspondence with the originally entered data. In both procedures, the user is alerted to each error as it is detected and given an opportunity to correct it. Finally, a table of errors and their specific locations in the data matrix is printed.

The FREQUENCIES procedure of SPSS/PC+ is also useful in error detection. This procedure prints the frequencies in all categories of recorded responses for all requested variables. Consequently, the number of errors and missing values for each variable are listed in the frequency distribution for that variable. Unfortunately, the user must still determine, by some other means, the exact location of an error in the data file, and then correct it.

Recording and Transforming Responses

Because it is easier to perform statistical manipulations on data in numerical than in alphabetic form, when responses to a series of questions are recorded as letters (a, b, c, d, etc.), it is wise to convert them to numbers before proceeding with the data analysis. The recoding or translation can be done using program D2 on the computer diskette or by means of the SPSS/PC+ AUTORECODE command. Program D2 recodes alphabetically-coded responses to numbers, or vice versa, and stores the recoded responses in a designated file. If only the responses to selected variables are to be recoded, program B2 on the diskette can be used to create a reduced data file. When running program B2 for this purpose, make the number of observations or cases in the output file equal to the number of cases in the input data file, and select a sequential rather than a random sampling procedure. Then the output file can be recoded by program D2.

As an illustration of the SPSS/PC+ AUTORECODE procedure, assume that the original data file contains alphabetic responses (a, b, c, d, e) for variables XVAR1, XVAR2, and XVAR3. An appropriate statement for changing these letters to consecutive integers prior to making statistical computations is:

```
AUTORECODE XVAR1 TO XVAR3/INTO YVAR1 to YVAR3.
```

To change numeric data into a form that is appropriate for certain statistical methods, the data may be subjected to a mathematical transformation. For example, depending on the nature of the original (raw) scores, converting them to square roots, arc sines, or logarithms tends to make the between-groups variances more homogeneous (Winer, Brown, & Michels, 1991). Homogeneity of group variances is an important assumption underlying the *t* test for independent groups and the between-groups analysis of variance. A logarithmic transformation also normalizes frequency distributions that are positively skewed.

Program D2 on the computer diskette includes subroutines for transforming a set of scores to square roots, arc sines, or logarithms. SPSS/PC+ makes these same transformations of X to Y by means of the COMPUTE statement. For making a square root transformation:

```
COMPUTE Y = SQRT(X).
```

For transforming X scores to natural logarithms:

```
COMPUTE Y = LN(X).
```

and for transforming X scores to common logarithms:

```
COMPUTE Y = LG10(X).
```

Although SPSS/PC+ has no arc sine function, the original (X) data can be transformed to arc sines by means of the statement:

```
COMPUTE Y = ARTAN(SQRT(X/(1-X))).
```

Winer, Brown, and Michels (1991, pp. 355–357) provide further details on appropriate transformations.

Frequency Distributions

One disadvantage, among many advantages, of the digital computer for data analysis purposes is that it often "distances" the investigator from his or her data. Responses are less likely to be scrutinized ("eye-balled") when they can be efficiently entered on a keyboard and analyzed at incredibly high speeds. Consequently, unanticipated glitches and other problems, and even interesting features of the data, may be overlooked.

A computer can assist in the careful inspection of data if one is willing to take the time prior to computing correlations or conducting statistical tests of hypotheses. One of the first steps in the statistical analysis of data obtained from questionnaires and inventories is to inspect the frequency distributions of responses to the various questions or items. As noted, such an inspection can reveal errors and omissions in responding and scoring. The observed frequencies in the several bona fide response categories of an item can also reveal something about how the item was interpreted and how common certain responses are. For example, Table 5.1 is a printout of results obtained from the following SPSS/PC+ statements:

```
GET FILE='A:GSS.SYS'.
SET PRINTER=ON.
FREQUENCIES VARIABLES = ABANY CAPPUN COURTS.
```

Note that, for some reason, item ABANY was not applicable to 110 of the 300 respondents, and that the yes and no responses to this item were fairly evenly split (94–90). Perhaps the most interesting finding regarding the CAPPUN variable is the large percentage of respondents (74.7%) who favored the death penalty for murder. A related finding on the COURTS variable is the large percentage (82.3%) of respondents who felt that the courts are not harsh enough in dealing with criminals.

Frequency distributions and related statistics, for all or any subset of the variables in a data bank, can also be obtained with program D3 on the computer diskette. Actually, program D3 is easier to use than SPSS/PC+ for this purpose. Unlike the SPSS/PC+ FREQUENCIES procedure, however, program D3 requires that the number of cases and variables in the original data bank, the total number and the identifying numbers of the selected subset of variables, and the numbers and codes of the selected variables be entered at run time.

TABLE 5.1. Frequency Distributions of Three GSS Variables

ABANY   ABORTION IF WOMAN WANTS FOR ANY REASON

Value Label	Value	Frequency	Percent	Valid Percent	Cum Percent
Not applicable	.00	110	36.7	36.7	36.7
Yes	1.00	94	31.3	31.3	68.0
No	2.00	90	30.0	30.0	98.0
Dont know	8.00	6	2.0	2.0	100.0
	Total	300	100.0	100.0	

Valid cases   300   Missing cases   0

CAPPUN   FAVOR OR OPPOSE DEATH PENALTY FOR MURDER

Value Label	Value	Frequency	Percent	Valid Percent	Cum Percent
Favor	1.00	224	74.7	74.7	74.7
Oppose	2.00	57	19.0	19.0	93.7
Dont know	8.00	19	6.3	6.3	100.0
	Total	300	100.0	100.0	

Valid cases   300   Missing cases   0

COURTS   COURTS DEALING WITH CRIMINALS

Value Label	Value	Frequency	Percent	Valid Percent	Cum Percent
Not applicable	.00	3	1.0	1.0	1.0
Too harshly	1.00	10	3.3	3.3	4.3
Not harshly enough	2.00	247	82.3	82.3	86.7
About right	3.00	24	8.0	8.0	94.7
Dont know	8.00	16	5.3	5.3	100.0
	Total	300	100.0	100.0	

DESCRIPTIVE AND INFERENTIAL STATISTICS

Central Tendency and Variability

Both the FREQUENCIES procedure of SPSS/PC+ and program D3 on the computer diskette will compute descriptive statistics such as category percentages and various measures of central tendency and variability. Although these statistics are no substitute for careful examination of the raw data, they provide an overall description of the data. One must be careful, however, not to include the numerical codes for responses such as "Not applicable," "Don't know," "No response," or "Missing datum" in the computations of statistics such as the mean and standard deviation. It is fairly easy to control for this problem with program D3 by selecting for entry only the numerical codes for answer options that are to be included in the computations. For example, only response options 1 and 2 are used for the ABANY and CAP-PUN variables, and only response options 1, 2, and 3 for the COURTS variable in the gss.dat file. With the COURTS variable, however, it makes sense to reverse the values of the "Not harshly enough" and "About right" responses. With all of these things considered, an appropriate set of SPSS/PC+ statements for determining the means, medians, modes, and standard deviations of the ABANY, CAPPUN, and COURTS variables is:

```
GET FILE='A:GSS.SYS'.
SET PRINTER=ON.
RECODE ABANY COURTS (0=8)/COURTS (2=3)(3=2).
MISSING VALUE ABANY CAPPUN COURTS (8).
VALUE LABELS COURTS 1 'Too Harshly' 2 'About Right'
3 'Not Harshly Enough'.
FREQUENCIES VARIABLES=ABANY CAPPUN COURTS
/STATISTICS=MEAN MEDIAN MODE STDEV.
```

The RECODE statement recodes option 0 of ABANY and COURTS as 8 and reverses options 2 and 3 of COURTS. Then 8 is set as the missing value for all three variables so it will not be included in the statistical computations. Note that a new VALUE LABELS statement must be included to reflect the switch in options 2 and 3 of the COURTS variable. In addition to new frequency distributions, the means, medians, modes, and standard deviations variables of the three variables are given in Table 5.2.

Measures of Association

A number of other descriptive statistics can be computed from the data in file gss.dat, among which are other measures of variability (range, semi-interquartile range, variance), measures of skewness and kurtosis, standard scores, and measures of relationship between

TABLE 5.2. Revised Frequency Distributions and Associated Statistics for Three Variables in Table 5.1

ABANY   ABORTION IF WOMAN WANTS FOR ANY REASON

Value Label	Value	Frequency	Percent	Valid Percent	Cum Percent
Yes	1.00	94	31.3	51.1	51.1
No	2.00	90	30.0	48.9	100.0
Dont know	8.00	116	38.7	Missing	
	Total	300	100.0	100.0	

Mean	1.489	Median	1.000	Mode	1.000
Std dev	.501				

Valid cases   184   Missing cases   116

CAPPUN   FAVOR OR OPPOSE DEATH PENALTY FOR MURDER

Value Label	Value	Frequency	Percent	Valid Percent	Cum Percent
Favor	1.00	224	74.7	79.7	79.7
Oppose	2.00	57	19.0	20.3	100.0
Dont know	8.00	19	6.3	Missing	
	Total	300	100.0	100.0	

Mean	1.203	Median	1.000	Mode	1.000
Std dev	.403				

Valid cases   281   Missing cases   19

COURTS   COURTS DEALING WITH CRIMINALS

Value Label	Value	Frequency	Percent	Valid Percent	Cum Percent
Too Harshly	1.00	10	3.3	3.6	3.6
About Right	2.00	24	8.0	8.5	12.1
Not Harshly Enough	3.00	247	82.3	87.9	100.0
	8.00	19	6.3	Missing	
	Total	300	100.0	100.0	

Mean	2.843	Median	3.000	Mode	3.000
Std dev	.452				

Valid cases   281   Missing cases   19

TABLE 5.3   GSS Variables at Three Levels of Measurement[a]

Nominal		Ordinal		Interval	
Variable	Categories	Variable	Categories	Variable	Range
1. ABANY	1-2	11. ATTEND	1-8	2. AGE	18–89
12. CAPPUN	1-2	13. COURTS	1-3	ALIKE[b]	0–16
16. GRASS	1-2	15. GOD	1-6	14. EDUC	6–20
17. GUNLAW	1-2	8. HAPPY	1-3	21. INCOME	1–12
22. LETDIE1	1-2	19. HEALTH	1-4	30. SEI	17.1–97.2
23. MARITAL	1-5	20. HOMOSEX	1-4	32. SIBS	0–25
26. PRAYER	1-3	24. MELTPOT	1-7		
27. RACE	1-3	25. PARTYID	1-6		
28. REGION	1-9	33. TAX	1-3		
29. RELIG	1-5				
31. SEX	1-2				

[a] Variable names from Davis, James Allan and Smith, Tom W.: *General Social Surveys, 1972–1994*. [machine-readable data file]. Principal Investigator, James A. Davis; Director and Co-Principal Investigator, Tom W. Smith. NORC ed. Chicago: National Opinion Research Center, producer, 1994; Storrs, CT: The Roper Center for Public Opinion Research, University of Connecticut, distributor. 1 data file (32,380 logical records) and 1 codebook (1073 pp.)
[b] ALIKE is the sum of variables 3–10 in file gss.dat on the computer diskette.

pairs of variables. The FREQUENCIES procedure of SPSS/PC+ will compute all of these statistics except the measures of relationship. The CROSSTABS, CORRELATIONS, and RANK procedures will compute almost any type of correlation coefficient between two variables. The programs in category E on the computer diskette will also compute a wide assortment of measures of relationship for data on nominal, ordinal, or interval scales. Application and implementation of these programs are discussed in the next section.

The variables in the gss.sys file, the level of measurement, and the number of response categories for each variable are listed in Table 5.3; detailed descriptions are given in Appendix B. The demographic variables in this list are measured on either a nominal or an interval scale, whereas the attitude variables are measured on a nominal or an ordinal level.

Nominal-Level Measures of Association

Three measures of association that are appropriate for the analysis of data on a nominal scale are phi, Cramer's V, and lambda. *Phi,* a chi square-based statistic, is an appropriate measure of the degree of relationship between two variables with two categories each. A second measure of association based on chi square—*Cramer's V*—is appropriate for variables having two or more categories.

Even more clearly interpretable than the results of measures of association based on chi square are those based on the concept of *proportional reduction in error (PRE)*. PRE coefficients reflect the decrease in errors of prediction occurring when an additional (independent) variable is taken into account in making predictions of an individual's standing on a second (dependent) variable. A PRE index of association between two variables measured on a nominal scale is *lambda* (Goodman & Kruskal, 1954).

Either program E1 on the computer diskette or the CROSSTABS procedure of SPSS/PC+ can be used to compute phi, Cramer's V, or lambda. To illustrate the computation and interpretation of these three coefficients by means of the CROSSTABS procedure, consider the following SPSS/PC+ statements:

```
GET FILE='A:GSS.SYS'.
SET PRINTER=ON.
RECODE GUNLAW (0=8)/RELIG (3 thru 9=8).
MISSING VALUE CAPPUN GUNLAW RELIG (8).
CROSSTABS TABLES=SEX BY CAPPUN GUNLAW/CELLS=COUNT ROW
/STATISTICS=PHI.
CROSSTABS TABLES=RACE BY RELIG/CELLS=COUNT ROW
/STATISTICS=LAMBDA.
```

The first CROSSTABS statement yielded a phi and a Cramer's V of .157 between SEX and CAPPUN and .187 between SEX and GUNLAW, both of which, though small, are statistically significant. Inspection of the SEX × CAPPUN and SEX × GUNLAW crosstabs tables reveals that a greater percentage of males than females favored capital punishment, but a greater percentage of females than males favored the gun law. The second CROSSTABS statement yielded a lambda value of .000 with RACE as the dependent variable and .023 with RELIGION as the dependent variable. These values indicate that taking either RACE or RELIGION into account does not appreciably improve the prediction of the other variable.

Ordinal-Level Measures of Association

Four measures of association for ordinal-level data are Spearman's rho, gamma, Somers' d, and Kendall's tau-b. In the first three, the data are collapsed into a two-way contingency table; in Spearman's rho, they are not. *Spearman's rho*—an "ordinalization" of the formula for Pearson's *r*—is the oldest of these coefficients. Gamma is the only PRE measure, in that it gives the proportional reduction in the error of predicting the dependent variable when the independent variable is taken into account. *Somers' d* is preferable to *gamma* when the independent and dependent variables can be clearly differentiated. *Kendall's tau* provides more information than either gamma or Somers' d, but it is limited to square contingency tables.

To illustrate the SPSS/PC+ procedures for computing these coefficients, consider the variables ATTEND, GOD, HAPPY, and SEI in file gss.dat. Including appropriate statements for eliminating the noncomputable options from consideration, we have:

```
GET FILE='A:GSS.SYS'.
SET PRINTER=ON.
RECODE EDUC (6 thru 11=1)(12=2)(13 thru 16=3)
    (17 thru 20=4)
/HEALTH (0=8)(4=3)/INCOME (1 THRU 11=1)(12=2)
    (0,13,98=8).
MISSING VALUE HEALTH INCOME (8).
VALUE LABELS EDUC 1 '6-11 Yr' 2 '12 Yrs' 3
    '13-16 Yr' 4 '17-20 Yr'
/HEALTH 1 'Excellent' 2 'Good' 3 'Fair/Poor'
/INCOME 1 'Low' 2 'High'.
CROSSTABS TABLES=HEALTH BY EDUC INCOME
    /CELLS=COUNT EXPECTED
/STATISTICS=CHISQ GAMMA D.
```

A portion of the printout of results of this program is given in Table 5.4, including three ordinal measures of association, along with values of chi square, one of the most frequently used statistics in the analysis of questionnaire data. As indicated by the two-tailed probability ("significance") values, the Pearson chi squares for both crosstabs tables (HEALTH by EDUC and HEALTH by INCOME) displayed in Table 5.4 are statistically significant. Therefore, without computing any other statistics, we can conclude that HEALTH is significantly related to EDUC and INCOME. The nature of this relationship can be clarified by a comparison of the cell "counts" with their corresponding "expected frequencies." The negative sign on the gamma and Somers' d coefficients is the result of the fact that HEALTH is ranked in the reverse

TABLE 5.4.   Crosstabs Analysis of Health by Education and Income

HEALTH CONDITION OF HEALTH by EDUC HIGHEST YEAR OF SCHOOL COMPLETED

EDUC

Count Exp Val	6-11 yr 1.00	12 yrs 2.00	13-16 yr 3.00	17-20 yr 4.00	Row Total
HEALTH					
1.00 Excellent	4 11.9	19 22.5	27 22.2	13 6.3	63 33.2%
2.00 Good	20 16.7	33 31.5	29 31.0	6 8.8	88 46.3%
3.00 Fair/Poor	12 7.4	16 14.0	11 13.8	0 3.9	39 20.5%
Column Total	36 18.9%	68 35.8%	67 35.3%	19 10.0%	190 100.0%

Pearson Chi Square = 23.37683   DF = 6   Significance = .00068
Gamma = -.42945   Significance = .07839
Somers' D with HEALTH dependent = -.27564   Significance = .05278
Somers' D with EDUC dependent = -.30534   Significance = .05935

HEALTH CONDITION OF HEALTH by INCOME TOTAL FAMILY INCOME

INCOME

Count Exp Val	Low 1.00	High 2.00	Row Total
HEALTH			
1.00 Excellent	14 20.8	42 35.2	56 33.5%
2.00 Good	32 29.7	48 50.3	80 47.9%
3.00 Fair/Poor	16 11.5	15 19.5	31 18.6%
Column Total	62 37.1%	105 62.9%	167 100.0%

Pearson Chi-Square = 6.59783   DF = 2   Significance = .03692
Gamma = -.34298   Significance = .12305
Somers' D with HEALTH dependent = -.21843   Significance = .08205
Somers' D with INCOME dependent = -.16352   Significance = .06143

order of EDUC and INCOME. In any event, respondents who indicated their health as being more positive tended to report having more education and higher incomes.

As an illustration of the computation of Spearman's rho coefficient by means of SPSS/PC+, consider the following statements:

```
GET FILE='A:GSS.SYS'.
SET PRINTER=ON.
RECODE HAPPY (0=8)/INCOME (0,13,98=8).
MISSING VALUE HAPPY INCOME (0).
RANK VARIABLES=HAPPY INCOME SEI/RANK.
CORRELATIONS VARIABLES=HAPPY INCOME SEI/OPTION 5.
```

This program computes Spearman's rho coefficient between HAPPY and INCOME, HAPPY and SEI, and INCOME and SEI, yielding the following values:

HAPPY with INCOME = −.109

HAPPY with SEI = −.218

INCOME with SEI = .336

The last two values, which are statistically significant, point to the (hardly surprising!) fact that both happiness and income are related to socioeconomic status. The negative sign on the correlation between HAPPY and SEI reflects the fact that HAPPY is measured in the opposite direction to SEI.

Interval-Level Measures of Association

The most popular measure of association between two variables measured on an interval or ratio scale is the Pearson product-moment r. In addition to requiring that the variables (X and Y) be measured on an interval scale, it is assumed in computing and interpreting r that: X and Y are linearly related; the underlying population distribution of Y values (marginal distribution) for each X value is normal; and all of the marginal Y distributions have the same variance (homoscedasticity). These assumptions can be verified to some extent by examining the X-Y scatterplots and making certain statistical computations. Because r is a robust statistic, minor violations of the normality and homoscedasticity assumptions are not considered serious, although departures from linearity can lead to misinterpretation of the results.

A number of special-purpose coefficients have been derived from the formula for r, one being the Spearman rho discussed in the previous section. Another coefficient derived from r is the ***point-biserial correlation*** (r_{pb}), which is appropriate when one of the variables is dichotomous and the other is continuous. If it can be assumed that the dichotomy is artificial and has an underlying continuous scale, computation of a ***biserial coefficient*** (r_b) may be appropriate. Unlike the point-biserial coefficient, however, the biserial coefficient is not derived from r. Both r_{pb} and r_b are computed frequently in item analyses involving the determining of the relationships between the dichotomous items on a questionnaire or inventory and performance on an external criterion. A third "biserial" coefficient—the ***rank-biserial*** (r_{rb})— is computed between a dichotomous variable and a ranked variable.

In computing r, the focus is often on determining how efficiently scores on one variable (Y) can be predicted from scores on another variable (X): The larger the value of r, the better the prediction of Y from X. The actual prediction process begins with the determination of a linear regression equation of the form Y'=bX + a, where a and b are constants, X is a person's score on the predictor (independent) variable, and Y' is the person's predicted Y score. A statistic known as the ***standard error of estimate*** can be added to and subtracted from Y' to provide a range of Y values within which one can be fairly confident that the person's actual Y score will fall.

Program E3 on the computer diskette determines r and the associated linear regression equation between two interval-level variables. Program E4 computes the biserial, point-biserial, and rank-biserial coefficients for a set of items on a questionnaire or inventory. The CORRELATIONS procedure of SPSS/PC+ can also compute r, and a scatterplot of the X-Y values can be obtained with the PLOT procedure. Most versatile of all SPSS/PC+ procedures for correlation and regression analysis, however, is REGRESSION.

To illustrate the SPSS/PC+ CORRELATIONS procedure, consider the following statements for finding the correlations among five variables in the gss.sys file:

```
GET FILE='A:GSS.SYS'.
SET PRINTER=ON.
RECODE INCOME (0,13,98=8).
MISSING VALUE INCOME (8).
CORRELATIONS VARIABLES = AGE EDUC INCOME SEI
    SIBS/OPTIONS=5.
```

TABLE 5.5.   Matrix of Correlations Among Five GSS Variables

	AGE	EDUC	INCOME	SEI	SIBS
AGE	1.0000	−.1412	−.0805	−.0585	.0470
	(262)	(262)	(262)	(262)	(262)
	P = .	P = .022	P = .194	P = .345	P = .449
EDUC	−.1412	1.0000	.3709	.6371	−.1449
	(262)	(262)	(262)	(262)	(262)
	P = .022	P = .	P = .000	P = .000	P = .019
INCOME	−.0805	.3709	1.0000	.3541	−.1514
	(262)	(262)	(262)	(262)	(262)
	P = .194	P = .000	P = .	P = .000	P = .014
SEI	−.0585	.6371	.3541	1.0000	−.1126
	(262)	(262)	(262)	(262)	(262)
	P = .345	P = .000	P = .000	P = .	P = .069
SIBS	.0470	−.1449	−.1514	−.1126	1.0000
	(262)	(262)	(262)	(262)	(262)
	P = .449	P = .019	P = .014	P = .069	P = .

The matrix of correlations among the five variables is given in Table 5.5. There are several statistically significant and interesting correlation coefficients in this group, including the negative correlations between AGE and EDUC, between EDUC and SIBS, and between INCOME and SIBS, and the positive correlations between EDUC and INCOME, EDUC and SEI, and INCOME and SEI. A significant correlation between INCOME and SEI is to be expected, because income is involved in determining the socioeconomic index (SEI).

Statistical Inference

If statistical methods were limited to the description of samples, they would be useful but much less so than is actually the case. From a research standpoint, the real value of statistics lies in making inferences or generalizations to populations on the basis of information contained in samples. This process, known as *statistical inference,* consists of two basic approaches: constructing confidence limits for population parameters and conducting tests of hypotheses concerning those parameters. Both approaches involve the application of probability theory and inductive logic to generalize from sample values *(statistics)* to the corresponding values in the population of interest *(parameters).*

Confidence Limits

Constructing confidence limits for a particular population parameter entails determining a range of values within which one can say with a certain degree of probability that the parameter actually falls. We begin by computing the standard error of the statistic—for example, the standard error of the mean—and then multiplying it by an appropriate tabled value of z or t. This product is next added to and subtracted from the sample mean to give a range of values within which it can be concluded with, say, 95% or 99% confidence, that the population mean falls. The construction of the p percent confidence limits for a population parameter is not limited to means; knowing the standard error of the particular statistic and applying a bit of statistical theory, we can find the confidence limits for almost any parameter. In addition to the confidence limits for a single parameter, the limits for the difference between corresponding parameters in two populations can be found.

Program F3 on the computer diskette computes the p-percent confidence limits for a proportion or mean in a single population or he difference between the proportions or means in two populations. The user must enter the sample size(s), the desired confidence level, and the sample proportion or the sample mean(s), and the estimated population standard deviation(s).

Tests of Hypotheses

Conducting tests of hypotheses is a somewhat more complex undertaking than constructing confidence limits, but the two processes are actually two sides of the same coin. In constructing confidence limits for a population parameter, or the difference between two population parameters, one is simultaneously testing multiple hypotheses concerning the parameter(s). For example, if we hypothesize that the population mean is some value, say 100, and the 95% confidence interval for the mean turns out to be 90 to 95, then we can reject the hypothesis at the .05 level in a two-tailed test. In fact, we can reject any hypothesis that the population mean is less than 90 or greater than 95.

On first exposure to the logic of statistical hypothesis testing, it seems a bit convoluted because it is different from how most people think. The logic of statistical inference involves the mathematical method of indirect proof: We assume that what we want to disprove is actually true. Then we try to demonstrate that, if it is true, a highly improbable event has occurred. In terms of statistical nomenclature, we begin by stating a null hypothesis and an alternative hypothesis (one-tailed or two-tailed). The null hypothesis is the "straw man" that we would like to disprove, while the alternative hypothesis is the comple-ment of the null hypothesis, and is what we would actually like to prove. We also need to state the probability (alpha, or α) that we are willing to accept of being wrong if we decide to reject the null hypothesis. Alpha may be a one-tailed or a two-tailed probability, depending on whether the alternative hypothesis is directional or nondirectional (greater than, less than, or greater or less than) some particular value. Another proba-bility that we must have in the back of our minds, even if we don't state it, is beta (β), the probability of being wrong if we decide not to reject the null hypothesis. Beta, and hence the power of our test (Power=$1 - \beta$), can't be controlled directly, but beta decreases and power increases as the size of the sample(s) increase(s). Alpha and beta also vary in oppo-site directions: When alpha increases, beta decreases, and vice versa. In any event, if the obtained probability associated with the statistical test of the null hypothesis is equal to or less than alpha, we conclude that the null hypothesis is false and accept the alternative hypothesis. Unfortu-nately, the outcome is not quite so clear when the obtained probability is greater than alpha. Despite occasional practice to the contrary, it is def-initely not correct to conclude in this case that the null hypothesis is true. Absence of evidence (that the null hypothesis is false) is not evi-dence of absence. When we fail to reject the null hypothesis, we are not justified in drawing any conclusion at all concerning its truth or falsity. We simply have to "sit on the fence" and await the outcome of the next investigation!

Even when the results of a statistical test are highly significant, it is important to bear in mind that *statistical significance is not equivalent to practical significance.* A statistically significant difference should serve as a kind of flag that alerts the researcher to the possibility but not the cer-tainty of practical significance. Factors such as cost, convenience, and the relative effectiveness of the products or procedures under investiga-tion contribute to decisions concerning the practical utility of research findings.

One of the biggest problems faced by a fledgling researcher who employs statistical inference is the decision as to what statistical test to apply: one-sample or two-sample? parametric or nonparametric? one-tailed or two-tailed? Table 5.6 is a "short list" of statistical tests employed by social scientists. Many of the tests in the Nominal and

TABLE 5.6. Statistical Significance Tests at Three Measurement Levels

One Sample		
Binomial	D test	z or t test for single samples

Two Samples					
Nominal Scale		Ordinal Scale		Interval Scale	
Dependent Samples	Independent Samples	Dependent Samples	Independent Samples	Dependent Samples	Independent Samples
Sign test	Fisher exact probability test	Wilcoxon signed-ranks test	Mann-Whitney U test	t test for correlated groups	t test for independent groups
McNemar test significance of changes	Chi square tests				

Multiple Samples					
Nominal Scale		Ordinal Scale		Interval Scale	
Dependent Samples	Independent Samples	Dependent Samples	Independent Samples	Dependent Samples	Independent Samples
Cochran Q test	Chi square test of goodness of fit and independence	Friedman two-way analysis of variance by ranks	Kruskal-Wallis H test	Repeated measures analysis of variance	Randomized groups analysis of variance

Ordinal categories are discussed in Chapter 4 of *Rating Scales and Checklists,* and programs for conducting these tests are provided in category G of the computer diskette accompanying that book. Programs for conducting chi square tests and the *t* tests and analyses of variance listed in the Interval column of Table 5.6 are in category G of this book's computer diskette. In addition to these tests of differences, the measures of association discussed previously in the chapter may all be tested for statistical significance by methods described in elementary statistics books (e.g., Healey, 1996; Pagano, 1994) and incorporated into several computer packages of statistical methods.

Analysis of Variance

Next to chi squares and correlations, ***analysis of variance*** (ANOVA) procedures are the most frequently employed of all statistical methods. Because of their versatility and the fact that cumbersome computations are no hindrance when one has a high-speed digital computer, multifactor, mixed, confounded, and even multivariate designs and analyses using ANOVA logic have become commonplace. It is not the purpose of this book to give a condensed course in statistics or computer programming and applications, although it may occasionally seem so to the reader; nevertheless, we will illustrate an application of one computer package, namely SPSS/PC+, in conducting a simple ANOVA. The following statements are entered, with the results given in Table 5.7.

```
GET FILE='A:GSS.SYS'.
SET PRINTER=ON.
RECODE GOD (0=8)/INCOME (0,13,98=8)
/AGE (18 THRU 33=1)(34 THRU 44=2)
     (45 THRU 58=3)(59 THRU 89=4).
MISSING VALUE GOD INCOME (8).
ONEWAY GOD BY SEX (1,2)/STATISTICS=1.
ONEWAY INCOME BY AGE (1,4)/STATISTICS=1
/RANGES=SCHEFFE.
```

The null hypothesis tested in this one-way, between-groups ANOVA is whether the group means are all equal. A significant F ratio indicates that at least one of the means is different from one of the other means. As shown by the significant F ratio between sex groups in the first panel of Table 5.7, the mean GOD (confidence in the existence of God) score of males (Group 1) is significantly lower than the mean GOD score of females (Group 2). Because only two groups are involved, a multiple-comparisons test between means to determine the source of the significant overall F ratio is unnecessary in this case. From the significant F ratio, we conclude that reported confidence in the existence of God is higher for females than for males.

The overall F ratio in the second analysis (INCOME by AGE) is also statistically significant, so we know that at least one of the four group means is significantly different from one of the others. As shown by the results of the multiple-comparisons (Scheffé) test, the reported mean family income of group 4 (ages 59–89) is significantly lower than the reported mean family income of group 2 (ages 34–44) and group 3 (ages 45–58).

For the first ANOVA analysis—GOD by SEX—we could have used an independent groups *t* test, but the *t* test has gradually been

TABLE 5.7. Results of Two One-Way ANOVAs Performed by SPSS/PC+

| Variable | GOD | RESPONDENT'S CONFIDENCE IN THE EXISTENCE |
| By Variable | SEX | RESPONDENT'S SEX |

Analysis of Variance

Source	D.F.	Sum of Squares	Mean Squares	F Ratio	F Prob.
Between Groups	1	6.1137	6.1137	4.3270	.0394
Within Groups	137	193.5697	1.4129		
Total	138	199.6835			

Group	Count	Mean	Standard Deviation	Standard Error	95 Pct Conf Int for Mean		
Grp 1	54	4.9815	1.2957	.1763	4.6278	To	5.3351
Grp 2	85	5.4118	1.1158	.1210	5.1711	To	5.6524
Total	139	5.2446	1.2029	.1020	5.0429	To	5.4463

| Variable | INCOME | TOTAL FAMILY INCOME |
| By Variable | AGE | AGE OF RESPONDENT |

Analysis of Variance

Source	D.F.	Sum of Squares	Mean Squares	F Ratio	F Prob.
Between Groups	3	105.8799	35.2933	6.0082	.0006
Within Groups	258	1515.5438	5.8742		
Total	261	1621.4237			

Group	Count	Mean	Standard Deviation	Standard Error	95 Pct Conf Int for Mean		
Grp 1	74	10.3514	2.6506	.3081	9.7373	To	10.9654
Grp 2	65	11.0615	2.2904	.2841	10.4940	To	11.6291
Grp 3	66	11.4545	1.6472	.2028	11.0496	To	11.8595
Grp 4	57	9.7544	2.9597	.3920	8.9691	To	10.5397
Total	262	10.6756	2.4925	.1540	10.3724	To	10.9788

Mean	Group	4 1 2 3
9.7544	4	
10.3514	1	
11.0615	2	*
11.4545	3	*

replaced by the two-groups ANOVA. Not only do ANOVA procedures permit the analysis of the main effects of between-groups and within-groups differences, but the effects of simple- and higher-order interactions between two or more independent variables on one (univariate) or multiple (multivariate) dependent variables can be analyzed. Furthermore, statistical control over one or more concomitant variables (covariates) can be exercised in the analysis. Finally, ANOVA procedures are so robust that minor violations of the underlying assumptions—interval- or ratio-level measurement, normality of data distributions, homoscedasticity of population group variances—do not have a pronounced effect on the computed F ratios and the associated probabilities. For this reason, with the exception of chi square, nonparametric procedures (Mann-Whitney U test, Wilcoxon signed-ranks test, Kruskal-Wallis H test, Friedman test, etc.) are employed much less frequently than one might expect in the analysis of responses to questionnaires and inventories.

Multiple Regression Analysis

Just as analysis of variance is a generalization of the *t* test, multiple regression is a generalization of simple linear regression. Instead of predicting a dependent variable from one independent variable, in *multiple regression analysis,* several independent variables are applied in combination to the prediction of the dependent variable. Partial regression weights are assigned to each of the independent (predictor) variables and tested for significance, and a *multiple correlation coefficient (R)* is computed as a measure of the overall efficiency of prediction.

Program E5 on the computer diskette performs a multiple-regression analysis with 2 or 3 independent variables; the correlations among all variables, their means, standard deviations, and the number of cases must be entered. In addition to determining the multiple regression equation, the program tests the weight (beta weight) for each independent variable for significance and determines R and the standard error of estimate. If raw scores or more than three independent variables are to be used, however, another statistical package, such as program REGRESSION of SPSS/PC+, must be used.

To illustrate program REGRESSION, consider the following statements for performing a stepwise multiple regression analysis to predict the GSS variable INCOME from the variables EDUC, RACE, SEX, and SIBS:

```
GET FILE='A:GSS.SYS'.
SET PRINTER=ON.
RECODE INCOME (0,13,98=8).
MISSING VALUE INCOME(8)/RACE(3)/SIBS(99).
REGRESSION VARIABLES=EDUC INCOME RACE SEX SIBS
/DEPENDENT=INCOME
/METHOD=STEPWISE.
```

The stepwise procedure begins by entering into the regression equation the independent variable having the highest correlation with the dependent variable. Each of the remaining independent variables is then entered into the equation, in stepwise fashion, if it makes an additional significant contribution to the prediction of the dependent variable. Only two steps were necessary in this case; EDUC was entered at the first step and SIBS at the second step. The other two independent variables (RACE and SEX) made no further contribution to the prediction of INCOME. The resulting equation for predicting INCOME from EDUC and SIBS is INCOME$'$=.2909 EDUC $-$ .1302 SIBS + 7.3318, and the associated multiple correlation coefficient is R=.408. The algebraic signs on the two statistically significant regression coefficients indicate that educational level is directly related to family income and that number of siblings is inversely related to family income.

SUMMARY

Research data may be collected for description and/or inference purposes. In using statistical methods for descriptive purposes, interest is limited to describing the central tendency, variability, and other characteristics of the data. Statistical inference goes beyond samples to make inferences concerning the characteristics of populations: statistics based on samples are computed to infer population parameters.

Prior to computing any statistics on data obtained from questionnaires and inventories, the data should be coded, transformed and weighted if desired, carefully checked, and stored in a data file. In coding the data and making computations from it, distinctions should be made between bona fide responses to questions, response errors, and data that are missing for various reasons.

The particular inferential procedure employed in the statistical analysis of data depends on the research question and whether the mathematical assumptions underlying the procedure can be met.

Answers to research questions concerning differences between populations are sought by comparing proportions, means, variances, and other relevant statistics computed on samples drawn at random from those populations. Answers to research questions concerning the relationships among population variables are sought by computing correlations or other measures of association between the variables. The choice of inferential statistics procedure depends not only on the research question but also on the nature of the sample data. If the data cannot meet the assumptions of interval-level measurement or of normality and homoscedasticity of group scores, a nonparametric procedure may be more appropriate than a parametric one. Still, parametric procedures are quite robust and not greatly affected by minor violations in the assumptions underlying them.

In general, there are two sides to the statistical inference "coin": constructing confidence limits for population parameters, and conducting tests of hypotheses. Confidence limits for a parameter such as the population mean are determined by: (1) computing the product of the standard error of that statistic and a specified critical value of an appropriate test statistics (e.g., z or t), and (2) adding the resulting value to and subtracting it from the corresponding sample statistic.

In hypothesis testing, null and alternative hypotheses are formulated, and an appropriate test statistic is computed and compared with a critical value of that statistic. The critical value of the statistic will vary with the significance level (α) and whether the alternative hypothesis is directional (one-tailed) or nondirectional (two-tailed).

Computer programs for all the descriptive and inferential statistical procedures described in this chapter are on the accompanying diskette. For large data sets, however, a commercially distributed package of programs such as SPSS/PC+ is recommended for its versatility and efficiency. Examples of SPSS/PC+ statements for computing various statistics are provided in the chapter. The data set on which these computations are based consists of a random sample of 300 cases of 33 variables per case selected from the responses of 2,992 cases to 863 variables in the General Social Survey of 1994.

QUESTIONS AND ACTIVITIES

1. Define each of the following terms used in this chapter in a sentence or two. Consult the Glossary at the back of the book and a dictionary if you need help.

analysis of variance
(ANOVA)
biserial coefficient
central tendency
chi square
coding frame
confidence limits
Cramer's V
gamma
inferential statistics
Kendall's tau
lambda
linear regression analysis
measurement
multiple regression
analysis
multiple correlation
coefficient

nominal scale
nonparametric procedure
ordinal scale
parameter
Pearson r
phi
point-biserial correlation
proportional reduction in
error (PRE)
rank-biserial
ratio scale
Somers' d
Spearman's rho
standard error of estimate
statistic
statistical inference
variability
z test

2. Compare the method of correlation with the method of experiment in terms of (1) their relative advantages and disadvantages in answering research questions, (2) the statistical methods that are most appropriate for each method. See Chapter 1 for further descriptions of these methods.

3. If SPSS/PC+ is available to you, compute the phi, Cramer's V and lambda coefficients between the GRASS and SEX variables and the lambda coefficients between the GRASS and MARITAL variables of the gss.dat file. Appropriate statements are:

```
GET FILE='A:GSS.SYS'.
SET PRINTER=ON.
RECODE GRASS (0=8).
MISSING VALUE GRASS (8).
CROSSTABS TABLES=SEX BY GRASS/STATISTICS=PHI.
CROSSTABS TABLES=MARITAL BY GRASS/STATISTICS=PHI LAMBDA.
```

If SPSS/PC+ is not available, use program B2 on the computer diskette to select a random sample of 50 cases of variables 16 (GRASS), 23 (MARITAL), and 31 (SEX). Then run program E1 on the diskette with these values, computing Cramer's V and lambda for the SEX-GRASS association and lambda for the MARITAL-GRASS association.

4. Find the association between the HEALTH and SEX, PARTYID and ABANY, HOMOSEX and RELIG, and INCOME and TAX variables in the gss.dat file. If SPSS/PC+ is not available, use program B2 on the computer diskette to select a random sample of 50 cases on these eight variables. Then use program E2 to find the values of lambda and Somers' d for each comparison. If SPSS/PC+ is available, the following statements will accomplish this task with the entire data set of 300 cases in file gss.dat:

```
GET FILE='A:GSS.SYS'.
SET PRINTER=ON.
RECODE ABANY HEALTH (0=8)/HOMOSEX (0,5=8)
/INCOME (0,13,98=8) (1 THRU 11=1)(12=2)
/PARTYID (7,9=8)/RELIG (3 thru 9=8)
/TAX (0,4=8).
MISSING VALUE ABANY HEALTH HOMOSEX INCOME
    PARTYID RELIG TAX (8).
CROSSTABS TABLES=ABANY BY PARTYID/HEALTH BY SEX
/HOMOSEX BY RELIG/TAX BY INCOME
/STATISTICS=GAMMA D.
```

Interpret the results.

5. Find the product-moment correlation coefficients between the following variables: ALIKE with EDUC, ALIKE with SEI. ALIKE is the sum of variables 3 to 10 in the gss.dat file; the questions for these eight variables (ALIKE1 to ALIKE8) are similar to those on the Similarities subtest of the Wechsler Adult Intelligence Scale—Revised and a fair measure of abstract thinking ability. If SPSS/PC+ is available, the required correlation coefficients may be obtained by means of the following statements:

```
GET FILE='A:GSS.SYS'.
SET PRINTER=ON.
MISSING VALUE ALIKE1 TO ALIKE8 (8).
COMPUTE ALIKE=ALIKE1+ALIKE2+ALIKE3+ALIKE4
    +ALIKE5+ALIKE6+ALIKE7+ALIKE8.
```

```
CORRELATIONS VARIABLES=ALIKE WITH AGE EDUC SEI
/OPTIONS=5.
```

6. Use program F3 on the computer diskette to find the 95% confidence limits for the population mean if the mean of a single random sample is 110, the sample size is 90, and the estimated population standard deviation is 15. Assume that the population is infinite, and set the value of the population mean under the null hypothesis equal to 100.

7. Use analysis of variance to test the hypothesis that the mean of the ALIKE scores (computed as in exercise 5) of men is equal to the mean ALIKE score of women and that the mean ALIKE score of blacks is equal to the mean ALIKE score of whites. If SPSS/PC+ is available, use the following statements:

```
GET FILE='A:GSS.SYS'.
SET PRINTER=ON.
MISSING VALUE ALIKE1 TO ALIKE8 (8).
COMPUTE ALIKE=ALIKE1+ALIKE2+ALIKE3+ALIKE4
    +ALIKE5+ALIKE6+ALIKE7+ALIKE8.
ONEWAY ALIKE BY SEX (1,2)/STATISTICS=1.
ONEWAY ALIKE BY RACE (1,2)/STATISTICS=1.
```

If SPSS/PC+ is not available, use program B2 on the computer diskette to select a random sample of 50 cases on variables 3 to 10 (ALIKE1 to ALIKE8), 27 (RACE), and 31 (SEX). Then use program G4 to conduct the two analyses of variance. Interpret the results.

8. If SPSS/PC+ is available, add the following statements to the list in exercise 5 and run it again. These statements will conduct an analysis of the regression of the independent variables AGE EDUC, and SEI on the dependent variable ALIKE.

```
REGRESSION VARIABLES=AGE ALIKE EDUC SEI
/DEPENDENT=ALIKE
/METHOD=STEPWISE.
```

If SPSS/PC+ is not available, use the following summary statistics, based on a sample size of 234, and program E5 to find the

multiple regression equation and multiple correlation coefficient for this problem:

Variable	Correlations			Means	Standard Deviations
	ALIKE	AGE	EDUC		
ALIKE				8.7735	3.1041
AGE	−.0488			45.1154	15.6677
EDUC	.3981	−.0010		13.7094	2.7873
SEI	.3175	.0379	.6275	50.0043	20.2820

Interpret the results.

SUGGESTED READING

Aiken, L. R. (1994). Some observations and recommendations concerning research methodology in the behavioral sciences. *Educational and Psychological
Measurement, 54,* 848–860.

Anderson, J., & Rosier, M. J. (1994). Data banks and data archives. In T. Husén &
T. N. Postlethwaite (Eds), *International encyclopedia of education (2nd ed.)* (Vol. 2,
pp. 1377–1381). New York: Elsevier.

Braitman, L. (1991). Confidence intervals assess both clinical and statistical significance. *Annals of Internal Medicine, 114,* 515–517.

Dawson-Saunders, B., & Trapp, R. G. (1990). *Basic and clinical biostatistics.* Engle-
wood Cliffs, NJ: Prentice-Hall.

Fink, A. (1995). *How to analyze survey data.* Thousand Oaks, CA: Sage Publications.

Healey, J. F. (1996). *Statistics: A tool for social research* (4th ed.). Belmont, CA:
Wadsworth.

Keeves, J. P. (1994). Longitudinal research methods. In T. Husén & T. N. Postlethwaite (Eds), *International encyclopedia of education (2nd ed.)* (Vol. 6, pp. 3512–3554).
New York: Elsevier.

Lietz, P., & Keeves, J. P. (1994). Cross-sectional research methods. In T. Husén &
T. N. Postlethwaite (Eds), *International encyclopedia of education (2nd ed.)* (Vol. 2,
pp. 1213–1220). New York: Elsevier.

Miller, D. C. (1991). *Handbook of research design and social measurement.* Newbury
Park, CA: Sage.

NOTES

1. Likewise, a perfect score on an achievement test does not indicate the highest
possible level of achievement in the subject with which the test deals. Not
only may the "floor" of the test be too high, but its "ceiling" may be too low.

2. Be careful with blanks; some statistical programs read blanks as 0s.

3. Program D2 also computes z scores, T scores, and normalized z and T scores.

6

Norms, Reliability, and Validity

Three requirements for a good psychological test or any other measure of human behavior or cognition is that it should be reliable and valid, and that appropriate norms have been obtained to serve as a basis for response interpretation. This chapter discusses these three requirements, particularly with respect to questionnaires and psychological inventories.

STANDARDIZATION AND NORMS

Both questionnaires and inventories are standardized instruments, in the sense that they have standard directions for administration and scoring. Most questionnaires and many psychological inventories, however, are not standardized in the sense of obtaining norms based on a representative sample of the target population for which the instruments were intended. *Norms* are percentile ranks, standard scores, or other transformed scores corresponding to the raw scores on a psychometric instrument. Because the raw scores on most questionnaires, inventories, and tests are interpreted with respect to the frequency distributions of scores on the items and sections (parts) as well as the total scores made by a large sample of people, it is important for the sample to be a representative one.

Norms themselves are not standards; they are simply averages. Rather than interpreting a person's scores with respect to each other—the *ipsative approach,* his or her scores are compared with those obtained by a norm group—the *normative approach.* It is still possible and important to compare a person's scores with each other, but norms are obtained for the purpose of relative interpretation; namely, how does the individual's performance or protocol compare with those of other people who have completed the instrument?

Local and National Norms

In some instances, norms are used to sort and interpret a person's performance with respect to the average performance of people of a given chronological age or in a given school grade in a particular locality. These are referred to as *local* or *regional* norms, and may be used to make selection, placement, or other kinds of decisions in a particular school, school district, or other local or regional administrative unit. Local or regional norms may also be used for making personnel decisions (hiring, firing, promotion, transfer, etc.) in a particular business or industry.

Unlike local norms, which are restricted to a particular locality, *national norms* have presumably been determined on a sample of individuals representative of the entire nation. These are the kinds of norms that are typically published in the technical manuals accompanying standardized tests, inventories, and scales. By referring to the table of norms appropriate for a person's age, sex, grade, geographical region, or other relevant demographic variable, the person's score(s) can be interpreted with respect to those of other members of the same demographic groups throughout the nation.

In addition to being appropriate in terms of age, sex, and other demographic variables for the individuals with whom an instrument is to be used, norms should be fairly current and based on a carefully selected sample. Various methods are employed in selecting a sample on which to standardize a test or any other psychometric instrument, but in most instances some form of probability sampling is most appropriate. *Stratified random sampling,* by which the population is stratified according to relevant demographic variables and a proportional sample is selected from each stratum, is perhaps most common in selecting a norm group.

Age and Grade Norms

If the selected sample is heterogeneous with respect to chronological age and school grade—that is, if it contains sizable numbers of individuals of different chronological ages and in different school grades—then age and grade norms on the variables measured by a instrument may be determined. An *age norm,* or *age equivalent score,* is the median score on the instrument made by individuals of a given chronological age. Age norms are expressed in years and months (e.g., 10–0 to 10–11 for the 10th year). A *grade norm,* or *grade equivalent score,* is the average of the scores on the instrument made by a group of students in a given school grade. Grade norms are expressed in grades and tenths of a grade (e.g., 5–0 to 5–9), the assumption being that there is no growth in the characteristic being measured (e.g., school achievement) during the summer months.

Although age and grade norms are popular, especially with teachers, they have a serious shortcoming: The units in which grade and age norms are expressed are not uniform across the entire range of ages or grades. The same difference between two age-equivalent scores or two grade-equivalent scores represents a greater real difference in achievement during the elementary school years than it does in secondary school. Consequently, how large a gain (or loss) is represented by a given numerical difference in grade or age equivalent scores depends on the grade- or age-level at which the change is observed. In any event, age and grade norms are not usually computed on questionnaires and inventories. Rather, chronological age and school grade are used to group the respondents, and then percentile ranks or standard scores on the variables being assessed by the psychometric instrument are determined separately for each age or grade group.

Percentiles and Percentile Ranks

Perhaps the most popular of all types of norms are *percentile norms.* It might be more precise to call them percentile rank norms, because a percentile is a score and a percentile rank is the percentage of people in the norm group who made that score or lower. Regardless of the range of the raw scores, percentile ranks range from 1 to 100. The median is the 50th percentile—the score below which 50% of the distribution of scores in the standardization sample falls.

The manuals for many psychological inventories contain a table that lists the raw scores and the corresponding percentile ranks for the various scales on the inventory. For example, Table 6.1 is a portion of a set of percentile rank equivalents, listed separately for adult males and adult females, on the Depression and Anxiety Scales of the Basic Personality Inventory (Jackson, 1989). Note that a raw score of 7 on the Depression scale is the 91st percentile for adult males and the 84th percentile for adult females. A raw score of 7 on the Anxiety scale is the 68th percentile for adult males and the 52nd percentile for adult females.

Despite their popularity, percentile norms are not viewed with great favor by specialists in psychological measurement. The problem is that the units in which percentile ranks are expressed vary with the location of the score on the percentile rank scale. Because percentile

TABLE 6.1.   Percentile Ranks Corresponding to Raw Scores on the Depression (Dep) and Anxiety (Anx) Scales of the Basic Personality Inventory*

| | Percentile Rank | | | |
| | Depression | | Anxiety | |
Raw Score	Male	Female	Male	Female
20	99	99	99	99
19	99	99	99	99
18	99	99	99	99
17	99	99	99	99
16	99	99	99	99
15	99	99	99	98
14	99	99	99	97
13	99	99	99	94
12	99	99	97	91
11	99	98	95	86
10	99	97	92	80
9	97	94	86	72
8	95	90	78	63
7	91	84	68	52
6	85	77	56	42
5	76	68	44	32
4	65	47	32	24
3	52	46	21	16
2	39	35	13	11

ranks bunch up in the middle of the scale, the difference between two percentile ranks, in terms of the variable being measured, is less at the middle than at the extremes of the scale. For example, a difference between a percentile rank of 50 and one of 55 (or 45) represents a much smaller difference in the variable being measured than does the difference between percentile ranks of 5 and 10 (or 90 and 95). Consequently, in interpreting the difference between two percentile ranks, we have to keep in mind where these ranks are situated on the percentile rank scale.

Standard Score Norms

Just as the gram and meter are standard units in physical measurement, the z score is a standard unit in statistical measurement. The z score corresponding to a given raw score (X) is computed by subtracting the arithmetic mean $(\overline{X})$ of the raw scores from X and dividing the remainder by the standard deviation (s) of the raw scores:

$$z = (X - \overline{X})/s \qquad (6.1)$$

Thus z scores are standard linear transformations of raw scores, and they allow us to compare scores of the same individuals on variables having different means and standard deviations.

The transformed scores obtained by formula 6.1 have a mean of 0, a standard deviation of 1, and a range of approximately −3 to +3. In order to dispense with decimals and negative numbers, it is common practice to multiply z by 10 and add 50 to the product.

$$T = 10z + 50 \qquad (6.2)$$

The resulting T scores have a mean of 50, a standard deviation of 10, and a range of approximately 20 to 80.

As an illustration of the conversion of raw scores to T scores, Table 6.2 lists the T scores separately for adult males and adult females on the Depression and Anxiety Scales on the Basic Personality Inventory (Jackson, 1989). Note that a raw score of 7 on the Depression scale converts to a T score of 64 for adult males and a T score of 60 for adult females. A raw score of 7 on the Anxiety scale converts to a T score of 55 for adult males and a T score of 51 for adult females.

TABLE 6.2.   Standard (T) Scores Corresponding to Raw
Scores on the Depression (Dep) and Anxiety (Anx) Scales of
the Basic Personality Inventory*

| | Standard (T) Score | | | |
| | Depression | | Anxiety | |
Raw Score	Male	Female	Male	Female
20	107	97	96	85
19	104	94	93	82
18	100	91	89	79
17	97	89	86	77
16	94	86	83	74
15	90	83	80	72
14	87	80	77	69
13	84	77	74	66
12	80	74	71	64
11	77	72	67	61
10	74	69	64	59
9	70	66	61	56
8	67	63	58	53
7	64	60	55	51
6	60	58	52	48
5	57	55	48	46
4	54	52	45	43
3	51	49	42	40
2	47	46	39	38

Normalized and Uniform T Scores

Unlike the unequal units problem of grade equivalents, age equivalents, and percentile ranks, T score units are equal across their entire
range. Therefore, we can say that the difference between a T score of 50
and a T of 55 is equal to the difference between a T of 20 and a T of 25
or between a T of 75 and a T of 80 on whatever variable is being measured. In addition, T scores retain the same shape as the original distribution of raw scores from which they were derived. This is no great
problem unless those distributions vary markedly in shape. When
they do, one possibility is to transform the scores to *normalized standard scores* by determining the percentile rank of each raw score and
then converting the resulting percentages to their corresponding z

scores on the normal curve. The z scores are then multiplied by 10 and 50 is added to the product to give standard normalized T (T_n) scores. T_n scores are not the only units to which normalized z (z_n) scores can be converted; others are stanine scores, sten scores, C scores, and NCE scores. **Stanine scores,** which have a mean of 5 and a standard deviation of 2, range from 1 to 9; sten scores range from 1 to 10, and C scores from 1 to 11. **NCE (normal curve equivalent)** scores, which have a mean of 50 and a standard deviation of 21, range from approximately 0 to 100.

On personality inventories designed to identify and diagnose psychopathology, transforming the frequency distributions of the measured variables to normal distributions is considered inappropriate. Psychopathology is positively skewed rather than normally distributed. An alternative approach is used in determining the T score equivalents for raw scores on the clinical scales of the Minnesota Multiphasic Personality Inventory-II (MMPI-II). To compensate for differences in the skewness of the frequency distributions of scores on the MMPI-II clinical scales, the following procedure was employed. First, the linear T-score value for each of the frequency distributions of the eight clinical scales for males and females (16 distributions in all) was determined by an equivalent percentile method. Then the resulting T scores for the 16 distributions were averaged, and those averages were used to derive regression formulas and look-up tables for the individual scales (Butcher et al., 1989).

Base Rate Scores

Another score conversion procedure takes the base rate of the measured variables into account. The **base rate** for a particular characteristic or behavior is the proportion of individuals in the population who have a particular characteristic or condition. In converting raw scores to **base rate scores,** as was done in standardizing the Millon Clinical Multiaxial Inventory-III (Millon, Millon, & Davis, 1994), raw scores on the various scales were weighted and converted so as to take into account the base rate of a particular characteristic or disorder in the general population. By determining the occurrence of a particular personality disorder or trait in the population, the raw scores were transformed in such a way as to maximize the ratio of the number of correct classifications (valid positives) to the number of incorrect classifications (false positives).

Computer Programs for Norms

Three programs on the computer diskette that can be used to correct raw scores to percentile ranks or standard score equivalents are programs H1, H2, and D2. Program H1 may be used to compute either the normal probability for a given z value or the z value corresponding to a given cumulative normal probability. Program H2, working from a frequency distribution of raw scores on a particular variable, computes the standard z scores, the normalized z scores, and the normalized and nonnormalized T-score equivalents of these scores. Program D2 performs much the same functions as program H2, but works with ungrouped rather than grouped raw scores.

To illustrate the computation of percentile ranks and standard scores by means of program H2, consider the following frequency distribution of 30 scores on a 20-item interest inventory:

Score	Frequency	Score	Frequency
1	1	11	2
2	1	12	2
3	1	13	2
4	1	14	2
5	1	15	1
6	1	16	3
7	1	17	2
8	2	18	1
9	2	19	1
10	2	20	1

Using program H2, we enter 20 for the number of score intervals, 1 for the midpoint of the first interval, and 1 for the interval width. Then we enter the number of scores (frequency) on each interval. The printout is given in Table 6.3. The entries in the Midpoint PR column are the percentile ranks of the corresponding interval midpoints $(1, 2, 3, \ldots, 20)$. The z scores and T scores corresponding to the interval midpoints are listed in columns 4 and 5, and the normalized standard scores (z_n and T_n) in columns 6 and 7.

RELIABILITY

Since the very beginnings of the scientific study of human behavior and its products, it has been obvious that some people are better observers

TABLE 6.3.   Percentile and Standard Score Norms for an Interest
Inventory

Midpoint	Frequency	Midpoint PR	z	T	z_n	T_n
1	1	1.666667	−2	30	−2.13	29
2	1	5	−1.8	32	−1.64	34
3	1	8.333334	−1.61	34	−1.38	36
4	1	11.66667	−1.41	36	−1.19	38
5	1	15	−1.21	38	−1.04	40
6	1	18.33333	−1.02	40	−.9	41
7	1	21.66667	−.82	42	−.78	42
8	2	26.66667	−.63	44	−.62	44
9	2	33.33334	−.43	46	−.43	46
10	2	40	−.23	48	−.25	48
11	2	46.66667	−.04	50	−.08	49
12	2	53.33334	.16	52	.08	51
13	2	60	.35	54	.25	53
14	2	66.66667	.55	55	.43	54
15	1	71.66666	.74	57	.57	56
16	3	78.33334	.94	59	.78	58
17	2	86.66666	1.14	61	1.11	61
18	1	91.66667	1.33	63	1.38	64
19	1	95	1.53	65	1.64	66
20	1	98.33334	1.72	67	2.13	71

and performers than others. Unfortunately, many people are not very accurate in what they observe and do. Whether they are measuring the transit time of a celestial body,[1] rating the productivity of an individual or group, or gauging the effectiveness of a training program or treatment, people make errors in their assessment or measurements. Some people and some measurements contain less error, and hence are said to be more dependable or reliable than others. Not only do errors determine the reliability with which something is measured, but they also affect the utility of those measurements, that is, for what purposes and how effectively they can be used.

It is a maxim of psychological and social measurement that reliability is a necessary but insufficient condition for validity. An implication of this maxim is that measurements can be reliable without being valid, but they cannot be valid without being reliable.[2] Thus, we may measure the lengths and widths of dozens of objects with a 37-inch yardstick today, tomorrow, and next year, and, barring failing eyesight, dipsomania, or a rubber yardstick, obtain very close to the same measurements each time. But these reliable measurements will be wrong because our measuring instrument is faulty; the measurements contain a constant error of 1 inch and thereby are not valid. Constant errors affect validity alone, but variable errors—which produce variable measurements of different objects or events at different times—affect both reliability and validity.

In classical measurement theory, the *reliability coefficient* (r_{11}) is defined as:

$$r_{11} = 1 - s_e^2/s_o^2, \tag{6.3}$$

where s_e^2 is the score variance due to errors of measurement and s_o^2 is the observed (total) variance in whatever is being measured. As error variance increases relative to observed variance, reliability decreases.

Sources of Measurement Error

Low reliability may be caused by instability in either the measuring instrument or the people being measured. The conditions, situation, or environment in which measurement take place can also affect the functioning of the measuring instrument and/or influence the responses of the people who are being assessed. Instability of a psychometric instrument such as a questionnaire or inventory can result from different questions being asked on different occasions. When questions are presented orally, the persons who are asking the questions are also a potential source of instability of measurement, as are the persons who are answering them. For example, an interviewer may speak in a different tone of voice, act less interested, or otherwise behave inconsistently on different occasions. Temperature, humidity, illumination, ventilation, and other conditions in the assessment environment can influence both the questioner and the respondents. Conditions internal to the respondents—hunger, thirst, fatigue, distracting thoughts—can also affect respondents' interest in the questions and their ability and willingness to answer them conscientiously.

The previous sources of measurement error would have no effect on reliability if they influenced all respondents in the same way. Remember, reliability is not affected by constant errors, only by variable errors. However, not all people react in the same way to changes in an instrument or administration procedure, or to different environmental conditions in which the instrument is administered.

Types of Reliability

In general, classical test theory distinguishes between four methods of determining reliability: the method of stability, the method of equivalence, the method of stability and equivalence, and the method of internal consistency. Each method takes into account somewhat different sources of measurement error in estimating reliability.

The *method of stability,* or *test-retest method,* takes into account error variance produced by different times or conditions of administration. This method is an operational expression of O. K. Buros's definition of reliability as "the consistency of relative differentiation." To obtain a *test-retest coefficient,* we administer the instrument to the same people on two different occasions and correlate the two sets of scores. The resulting correlation coefficient is an estimate of the stability of the scores over time. This is a simple, straightforward procedure, but it has a drawback: the practice effect of taking the instrument the first time on taking it a second time. This practice effect would not influence the test-retest coefficient if it benefitted everyone by the same amount. Unfortunately, some people will remember more of the items and their answers from the first administration when they are retested. Because other people remember less, the error is a variable rather than a constant one and consequently reduces the estimated reliability.

The *method of equivalence* involves more work than the method of stability, in that two equivalent (parallel, alternate) forms of the same instrument must be constructed. Each form consists of the same number and kinds of items as on the other form, and it has the same mean, variance, and correlations among items as the other. An estimate of the equivalent forms reliability of a questionnaire or psychological inventory is obtained by administering both forms of the instrument to the same individuals and determining the correlation between their scores on the two forms. When both forms are administered during the same time period, the equivalent forms coefficient takes into account only error variance due to differences in the composition of the two forms. Frequently, however, some time passes before the second form is administered, yielding a coefficient that takes into account error variance due to different items and different conditions of administration. The result is a *coefficient of stability and equivalence.* In order to control for the confounding of time of administration with the form of the instrument that is administered, the usual procedure is to counterbalance forms and times by administering Form A at time 1 and Form B at time 2 to half of the respondents while administering Form B at time 1 and Form A at time 2 to the remaining respondents.

Realizing the laboriousness of developing equivalent forms for psychometric instruments, and as a way of controlling for the practice effect inherent in the test-retest method, pioneer psychologist C. E. Spearman proceeded as follows: Only one test was administered at one time, but everyone who took the test was assigned two scores. The first score was the number of correct responses given by a person to the odd-numbered items, and the second score was the number of correct responses given by the same person to the even-numbered items. These "odds" and "evens" scores were then correlated, and the resulting coefficient (r_{oe}) was "corrected" by the following *Spearman-Brown formula* to estimate the reliability of the total length test:

$$r_{11} = 2r_{oe}/(1 + r_{oe}) \qquad (6.4)$$

Because there are many different ways to divide a test into two halves, and each may provide a somewhat different coefficient, two refinements in this split-half procedure were developed by later psychologists. G. F. Kuder and M. W. Richardson began by expanding Spearman's technique into two formulas that estimate the mean of all the reliability coefficients that could be computed from splitting the test into two halves in all possible ways. These *internal consistency*, or *Kuder-Richardson*, *formulas* are given in most introductory texts on psychological testing (e.g., Aiken, 1997) and will not be reproduced here. Program H3 on the computer diskette will perform the necessary computations for both of these formulas (KR-20 and KR-21).

The Kuder-Richardson formulas can be applied only to instruments consisting of a series of items that are scored dichotomously (0 or 1). However, Cronbach's *coefficient alpha* represents a generalization of these formulas to multipoint items such as rating scales having several response categories. Coefficient alpha is computed as:

$$\alpha = k(1 - \Sigma s_i^2/s_t^2)/(k - 1), \qquad (6.5)$$

where k is the number of items, s_t^2 is the variance of total scores, and Σs_i^2 is the sum of the individual item variances.

Program H4 on the computer diskette and the RELIABILITY procedure of SPSS/PC+ will compute coefficient alpha for subsets of items thought to be fairly homogeneous (i.e., highly intercorrelated

TABLE 6.4. Items on Attitude Toward Abortion Scale from GSS Data File*

1. ABANY: Do you think it should be possible for a pregnant woman to obtain a *legal* abortion if the woman wants it for any reason?
1 = Yes, 2 = No

2. ABDEFECT: Do you think it should be possible for a pregnant woman to obtain a *legal* abortion if there is a strong chance of serious defect in the baby? 1 = Yes, 2 = No.

3. ABHLTH: Do you think it should be possible for a pregnant woman to obtain a *legal* abortion if the woman's own health is seriously endangered by the pregnancy?
1 = Yes, 2 = No

4. ABNOMORE: Do you think it should be possible for a pregnant woman to obtain a *legal* abortion if she is married and does not want any more children?
1 = Yes, 2 = No

5. ABPOOR: Do you think it should be possible for a pregnant woman to obtain a *legal* abortion if the family has a very low income and cannot afford any more children?
1 = Yes, 2 = No

6. ABRAPE: Do you think it should be possible for a pregnant woman to obtain a *legal* abortion if she became pregnant because of rape?
1 = Yes, 2 = No

7. ABSINGLE: Do you think it should be possible for a pregnant woman to obtain a *legal* abortion if she is not married and does not want to marry the man?
1 = Yes, 2 = No

*Reprinted from Davis, James Allan and Smith, Tom W.: *General Social Surveys, 1972–1994.* [machine-readable data file]. Principal Investigator, James A. Davis; Director and Co-Principal Investigator, Tom W. Smith. NORC ed. Chicago: National Opinion Research Center, producer, 1994; Storrs, CT: The Roper Center for Public Opinion Research, University of Connecticut, distributor. 1 data file (32,380 logical records and 1 codebook (1073 pp.)

or internally consistent) on a questionnaire or psychological inventory. As an illustration, let us compute coefficient alpha for the ABANY, ABDEFECT, ABHLTH, ABNOMORE, ABPOOR, ABRAPE, and ABSINGLE item set in the complete GSS data file of 2,962 cases (see Table 6.4). The appropriate SPSS/PC+ procedure statement is:

```
RELIABILITY VARIABLES = ABANY ABDEFECT TO ABSINGLE.
```

The resulting alpha coefficient is .898, a fairly high reliability coefficient. Thus, the Attitude Toward Abortion Scale consisting of these seven items has fairly good internal consistency reliability.

How large should a reliability coefficient be? The answer to this question depends on what the instrument is being used for, that is, the kinds of decisions that are to be made on the basis of scores on the instrument. If interest is limited to differentiating between groups of people, then a coefficient of .70 may be sufficient. But if we want to differentiate between or within individuals, then a coefficient of at least .85 is probably necessary. Of course, a particular instrument does not have a single reliability. As emphasized previously, the reliability of a psychometric instrument may vary with a wide range of personal and situational variables.

Reliability of Nominal- and Ordinal-Level Measures

Applications of the methods of stability, equivalence, and internal consistency are not limited to item composites; they are also applicable to the determination of the reliability of processes and products evaluated in terms on two or more categories. The evaluative categories may be nominal-level dichotomies such as pass/fail, accept/reject, or above average/below average. The categories may also be ranks or ratings on some kind of order-of-merit scale. Both checklists, which are typically scored on a checked/not checked dichotomy, and rating scales, which are scored on an ordered set of several rating categories, are popular psychometric instruments whose reliability must be determined by some method.

One popular procedure for estimating the consistency of responses to single items on questionnaires or inventories is to repeat the item, or present a variant of it, elsewhere on the instrument. Consider the following two items appearing in different sections of the General Social Survey for 1994:

1. ABANY: Do you think it should be possible for a pregnant woman to obtain a *legal* abortion if the woman wants it for any reason? 0 = Not applicable, 1 = Yes, 2 = No, 8 = Don't know, 9 = No answer

2. ABCHOOSE: A pregnant woman should be able to obtain a legal abortion for any reason whatsoever, if she chooses not to have the baby. 0 = Not applicable, 1 = Strongly agree, 2 = Agree, 3 = Neither agree nor disagree, 4 = Disagree, 5 = Strongly disagree, 8 = Can't choose, 9 = No answer

The gamma and Somers' d coefficients for these two items, based on the entire data set of 2,962 cases, are .935 and .869, respectively, (with ABCHOOSE dependent), indicative of a high degree of reliability.

Statistics for evaluating the consistency with which two or more groups of judges or raters evaluate persons, objects, or events include the *intraclass* (interrater, interobserver) *reliability coefficient* and the *coefficient of concordance.* Computer programs for determining these indexes of agreement among the ratings assigned by two or more observers or judges are contained in the diskette (category E) accompanying *Rating Scales and Checklists.* Two other nominal- and ordinal-level coefficients, the author's R (repeatability) and H (homogeneity) *coefficients,* can be computed by program H6 on the computer diskette accompanying the current volume. R is a measure of the stability of ratings assigned by several judges to one person or product, or the ratings assigned by one judge to several people or products. H is a measure of the extent to which one judge assigns the same ratings to several people or products, or several judges assign the same ratings to one person or product.

One of the best indexes for assessing the level of agreement among the evaluations of several observers or judges is the *kappa coefficient* (Cohen, 1968; Fleiss, 1971). This coefficient, in addition to the coefficient of agreement and the associated probabilities for both coefficients, can be computed by program H5 on the computer diskette.

VALIDITY

Validity, the extent to which a psychometric instrument measures what it was designed to measure, is a more important characteristic than reliability. Validity is affected by reliability,[3] but it is not enough for an instrument to be reliable in order to be valid: It must do what it is supposed to, that is, distinguish among people, objects, or events in terms of some characteristic of interest. An instrument designed to measure a particular ability or personality trait is not a valid measure of that trait unless it effectively differentiates among people possessing different amounts of the trait. And if an instrument was designed to predict performance on some criterion of interest, such as academic or job success, then it must do so in a significant way.

Like reliability, validity is not a general characteristic of a questionnaire, a psychological inventory, or any other psychometric instrument. The validity of an instrument varies with the purpose for which it is used; a test or questionnaire, for example, may be valid for one purpose—say, as a measure of reading ability—but not for another purpose—say, as a measure of intelligence. Validity also depends to a degree, and sometimes to a great degree, on the characteristics of the individuals being assessed and the situation or environmental context in which the assessment takes place. Higher-validity coefficients are obtained with more heterogeneous groups in which a wide range of abilities, personalities, attitudes, opinions, or whatever else is being measured exists. With respect to the situational generality of validity, some instruments show an appreciable amount of cross-situational validity while others are more situation-specific in what they measure. In any event, the validity of responses to any questionnaire, inventory, or other psychometric procedure should be verified in every situation in which it is used. This is particularly important, and legally required in many cases, when the responses or scores contribute to selection and placement decisions regarding employees and students. The validity of diagnostic instruments used for classification and treatment assignments and for evaluating the effectiveness of treatment or educational programs must also be substantiated.

Because of the multiple purposes, individuals, and contexts that can affect validity, it is misleading to conclude that an instrument or procedure designed for a particular purpose is "valid" without specifying the characteristic of the group of people who were assessed and the context in which the assessment took place. In addition to varying with persons and situations, validity depends on the method by which the relevant information was obtained. According to tradition, there are three types of validity: content, criterion-related, and construct validity, each of which is discussed in the following subsections.

Content Validity

The most straightforward approach to evaluating the validity of a psychometric instrument is simply to look at it. Determining whether a questionnaire or inventory possesses content validity, however, requires going beyond the *face validity* approach of superficially examining its external features. Establishment of content validity for an instrument requires careful inspection and analysis by experts in the topic with which the instrument is concerned. The experts may begin by comparing the content of the instrument with a detailed outline or table of specifications from which the instrument was developed and with their own judgments as to what kinds of items the instrument should contain and other structural features. The experts may then rate the instrument on various qualities, and the degree of agreement among the various experts may be determined. The author's *V index*, which can be computed and evaluated for its statistical significance by means of program H6 on the computer diskette, may serve this purpose.

Although content validity is of greatest concern with respect to achievement tests, all psychometric devices and procedures should be examined for content validity by several experts. In general, instruments that look like they measure what they were designed to measure actually do so more effectively than instruments whose content provides fewer clues as to what they are trying to measure (Wolfe, 1993).

Criterion-Related Validity

The most pragmatic of all types of validity is *criterion-related validity*, which is widely applied in evaluating instruments designed to assist in personnel decision-making in education, business, and other organizational settings. This type of validity is concerned with the extent to which scores on an assessment instrument are correlated with some criterion of behavior or cognition. The criterion scores may be obtained at the same time as the scores on the assessment instrument, or they may not become available until some time later. In the former case, we speak of *concurrent validity*, and in the latter case of *predictive validity*. In either case, the higher the correlation between the two sets of scores, the greater the criterion-related validity of the assessment instrument.

As an example of the statistical computations involved in determining the criterion-related validity of a psychometric instrument, let the ALIKE variable, created as the sum of variables ALIKE1 through ALIKE8 in file gss.dat, be the predictor variable, and let SEI (socioeconomic index) be the criterion variable. SPSS/PC+ REGRESSION procedure or program E3 on the computer diskette yields a Pearson r of .369 and the following linear regression equation for predicting SEI from ALIKE:

$$SEI' = 2.1593(ALIKE) + 30.0261.$$

Another important statistic obtained from this analysis is the standard error of estimate (s_{est}), which allows us to determine a range of values within which we can be 68%, 90%, 95%, or any percent confident that a given person's actual criterion score will fall. As an illustration, suppose that Joe's ALIKE score is 10. Then his predicted SEI score is SEI' = 2.1593(10) + 30.0261 = 51.62. Although it is very unlikely that Joe's actual SEI will be equal to his predicted score, by subtracting the s_{est} from SEI' and adding s_{est} to SEI', we obtain an interval within which we can be 68% percent confident that Joe's actual SEI will fall. For this problem, $s_{est} = 18.26$, so we are 68% sure that Joe's actual SEI score is between $51.62 - 18.26 = 33.36$ and $51.62 + 18.26 = 69.88$. The broadness of this interval is due to the relatively small correlation coefficient. When r is larger, the interval will be smaller, and the accuracy of prediction will be greater.

Whenever the absolute value of the correlation coefficient is less than 1.00, there will be errors in predicting criterion scores from scores on the predictor variable. These errors are of two kinds: false positives and false negatives. A *false positive error* occurs when the individual's predicted score falls above the cutoff score on the criterion but his or her observed score on the criterion falls below the cutoff. On the other hand, a *false negative error* occurs when the predicted criterion score falls below the cutoff score but the observed criterion score falls above the cutoff. The relative seriousness of these two kinds of errors depends on the monetary, personal, and other costs incurred as a result of the error. In academic selection situations, for example, false negative errors are usually considered more serious than false positive ones. But in selecting people for a highly dangerous job, false positive errors are usually more serious than false negative ones. In any event, the decision as to where to set the cutoff score on the criterion, and consequently on the predictor variable, depends not only on the size and quality of the applicant pool but also on the relative seriousness of false positive and false negative errors.

Construct Validity

The most general, and the most abstract, type of validity is *construct validity*. The variables in which researchers conceptualize the subject matter of their investigations are referred to as *constructs*. Anxiety is a construct, hostility is a construct, and so are repression, reinforcement, stress and frustration. These are the kinds of variables that psychologists and other social scientists measure and theorize about in their efforts to predict and explain behavior and cognition. Constructs are not objects or "things"; they are abstractions based on observations that hopefully assist in efforts to understand the causes and consequences of human actions.

As variables, constructs must be measured. Innumerable tests, inventories, questionnaires, scales, and checklists have been designed to measure abilities, personality traits, interests, attitudes, and other psychological constructs. The extent to which a particular instrument is an effective measure of the construct it was designed to measure is determined from various kinds of supporting evidence.

The construct validity of a psychometric instrument is not established by a single demonstration or investigation. Rather, it involves a series of interlocking studies: detailed analyses of the content of the instrument; predictions made from scores on the instrument; correlations between these scores and other measures; and studies of the relationships of scores on the instrument to the results of experimental or nonexperimental procedures for demonstrating the influence of the construct.

As an illustration of how some evidence of the construct validity of a psychometric instrument might be obtained, consider the matrix of correlations in Table 6.5. If we conceptualize the eight-item ALIKE scale as a measure of logical or abstract thinking—the ability to categorize and generalize—we would expect scores on the ALIKE scale to be positively correlated with education, income, and socioeconomic status. Generalizing from the research literature on general intelligence (see Aiken, 1996a), we might also expect the ALIKE variable to be correlated with health, race, and number of siblings. All of these

TABLE 6.5.   Correlations among Selected Variables from GSS Data File

	ALIKE	EDUC	HAPPY	HEALTH	INCOME	RACE	SEI	SEX
EDUC	.4882**							
HAPPY	−.0855	−.2652**						
HEALTH	−.2300*	−.3210**	.3423**					
INCOME	.2540*	.4127**	−.0750	−.2238*				
RACE	−.2448*	−.2275*	.1724	.0945	−.0710			
SEI	.3914**	.6090**	−.1574	−.3801**	.3676**	−.1800		
SEX	.0720	−.0195	.0260	−.0566	−.1467	−.0177	−.1373	
SIBS	−.2599**	−.2323*	.0634	.0447	−.2182*	.3929**	−.1835	−.0143

N of cases: 159   2-tailed Signif: *−.01   **−.001

relationships are significant in this case, providing support for the construct validity of the ALIKE scale.

Factor Analysis

As indicated, various methods and procedures can provide evidence for the construct validity of a psychometric instrument. For example, factor analysis, a mathematical procedure for analyzing the relationships among a set of items or variables to determine which factors or constructs account for the relationships is an important tool in construct validation. The end result of a factor analysis of scores on m variables is a set of loadings (correlations) of the variables on each of the factors extracted by the procedure. By way of illustration, let us conduct a principal axis factor analysis and an associated varimax rotation of the extracted factor matrix of the responses of the entire GSS sample to the seven items in Table 6.4. The loadings of these variables on the two extracted factors are given in Table 6.6. These two factors account for over 80% of the variance in the scores on the seven variables.

To interpret the rotated factor matrix in Table 6.6, we begin by identifying those variables with high loadings (greater than .50) on a factor. Variables ABANY, ABNOMORE, ABPOOR, and ABSINGLE have high loadings on factor 1, while ABDEFECT, ABHLTH, and ABRAPE have high loadings on factor 2. Referring to the descriptions in Table 6.4 of the seven variables, we see that the four variables having high loadings on factor 1 involve nonmedical or nontraumatic reasons, whereas the three variables having high loadings on factor 2 involve medical or traumatic reasons. Therefore, the construct measured by items 1, 4, 5, and 7 may be labeled Nontraumatic Reasons

TABLE 6.6. Rotated Factor Matrix for Seven Abortion Items

Item (Variable)	Factor 1	Factor 2
ABANY	.90004	.20859
ABDEFECT	.28142	.82166
ABHLTH	.11874	.87146
ABNOMORE	.89823	.23640
ABPOOR	.88661	.25674
ABRAPE	.28216	.80809
ABSINGLE	.90344	.23362

and the construct measured by items 2, 3, and 6 may be labeled Traumatic Reasons for abortion.

SUMMARY

A questionnaire or inventory is standardized by administering it to a representative sample of the target population for the purpose of deriving norms to serve as a basis for interpreting scores on the instrument. The standardization sample is typically selected by a probabilistic procedure, most notably, stratified random sampling. Age norms and grade norms are rarely used with questionnaires and inventories; percentile and standard score norms are much more common. All standard scores are derivatives of z scores, which are obtained by subtracting the mean from each raw score and dividing the remainder by the standard deviation. T-score norms, obtained by multiplying z scores by 10 and adding 50 to the products, are the most popular. Other types of standard scores are normalized z and T scores, stanine scores, sten scores, C scores, and NCE scores. Uniform T scores and base-rate scores are also used in scoring and interpreting certain psychological inventories.

The reliability of a psychometric instrument refers to the extent to which scores on the instrument are free from errors of measurement. A reliable instrument consistently differentiates between people in terms of the variables it purportedly measures. Reliability is affected by the characteristics of the measuring instrument, the conditions of measurement, and the individuals being measured. An instrument must be reliable in order to be valid, but it is not necessarily valid because it is reliable.

Four methods for evaluating reliability were discussed in this chapter: stability, equivalence, stability and equivalence, and internal consistency. A stability coefficient is obtained by a test-retest procedure, an equivalence coefficient by administering parallel forms of an instrument, and a stability and equivalence coefficient by administering parallel forms on two different occasions. An internal consistency coefficient may be obtained by the split-half procedure or by the application of the Kuder-Richardson formulas (for dichotomously scored items) and coefficient alpha (for multipoint items). Methods for determining the reliability of ratings (interrater reliability, coefficient of concordance, kappa coefficient) and for evaluating the reliability of single items on a questionnaire or inventory were also discussed. Procedures for computing reliability coefficients with the programs on the diskette accompanying this book and the SPSS/PC+ software were described.

Validity, the extent to which an instrument measures what it was designed to measure, varies not only with the composition of the instrument but also with the individuals being assessed and the situation or context in which the assessment takes place. Traditionally, three types of validity, or rather, three methods of obtaining validity information, have been employed. The first of these is content validity, consisting of a detailed analysis of the content of the instrument by reference to a comprehensive outline or table of specifications. A second type, criterion-related validity, is concerned with the extent to which scores on an instrument predict scores on a criterion measure obtained at the same time as scores on the predictor variable (concurrent validity) or some time later (predictive validity). The statistics of criterion-related validity include correlations, linear regression equations, and standard errors of estimate. Scores on a criterion variable cannot be predicted precisely from scores on a predictor variable, but the degree of error in prediction can be estimated and a confidence interval within which the obtained criterion scores are expected to fall can be constructed. When the predicted criterion score is higher and the obtained criterion score lower than the cutoff score, a false positive error has occurred; when the predicted criterion score is lower and the obtained criterion score higher than the cutoff score, a false negative error has occurred. The relative seriousness of these two kinds of errors depends on the nature of the situation in which the predictions are made.

The most complex type of validity is construct validity, which is concerned with evidence indicating that the instrument is a measure of the construct it is supposed to measure. Evidence from a variety of sources—observational, correlational, experimental, and others—is brought to bear in establishing the construct validity of a psychometric instrument. Correlations between scores on the instrument and other measures of the same construct, and factor analyses of scores on the items and item subsets of which the instrument is composed, are especially important in this regard.

QUESTIONS AND ACTIVITIES

1. Define each of the following terms used in this chapter in a sentence or two. Consult the Glossary at the back of the book and a dictionary if you need help.

age equivalent score
age norm
base rate
base rate scores
coefficient alpha
coefficient of concordance
coefficient of stability and
   equivalence
concordance reliability
concurrent validity
construct validity
content validity
criterion-related validity
face validity
factor analysis
false negative error
false positive error
grade equivalent score
grade norms
H coefficient
internal consistency
intraclass reliability
   coefficient
ipsative approach
kappa coefficient

Kuder-Richardson formulas
local norms
method of equivalence
national norms
normal curve equivalent (NCE)
   scores
normalized standard scores
normative approach
norms
percentile norms
predictive validity
R coefficient
regional norms
reliability
reliability coefficient
Spearman-Brown formula
standard score norms
stanine
stratified random sampling
T score
test-retest reliability
uniform T scores
V index
validity
z score

2. Store the following scores of 30 individuals on one variable in a data file named data. Then use program D2 on the computer diskette to find the percentile ranks, z, T, and stanine scores, and the NCEs corresponding to the following raw scores:

74	79	83	84	89	92	89	83	93	85
81	86	96	80	73	87	77	87	90	86
79	95	82	78	88	75	91	70	85	82

Name the transformed (output) file "results," and print it out after each of the three runs. One way to accomplish this is by running file Print.

3. The following is a frequency distribution of the scores on an ALIKE (ALIKE1+ALIKE2+ALIKE3+ALIKE4+ALIKE5+ALIKE6 +ALIKE7+ALIKE8) variable of 232 cases from the gss.dat file for which there were valid scores on the eight items.

ALIKE Score	Frequency
0	4
1	4
2	13
3	7
4	20
5	17
6	30
7	28
8	34
9	34
10	36
11	25
12	16
13	20
14	8
15	4
16	0

Use program H2 on the computer diskette to transform these raw ALIKE scores (midpoints of 17 intervals with interval width of 1) to percentile ranks, z scores, T scores, normalized z scores, normalized T scores.

How would you describe the shape of the original raw score distribution of the ALIKE variable? Do you believe that transforming the raw scores to normalized scores is justified, in that it can be assumed that the distribution of the underlying cognitive ability variable measured by the ALIKE scale is actually normal? Why or why not?

4. Find the Kuder-Richardson reliabilities (formulas 20 and 21) and coefficient alpha for the following responses of a sample of 10 people on 10 questionnaire items.

Respondent	Item									
	1	2	3	4	5	6	7	8	9	10
1	y	y	y	y	y	y	y	y	y	y
2	y	n	y	y	n	y	n	y	y	y
3	n	n	y	y	y	y	y	y	n	y
4	y	n	y	n	y	n	y	n	y	y
5	y	n	y	n	n	y	n	y	y	y
6	n	y	n	y	n	y	n	y	y	n
7	y	n	y	n	n	y	y	n	n	n
8	n	n	n	y	n	n	y	n	y	n
9	y	n	n	n	n	n	n	y	n	y
10	n	y	n	n	n	n	y	n	n	n

Record the responses in a data file, and then use program D2 to transform the y and n responses to 1s and 0s, respectively. Use program H3 to find the Kuder-Richardson reliabilities from the recorded file of 1s and 0s. Compare the results with coefficient alpha obtained from program H4.

6. Compute coefficient alpha for a Similarities test consisting of the ALIKE1, ALIKE2, ALIKE3, ALIKE4, ALIKE5, ALIKE6, ALIKE7, and ALIKE8 variables in the gss.sys file. If the SPSS/PC+ software is available, use the following statements:

```
GET FILE='A:GSS.SYS'.
SET PRINTER=ON.
RECODE ALIKE1 TO ALIKE8 (8=0).
RELIABILITY VARIABLES=ALIKE1 TO ALIKE8.
```

Note that a value of 0 has been assigned to any of the eight items to which a response was "Don't know" (8). If SPSS/PC+ is not available, use program B2 on the computer diskette to select the scores on the eight variables (ALIKE1 to ALIKE8) and store the output in file named results. You will have to edit this file to change the value of 8 to 0. Then use program H4 to compute coefficient alpha on these eight variables.

7. We have used the ALIKE variable as an independent (predictor) variable in several examples. Now let us use it as a dependent (criterion) variable. The problem is to predict ALIKE scores from EDUC, RACE, and SEX by means of a multiple

regression analysis. If SPSS/PC+ is available to you, type and enter the following statements after you get into SPSS/PC+:

```
GET FILE='A:GSS.SYS'.
SET PRINTER=ON.
RECODE ALIKE1 TO ALIKE8 (8=0).
MISSING VALUE RACE (3).
COMPUTE ALIKE=ALIKE1+ALIKE2+ALIKE3
+ALIKE4+ALIKE5+ALIKE6+ALIKE7+ALIKE8.
REGRESSION VARIABLES=ALIKE EDUC RACE SEX
/DEPENDENT=ALIKE
/METHOD=ENTER.
```

If SPSS/PC+ is not available, use the 226 data sets in file alike.dat and program E3 on the computer diskette to compute the required correlation coefficients and program E5 to determine the multiple regression equation. The order in which the variables are scored in file alike.dat is EDUC, RACE, SEX, ALIKE. Which independent variables in the regression equation made significant contributions to the prediction of the ALIKE variable?

8. The following five questions from the General Social Survey were scored for the total sample, coefficient alpha was computed on the scores, the scores were factor-analyzed (principal axis solution), and the resulting factors rotated (varimax procedure).[4]

LIBATH: There are always some people whose ideas are considered bad or dangerous by other people. For instance, somebody who is against all churches and religion . . .
If some people suggested that a book he wrote against churches and religion should be taken out of your public library, would you favor removing this book, or not? 1 = Favor, 2 = Not favor

LIBCOM: Now, I should like to ask you some questions about a man who admits he is a Communist.

Suppose he wrote a book which is in your public library. Somebody in your community suggests that the book should be removed from the library. Would you favor removing it, or not? 1 = Favor, 2 = Not favor

LIBHOMO: And what about a man who admits that he is a homosexual?
If some people in your community suggest that a book he wrote in favor of homosexuality should be taken out of your public library, would you favor removing this book, or not? 1 = Favor, 2 = Not favor

LIBMIL: Consider a person who advocates doing away with elections and letting the military run the country. Suppose he wrote a book advocating doing away with elections and letting the military run the country. Somebody in your community suggests that the book be removed from the public library. Would you favor removing it, or not? 1 = Favor, 2 = Not favor

LIBRAC: Or consider a person who believes that Blacks are genetically inferior. If some people in your community suggested that a book he wrote which said Blacks are inferior should be taken out of your public library, would you favor removing this book, or not? 1 = Favor, 2 = Not favor

Alpha = .8759

Rotated Favor Matrix:

Variable	Factor 1
LIBATH	.70206
LIBCOM	.72753
LIBHOMO	.61324
LIBMIL	.66964
LIBRAC	.63323

This one factor accounts for 67% of the variance in the scores of all five variables. Interpret these results.

SUGGESTED READING

Angoff, W. H. (1992). Norms and scales. In M. C. Alkin (Ed.), *Encyclopedia of educational research* (6th ed., pp. 909–921). New York: Macmillan.

Felner, R. D. (1994). Reliability of diagnoses. In R. J. Corsini (Ed.), *Encyclopedia of psychology* (2nd ed., pp. 299–300). New York: Wiley.

Green, K. E. (1991). Measurement theory. In K. E. Green (Ed.), *Educational testing: Issues and applications* (pp. 3–25). New York: Garland Publishing.

Litwin, M. S. (1995). *How to measure survey reliability and validity.* Thousand Oaks, CA: Sage.

Ozer, D. J. (1989). Construct validity in personality assessment. In D. M. Buss & N. Cantor (Eds.), *Personality psychology: Recent trends and emerging directions* (pp. 224–234). New York: Springer-Verlag.

Shavelson, R. J., Webb, N. M., & Rowley, G. L. (1989). Generalizability theory. *American Psychologist, 44,* 922–932.

Tulsky, D. S. (1990). An introduction to test theory. *Oncology, 4,* 43–48.

NOTES

1. An oft-quoted anecdote pertaining to individual differences in behavior concerns the error made during the late 18th century by an assistant to the royal astronomer at the Greenwich observatory in measuring the transit time of Venus. The error was a relative one, in that the assistant's time measurements differed from those of his superior. Unfortunately, it resulted in the assistant being fired. After hearing about this incident, certain scientists attributed it to the so-called *personal equation,* or individual differences in the perception and response to stimuli. Their observations and formulations led to extensive research by 19th-century psychologists on individual differences in response times to various stimuli.

2. It is possible, of course, for measurements to change, as a result of training or treatment for example, and hence appear to be unreliable but not necessarily invalid. The maxim assumes, however, that reliability and validity are both evaluated during the same time frame.

3. The validity of a psychometric instrument cannot be greater than the square root of its parallel forms reliability coefficient.

4. Reprinted from Davis, James Allan and Smith, Tom W.: *General Social Surveys, 1972–1994.* [machine-readable data file]. Principal Investigator, James A. Davis; Director and Co-Principal Investigator, Tom W. Smith. NORC ed. Chicago: National Opinion Research Center, producer, 1994; Storrs, CT: The Roper Center for Public Opinion Research, University of Connecticut, distributor. 1 data file (32,380 logical records and 1 codebook (1073 pp.)

7

Standard Questionnaires

Most questionnaires are ad hoc devices designed for a particular research investigation or application. Many of these are in-house instruments completed by patients, applicants, clerks, or interviewers in an office or organization. Still others are unpublished but are administered repeatedly, with some modifications, in periodic surveys. Examples are the questionnaires designed for the U.S. Department of Labor's Current Population Survey (CPS) and the National Opinion Research Center's General Social Survey (GSS). The former (CPS) survey is an important source of information on the labor force, employment, and unemployment in the United States. The results provide government policy makers, business executives, and academic researchers with an empirical basis for making economic forecasts and decisions. Data obtained from the latter (GSS) survey, which was used in many of the statistical computations in Chapters 5 and 6 of this book, is examined and interpreted by many social scientists. In addition to designating a particular research project or investigation, the term *survey* is often included in the title of a questionnaire designed for obtaining data on groups or individuals. A representative list of such survey questionnaires is given in Table 7.1. A majority of these instruments are directed at work or industrial/organizational situations, although many are also used in educational contexts.

Unless they are designed impromptu or "on-the-spot," questionnaires are typically standardized to some degree. In the "weak" sense, **standardization** refers to the fact that an instrument consists of

TABLE 7.1.   Instruments Designated as Surveys in the 11th and 12th
Mental Measurements Yearbooks

Access Management Survey
The ACT Evaluation/Survey Service
  High School Opinion Survey, Student Needs Assessment Questionnaire, High
  School Follow-Up Survey, Adult Learner Needs Assessment Survey, Alumni
  Survey, Alumni Survey (2-Year College Form), Alumni Outcomes Survey,
  College Outcomes Survey, College Student Needs Assessment Survey,
  Entering Student Survey, Student Opinion Survey, Student Opinion Survey
  (2-Year College Form), Survey of Academic Advising, Survey of Current
  Activities and Plans, Survey of Postsecondary Plans,
  Withdrawing/Nonreturning Student Survey, Withdrawing/Nonreturning
  Student Survey (short form)
Alienation Index Survey
Arlin-Hills Attitude Surveys
The American Drug and Alcohol Survey
Attitude Survey Program for Business and Industry (Managerial Survey,
  Organization Survey, Professional Survey, Sales Survey)
Bloom Sentence Completion Attitude Survey
Campbell Interest and Skill Survey
Campbell Organizational Survey
Conflict Management Survey
Employee Involvement Survey
Fleishman Job Analysis Survey
Guilford-Zimmerman Aptitude Survey
Guilford-Zimmerman Temperament Survey
Interpersonal Relationship Survey
Jackson Vocational Interest Survey
Jenkins Activity Survey
Kilmann-Saxton Culture-Gap Survey
Kuder General Interest Survey, Form E
Kuder Occupational Interest Survey, Form DD
Management Relations Survey
The Marriage and Family Attitude Survey
Meyer-Kendall Assessment Survey
Parent Awareness Skills Survey
Participative Management Survey
Personnel Relations Survey
Reality Check Survey
Rokeach Value Survey
School Situation Survey
Student Satisfaction Survey
Study Attitudes and Methods Survey
Styles of Leadership Survey
Survey of Basic Skills
Survey of Educational Leadership Practices

TABLE 7.1. *(Continued)*

Survey of Employee Access
Survey of Functional Adaptive Behaviors
Survey of Interpersonal Values
Survey of Management Practices
Survey of Organizational Climate
Survey of Organizational Culture
Survey of Organizational Stress
Survey of Personal Values
Survey of School Attitudes
Survey of Student Opinion of Instruction
Survey of Study Habits and Attitudes
Survey of Work Values, Revised
Surveys of Problem-Solving and Educational Skills
Team Effectiveness Survey
Teamwork Appraisal Survey
The Wilson Battery of Multi-Level Management & Organization Surveys

a predetermined set of questions presented in a fixed sequence and with specific directions; if scored, the scoring process should also be standard. In the "strong" sense, standardization has the further meaning that norms have been collected by administering the questionnaire to a representative sample of the population for which it is intended. Although norms provide a basis for interpreting responses to the items on a questionnaire, they are expensive and time-consuming to obtain. For these reasons, not all published and/or commercially available questionnaires have norms.

All of the instruments cited and described in this chapter are standardized in the weak sense, but norms are not available for many of them. Even when norms are available, they are frequently unrepresentative of the population for which the instrument was intended. Information pertaining to the norms and other psychometric characteristics (validity, reliability, etc.) of these instruments, which are given in the accompanying manuals or other technical materials and in professional journals and books, should be studied closely. Reviews in the *Mental Measurements Yearbook, Test Critiques,* and other sources also provide information that will help in deciding whether to employ a questionnaire for a particular purpose.

The great majority of the questionnaires discussed in this chapter are available from commercial publishers. Appendix C lists several dozen commercially available questionnaires, which can be ordered

TABLE 7.2.   The 25 Most Frequently Cited Questionnaires in the
Psychological Research Literature, 1990–1996

Name of Questionnaire	Number of Articles Citing Questionnaire	Citation Rank
Attributional Style Questionnaire	104	4½
Children's Personality Questionnaire	21	17
Client Satisfaction Questionnaire	19	18
Clinical Analysis Questionnaire	23	16
Defense Style Questionnaire	25	14½
Depressive Experiences Questionnaire	32	10½
Eysenck Personality Questionnaire	571	1
General Health Questionnaire	539	2
High School Personality Questionnaire	33	9
Infant Temperament Questionnaire	18	20
IPAT Anxiety Scale Questionnaire	15	22
Leader Behavior Description Questionnaire	11	24
McGill Pain Questionnaire	104	4½
Menstrual Distress Questionnaire	32	10½
Minnesota Satisfaction Questionnaire	27	13
Offer Self-Image Questionnaire, Revised	41	7
Personal Questionnaire	18	20
Preschool Behavior Questionnaire	31	12
Questionnaire on Resources and Stress	25	14½
Self-Description Questionnaire	34	8
Self-Esteem Questionnaire	18	20
16 Personality Factor Questionnaire	322	3
Student Adaptation to College Questionnaire	10	25
Study Process Questionnaire	14	23
Ways of Coping Questionnaire	45	6

The second column is the number of articles in PsycLit during the period 1/90–6/96.

from the addresses given in Appendix E. In addition to a brief description of the questionnaire's content, the age level or group for which the questionnaire is appropriate, the author(s) and publisher, and the locations of reviews in the *Mental Measurements Yearbook* (MMYB) and *Test Critiques* (TC) are provided. Although most of them are American products, a number of these questionnaires were developed in Australia, Canada, England, and South Africa. In addition, adaptations and translations of questionnaires developed in the United States have been used extensively in other countries.

A questionnaire may be widely administered for research purposes but prove less popular for making practical decisions concerning individuals, groups, and programs. As a general rule, however, research and practice interact to influence the popularity of a psychometric instrument: Research influences practice, practice stimulates research, and both processes are facilitated by the availability of effective measuring instruments. For this reason, the most frequently researched questionnaires, as indicated by the number of citations in computer banks such as PsycLit, ERIC, and SSCI, also tend to be employed most often for practical decision-making purposes (see Table 7.2).

The commercially available questionnaires listed in Appendix C are in alphabetical order, but the discussion of these and other questionnaires in this chapter follows a topical outline. We begin by considering questionnaires designed to measure aspects of health and illness, followed by questionnaires for evaluating students, teachers, and other aspects of the educational environment. Next is a discussion of questionnaires administered in business/industrial contexts for purposes related to jobs, management, and other aspects of the world of work. Finally, questionnaires designed for research and applications concerned with personality and the diagnosis and treatment of psychological problems and disorders are described.

HEALTH AND ILLNESS

Familiar to anyone who has ever had a doctor's appointment are questionnaires like the one in Figure 7.1, typically nonstandardized forms devised by general practitioners, specialists, or hospitals to obtain patient intake information. In addition to identifying data and associated demographic facts, the forms may ask for information on current symptoms, previous illnesses, injuries, surgeries, allergic reactions to specific medications, and the like. Some forms are fairly long and detailed, but most consist of only a page or two.

Among the standard health and illness questionnaires designed for research concerning the etiology, diagnosis, and treatment of various medical disorders are the following baker's dozen:

Adult Neuropsychological Questionnaire

American Thoracic Society Adult Questionnaire

Behavioral Assessment of Pain Questionnaire

Child Neuropsychological Questionnaire

Diabetes Treatment Satisfaction Questionnaire

Name: _____   Date: _____
      Last   First   M.I.

Right _____ Left _____ Handed   Age: _____ Height: _____ Weight: _____

For what **problem, symptom,** or **condition** are you being seen today?	
When was the **first time** the problem was noted (if an injury, **when** and **where** were you injured?)	
Describe **how** the symptoms developed, and any **treatments** received so far, including the names of any other **doctors** you have seen for this problem.	
Describe any **prior occurrences** or similar symptoms before the current condition began.	
List other significant **musculoskeletal** problems you have had in the past.	

List any current or previous **medical problems** such as: diabetes, high blood pressure, heart or lung problems, cancer, ulcers, gout, hepatitis, AIDS, bleeding problems, or other significant illness:

List any **hospitalizations** or **surgery**:	
List any **drug allergies** or **drug reactions** in the past:	
List any pills or other **medications** you use now or have taken recently:	
List any other medical information that may be helpful to the doctor:	

Cigarettes: Packs/day for   Years
Alcohol: Drinks/day or   Occasionally
Are you possibly pregnant?

Figure 7.1. An example of a medical patient intake questionnaire.

Illness Behavior Questionnaire

McGill Pain Questionnaire

McMaster Health Index Questionnaire

Patient Assessment Questionnaire

Philadelphia Head Injury Questionnaire

Sleep History Questionnaire

The Stanford Arthritis Center Health-Assessment Questionnaire

Well-Being Questionnaire

These and other questionnaires in the field of health care deal with subjective experiences such as feelings of pain, distress, well-being, and energy/fatigue, as well as behavioral symptoms such as sleeplessness, limitations in physical functioning and social activity, and changes in cognition (alertness, memory, problem-solving ability, etc.), motivation, and temperament. They provide detailed information on the patient's physical condition, how satisfied the patient is with the medical care received, and his or her everyday functioning, feelings, and rated health. Physical and mental functioning, feelings of well-being, and quality of life in general can be assessed before, during, and after treatment and yield data on treatment effectiveness.

Quality of Life

Standard forms such as the Patient Assessment Questionnaire (PAQ), the Short Health Survey, and the General Health Survey provide information of the current health perceptions, pain level, physical functioning, psychological distress, social functioning, and work role functioning of the patient. Some health questionnaires, such as the PAQ, are fairly long and detailed, whereas others, such as the Short Health Survey (see Figure 7.2) or the six-item General Health Survey, are much shorter (Stewart & Ware, 1992). More recent questionnaires designed to assess general health emphasize the concept of *positive wellness*, that health is a subjective as well as an objective phenomenon. According to this definition, **health** is more than the absence of functional limitations and pain; it is concerned in a more holistic sense with the patient's *quality of life*. A result of the focus on quality-of-life aspects of treatment has been the appearance of several new psychometric instruments (Migraine Quality of Life Questionnaire, Health-Related Quality of

1. In general, would you say your health is:
   a. Excellent
   b. Very Good
   c. Good
   d. Fair
   e. Poor

2. For how long (if at all) has your *health limited you* in *each* of the following activities? (Mark *One* Circle on *Each* line)

	1 Limited for more than 3 months	2 Limited for 3 months or less	3 Not limited at all
a. The kinds or amount of *vigorous* activities you can do, like lifting heavy objects, running or participating in strenuous sports	0	0	0
b. The kinds or amounts of *moderate* activities you can do, like moving a table, carrying groceries or bowling	0	0	0
c. Walking uphill or climbing a few flights or stairs	0	0	0
d. Bending, lifting or stooping.	0	0	0
e. Walking one block.	0	0	0

3. How much *bodily* pain have you had *during the past 4 weeks?*
   1–0   None
   2–0   Very mild
   3–0   Mild
   4–0   Moderate
   5–0   Severe
   6–0   Very Severe

4. Does your health *keep* you from working at a job, doing work around the house, or going to school?
   1–0   YES, for more than 3 months
   2–0   YES, for 3 months or less
   3–0   NO

5. Have you been unable to do *certain kinds or amounts* or work, housework, or schoolwork because of your health?
   1–0   YES, for more than 3 months
   2–0   YES, for 3 months or less
   3–0   NO

Figure 7.2.   Short-Form Health Survey. (From Stewart, Hays, & Ware, 1988. Reprinted with permission.)

For *each* of the following questions, please mark the circle for the *one* answer that comes *closest* to the way you have been feeling *during the past month.*

	1 All of the time	2 Most of the time	3 A good bit of the time	4 Some of the time	5 A little of the time	7 None of the time
6. How much of the time, during the past month, has your *health limited your social activities* (like visiting with friends or close relatives)?	0	0	0	0	0	0
7. How much of the time, during the past month, have you been a *very nervous person?*	0	0	0	0	0	0
8. During the past month, how much of the time have you felt *calm and peaceful?*	0	0	0	0	0	0
9. How much of the time, during the past month, have you felt *downhearted and blue?*	0	0	0	0	0	0
10. During the past month, how much of the time have you been a *happy person?*	0	0	0	0	0	0
11. How often, during the past month, have you felt so *down in the dumps that nothing could cheer you up?*	0	0	0	0	0	0

12. Please mark the circle that *best* describes whether each of the following statements is *true* or *false* for you. (Mark *One* Circle on Each Line)

	1 Definitely true	2 Mostly true	3 Not sure	4 Mostly false	5 Definitely false
a. I am somewhat ill	0	0	0	0	0
b. I am as healthy as anybody I know	0	0	0	0	0
c. My health is excellent	0	0	0	0	0
d. I have been feeling bad lately	0	0	0	0	0

Figure 7.2. *(Continued)*

Life Questionnaire, Cuestionario de Calidad de Vida, Quality of Life Questions) and a new journal, *Quality of Life Research: An International Journal of Quality of Life Aspects of Treatment*. In addition, a number of anthologies and compendia concerned with the measurement of quality of life and well-being have been published in the past few years (e.g., Bowling, 1991; Stewart & Ware, 1992).

McGill Pain Questionnaire

Two of the principal indicators of a medical problem are limitations in physical functioning and feelings of pain. Of these, pain is often the most misleading and difficult to combat. The quality and intensity of the pain experience is not only a function of the sensory stimulus per se, but is also affected by the patient's emotional state and interpretation of the pain. In particular, the degree of stress that the individual is experiencing because of other events, and his or her general optimistic/pessimistic outlook, can affect the perceived quality and intensity of a pain experience.

Because pain cannot be directly observed but must be reported by the patient, rating scales and questionnaires designed to assess the quality, intensity, persistence, and locus of pain have been used extensively in research and practice. Perhaps the most common method of assessing pain are *visual analogue scales* (Wewers & Lowe, 1990). Next in order of frequency is the McGill Pain Questionnaire (MPQ) (Melzack, 1975, 1983, 1987). Reports of more than 100 research studies employing the McGill Pain Questionnaire (MPQ) were published in scientific journals during 1990 to 1996. These articles dealt with back pain, cancer pain, pelvic pain, postmastectomy pain, osteoarthritis and rheumatoid arthritis pain, acute myocardial infarction pain, labor pain, and musculoskeletal pain.

On the full-length form of the MPQ, the patient is presented with three major classes of word descriptions (sensory, affective, evaluative) and 78 descriptors; one descriptor in each of 20 classes is used by the patient to indicate his or her present experience of pain. Four forms of the MPQ are available, including a short form consisting of the following 15 descriptors: aching, cramping, fearful, gnawing, heavy, hot-burning, punishing-cruel, sharp, shooting, sickening, splitting, stabbing, tender, throbbing, and tiring-exhausting.

The full-length form of the MPQ takes 5 to 15 minutes to complete, and the short form 2 to 5 minutes. On all forms, the patient is asked to select those words from the list of descriptors that describe the pain being experienced. Each descriptor is weighted according to the reported severity of the patient's pain, and pain scores are determined by combining the weights (0 = no pain, 1 = mild pain, 2 = discomforting, 3 = distressing, 4 = horrible, 5 = excruciating) assigned to the selected descriptors. Separate scores may be determined on the sensory and evaluative scales, which designate the perception of pain, and on the affective scale, which denotes the emotional response to the pain. Scores may be obtained either according to the number of words chosen, or by summing the scale values for all the words in a given category or categories combined. Also available with the MPQ package are a revised pain assessment questionnaire for use in pain clinics and a card to record pain levels at home.

An earlier validity study by Dubuisson and Melzack (1976) found that the MPQ classified 73 out of a sample of 95 patients into their correct diagnostic groups. Evidence for the validity of the MPQ was also found in the moderate correlations with scores on visual analogue scales, and from the results of factor analysis supporting the distinction between the affective and sensory dimensions of pain. Additional evidence for the validity and reliability of the MPQ was reported by Chapman, Casey, Dubner, et al. (1985) and Melzack (1987). An update and evaluation are provided by Melzack and Katz (1992) and a revised format by Hase (1992).

Two other popular questionnaire measures of pain are the Wisconsin Brief Pain Questionnaire (Daut, Cleeland, & Flanery, 1983) and the Behavioral Assessment of Pain Questionnaire. The former is a relatively short (19-item) instrument focusing on the frequency, severity, and effects of pain in cancer and other diseases. The latter is a longer instrument designed to provide an understanding of factors that contribute to the subacute and chronic experience of pain in noncancerous disorders.

Menstrual Distress

Reflective of the current interest in women's studies, and specifically the health problems of women, is the increase in research on menstrual disorders, breast and ovarian cancer, and osteoporosis in particular. To consider only one of these conditions, several dozen reports on menstrual distress were published in the medical and psychological literature during the early 1990s. The most common psychometric instrument administered in these studies was the Menstrual Distress Questionnaire (MDS), an older, 47-item self-report instrument designed to identify the type and intensity of symptoms experienced during the three phases of the menstrual cycle: four days prior to menstrual flow, menstruation, and the remainder of the cycle. The two forms (Cycle and Today) of the MDS can be scored on eight scales (Pain, Water Retention, Autonomic Reactions, Negative Affect, Impaired Concentration, Behavior Change, Arousal, Control). Though the norms and validity data on the MDS are rather skimpy, Fager (1995) and Sundre (1995) gave it good marks in terms of the information that it provides in comparison with competing instruments.

Many other questionnaires have been devised for surveys and investigations directed toward the health problems of women; for example, the National Lesbian Health Care Survey (Ryan & Bradford, 1993). Standard questionnaires have also been developed for studies concerned with health risks posed by particular environments, such as specific occupations (e.g., Ehrenberg & Sniezek, 1989).

HOME AND SCHOOL

Human beings are born with relatively few ready-made sensory and motor capacities but with a multitude of potentialities. The extent to which those potentialities are fulfilled depends on experiences in the various physical and social environments in which the person develops. The examples and lessons provided by other people—at home and school, in work and play—combine with abilities and personality traits to mold and shape behavior into something that is approved or disapproved of or rewarded or punished by the people and organizations with which the individual comes into contact in attempting to survive and prosper.

The life experiences of most children in Western culture begin in a family group. This is a child's first psychological environment, the pressures and sanctions of which stamp an indelible mark on growth and development. Instruments such as the Home Environment Questionnaire and the Home Screening Questionnaire were designed to measure certain significant parameters of the home environment.

Even under the best of conditions children and parents experience problems at home. The Nisonger Questionnaire for Parents and related measures can help identify and establish the characteristics and causes of these problems. Questionnaires that focus on the interaction between parents and children (e.g., Parental Acceptance-Rejection Questionnaire, Offer Parent-Adolescent Questionnaire) are also useful. Identification of emotional/behavioral and other problems of development can be facilitated by questionnaires such as the Revised Denver Prescreening Developmental Questionnaire and the Preschool Behavior Questionnaire. The latter, a popular screening tool for identifying emotional and behavioral problems in children aged 3 to 6 years, is completed by a parent, a teacher, or another adult who knows the child well. Four scores are provided: Hostile-Aggressive, Anxious-Fearful, Hyperactive-Distractible, and Total.

ADHD and Other Developmental Disabilities

Of particular concern with regard to children's behavior at home and school are conditions such as *attention-deficit hyperactivity disorder (ADHD),* which can affect not only the child but everyone with whom he or she comes in contact. Among the psychometric instruments for analyzing and assisting children who have ADHD are the Conners Teacher Questionnaire, the Conners-March Developmental Questionnaire, and the Conners Abbreviated Symptom Questionnaire.

ADHD is only one of many illnesses and disabilities that cause or exacerbate adjustment problems in families. Mental retardation, hearing disorders, traumatic brain injury, autism, cystic fibrosis, and diabetes are others. The Questionnaire on Resources and Stress is one widely researched instrument that can provide assistance in dealing with these problems. The Adaptive Behavior: Street Survival Skills Questionnaire can also contribute to the assessment of the extent to which physical, mental, and developmental disabilities produce functional impairments in the living skills of children, adolescents, and adults. Appropriate vocational and residential placement can then be recommended on the basis of the results.

Adjusting to School

Most children adjust fairly well to the school environment. The influence of peers and adults who are less manipulable than parents can shape a "problem child" into a more socially acceptable and responsible individual. The development of positive attitudes toward oneself and other people is a particularly important goal for schoolchildren.

The Katz-Zalk Opinion Questionnaire and other measures of social attitudes can assist in this process. In addition to learning to get along with a host of new people, the school-age child must respond appropriately to the demand that he or she acquire new motivations and cognitive skills. Not only does the child have to acquire knowledge and skills, but must also *learn how to learn:* how to take tests and other evaluative requirements; how to be prompt, attentive, and orderly; and how to win and lose, succeed and fail graciously.

Individual Differences in Learning

The school situation demands conformity and, to a large extent, a lock-step method of getting things done. Individual differences among students are, of course, recognized and provided for to some extent. Educational research on adapting instruction to the individual characteristics of students has led to the construction of a number of questionnaires, including the Student Styles Questionnaire and the Learning Process Questionnaire for elementary and high school students, and the Motivated Strategies for Learning Questionnaire and the Study Process Questionnaire for college students. The last of these, an Australian product, is the most extensively researched. It measures the extent to which college students apply different approaches to learning and the motives and strategies involved in those approaches.

Evaluating Classes and Courses

A number of questionnaires have been designed to assess classroom atmosphere and activities in elementary and secondary school; for example, the Class Activities Questionnaire, the Classroom Atmosphere Questionnaire, the Educational Process Questionnaire, and the Individualised Classroom Environment Questionnaire. At the college level, the publication and distribution of questionnaires for evaluating courses and professors has become widespread during the past three decades. Examples are the Course Evaluation Questionnaire and the Illinois Course Evaluation Questionnaire. Many colleges and universities, however, have opted to design and administer their own questionnaires, such as the one in Figure 7.3.

Less popular than course evaluation questionnaires but also widely administered in higher education contexts are instruments designed to determine how well freshmen adapt to the demands of the

Course and Instructor Evaluation Questionnaire

Directions: For each item on this questionnaire, indicate whether you Strongly Disagree (SD), Disagree (D), are Undecided (U), Agree (A), or Strongly Agree (SA) with it by circling the appropriate letter(s).

1. The course is well organized.	SD	D	U	A	SA
2. The course objectives have been defined and met.	SD	D	U	A	SA
3. The textbook and other readings are appropriate in content.	SD	D	U	A	SA
4. The papers, reports and/or other written or oral assignments are reasonable and fair.	SD	D	U	A	SA
5. The tests and other evaluations are appropriate and fair.	SD	D	U	A	SA
6. The instructor shows interest and enthusiasm for the course.	SD	D	U	A	SA
7. The instructor has been available when needed outside of class during posted office hours.	SD	D	U	A	SA
8. The instructor has provided quality advising during office hours.	SD	D	U	A	SA
9. The instructor is prepared for class and makes good use of class time.	SD	D	U	A	SA
10. Lecture and course material is clearly explained.	SD	D	U	A	SA
11. The workload in the course is demanding.	SD	D	U	A	SA
12. The course material is challenging.	SD	D	U	A	SA
13. Overall, the instructor is an excellent teacher.	SD	D	U	A	SA
14. Overall, this is an excellent course.	SD	D	U	A	SA

Comments:

Figure 7.3.   College Course and Instructor Evaluation Questionnaire.

college experience. An example is the Student Adaptation to College Questionnaire, a useful tool for counseling interventions and research related to the influence of various factors on college life.

As in all groups or organizations, interpersonal relations are a critical component of effective functioning in educational contexts. Getting along with other people is an important learned skill in its own right, but it can affect other areas of learning and motivation as well. Whether it is a matter of students relating to each other and to the school faculty and staff, or of faculty and staff relating to their colleagues and coworkers, relationships with people are crucial to a

Questionnaire

Directions: Mark T in the marginal dash if the statement is *true;* mark F if the statement is *false.* Feel free to explain your answer or elaborate on it in the space below the question.

_____   1. In general, do your professors know your name?

_____   2. Are you on a first-name basis with one or more of your professors?

_____   3. Have you made an effort to become personally acquainted with your professors?

_____   4. Have you ever made an appointment with a professor for academic assistance?

_____   5. Have you ever made an appointment with a professor for nonacademic assistance?

_____   6. In general, have your interactions with professors been satisfactory?

_____   7. Have you ever visited a professor in his or her home?

_____   8. Do you have the feeling that most professors are genuinely interested in students?

_____   9. Do you feel that you could drop by a professor's office at almost any time for assistance or just to chat?

_____   10. In your opinion, do most students seem to get along well with their professors?

Note: This questionnaire can be taken by running program I4 on the diskette of computer programs accompanying this book.

Figure 7.4. Questionnaire for evaluating student interactions with professors.

healthy educational environment. Nonstandardized questions such as the one in Figure 7.4 yield information on interpersonal relations on a college campus. Standard questionnaires such as Relating to Each Other: A Questionnaire for Students and Relating with Colleagues: A Questionnaire for Faculty Members can also provide valuable data.

JOBS AND ORGANIZATIONS

Modern society is characterized by a large number of diverse organizations, public and private, that manufacture products and provide services to people. Becoming familiar with the existence of those organizations and how and when to use them to get what one wants and needs is a necessary part of growing up. Few people choose to live in isolation from the business, industrial, governmental, and other organizations that they come to depend upon to help them survive and enjoy life. People are fed, clothed, protected, warmed, cooled, illuminated, entertained, counseled, employed, trained, and treated by those organizations, and eventually buried by them.

Because of the importance of organizations of all kinds for efficient functioning of society, a great deal of human time and energy is spent in trying to make organizations more productive, efficient, safe, and personally rewarding. Investigations of selection, training, placement, promotion, evaluation, and termination of employees, as well as job analysis, accidents and safety, industrial health and pollution, job design, production efficiency, and marketing are some of the purposes for which questionnaires and other psychometric devices have been used to help make decisions concerning organizational activities.

Vocational Interests

Preparation and planning for entry into the world of work may begin earlier, but it typically becomes more serious in high school. The process of vocational counseling can be facilitated by interest questionnaires and inventories. Interest questionnaires, which are basically the same as the more popular interest inventories discussed in Chapter 8, are usually administered to seniors in high school to provide a basis for discussion, consideration, and counseling concerning various career possibilities. Examples are The Edinburgh Questionnaires and the Personal Questionnaire in the United Kingdom, the High School Interest Questionnaire and the Picture Vocational Interest Questionnaire for Adults in South Africa, and the Job Activity Preference Questionnaire in the United States. Questionnaires that focus on specific occupational areas, such as the Purdue Interest Questionnaire for identifying possible specializations within the field of engineering, are also available. Furthermore, certain questionnaires are directed toward the employment of specific groups of individuals, such as the disabled (e.g., the Preliminary Diagnostic Questionnaire). In recognition of the relationships of vocational interests to values, personality characteristics, and other affective variables, measures such as the Jung Personality Questionnaire, which is based on Carl Jung's personality typology, have been constructed.

Leadership and Management

Many researchers in business and the social sciences spend a substantial portion of their professional lives investigating the leadership/management process and the characteristics and behaviors of effective leaders and managers. One of the oldest questionnaires concerned with the analysis of leadership is the Leadership Opinion Questionnaire, which differentiates between the "consideration" and "structure" dimensions of leadership. Among more recently developed instruments for selecting leaders are the Leatherman Leadership Questionnaire, the Managerial Style Questionnaire, and the Multifactor Leadership Questionnaire. Measures of attitudes and personality, such as the Work Attitudes Questionnaire, which was designed to differentiate the "workaholic" or *Type A personality* from the highly committed worker, have also been administered to prospective managers. Instruments like these may be combined with observations, interviews, situational tests, and management games in the *assessment center* approach to management selection. Employed supervisors or managers may be evaluated by their subordinates on the Leader Behavior Description Questionnaire. Specific leader behaviors (e.g., mentoring, decision-making) can be studied by means of instruments such as the Alleman Leadership Development Questionnaire and the Inquiry Mode Questionnaire.

Most managers realize that the effectiveness of particular leadership or management styles depends on the situation. A given style may be more effective in one situation—with a particular task or group of people—and another style in another situation. For example, some situations require more structure and others more consideration on the part of the leader. Based on this truism, the Situation Diagnosis Questionnaire was designed to help employees and managers understand the concept of *situational management,* to recognize situations in which various management styles are appropriate, to identify the management style that is best for a particular situation, and to develop a plan for using that style on the job.

As noted, attitudes and personality characteristics are important to success in many jobs. This is especially true in jobs where there is a great deal of contact with other people, such as sales. One of several instruments developed to assess the personality characteristics necessary for sales success is the Sales Personality Questionnaire. Two other representative questionnaires that have been administered for personnel selection and evaluation purposes are the Minnesota Importance Questionnaire and the Minnesota Satisfaction Questionnaire. The former instrument measures 20 psychological needs and six values that are relevant to adjustment to work and satisfaction with it. The latter questionnaire, which can be scored on 21 variables, is a measure of satisfaction with the job.

Evaluating Positions and Organizations

Questionnaires are used not only to select and evaluate employees but also to analyze and evaluate the positions filled by those employees. One of these instruments is the time-honored Position Analysis Questionnaire, which was designed to analyze jobs in terms of work activities and work situations on 45 dimensions in seven divisions. More specific to managerial positions is the Professional and Managerial Position Questionnaire. This questionnaire is used to evaluate professional positions on several job elements: communicating, planning, exercising judgment, required personal characteristics, number of people supervised, and the amount of supervision needed. A final example of a job or position analysis questionnaire is the Minnesota Job Description Questionnaire, which provides 21 reinforcer scores for assessing the reinforcement characteristics of a job.

Going beyond the individual employee and the job itself are questionnaires for analyzing and evaluating an organization as a whole. An illustrative instrument, the Oliver Organizational Description Questionnaire, describes an occupational organization in terms of four roles: H (Hierarchy), P (Professional), T (Task), and G (Group). These are roles that individuals or subunits of an organization must perform to direct and sustain efforts toward attainment of the goals of the organization.

PERSONALITY CHARACTERISTICS AND DISORDERS

Due in large measure to the predominance of clinical and counseling psychology among psychological specialties, more paper-and-pencil instruments for assessing personality are published than any other psychometric device. These instruments, which are referred to as questionnaires, inventories, scales, or related terms, are administered in clinical, counseling, educational, occupational, and other settings. In these settings, they provide data for research, personnel decisions, diagnosis, assignment to intervention programs, and evaluation of the effectiveness of treatment or training. Whether it is called a questionnaire, an inventory, or a scale makes almost no difference in what is presumably being measured by a paper-and-pencil personality assessment device. A personality questionnaire in the United Kingdom is much the same as a personality inventory in the United States. For reasons of convenience and consistency rather than any difference in substance, the following discussion will be limited to instruments specifically designated as personality questionnaires; the description of personality inventories will be left to the next chapter.

Clinically Based Questionnaires of Single Constructs and Behaviors

The first standardized personality questionnaire, the Woodworth Personal Data Sheet, could be characterized as a measure of adjustment, neuroticism, or stress tolerance. Many other single-score personality questionnaires have been constructed during this century, including those designed to measure anxiety, depression, frustration tolerance, gender identity, self-concept, stress and strain, and suicidal ideation. Questionnaires for identifying certain behaviors or behavior patterns associated with specific personality characteristics have also been constructed, including attributions, alcoholism, eating disorders, smoking, substance abuse, and violence. Representative of the many questionnaires for assessing a specific clinical construct or behavior are the:

> Adult Suicidal Ideation Questionnaire
>
> Depressive Experiences Questionnaire
>
> Drug Use Questionnaire
>
> General Health Questionnaire
>
> IPAT Anxiety Questionnaire
>
> Offer Self-Image Questionnaire, Revised
>
> Penn State Worry Questionnaire
>
> Questionnaire Measure of Trait Arousability
>
> SAQ-Adult Probation (Substance Abuse Questionnaire)

Self-Administered Dependency Questionnaire

Self-Esteem Questionnaire

The Strain Questionnaire

Stress Management Questionnaire

Suicidal Ideation Questionnaire

Ways of Coping Questionnaire

Well-Being Questionnaire

All of these and others are described briefly in Appendix C.

Self-Concept Questionnaires

Although a majority of clinically based questionnaires stem from a trait-factor and/or psychoanalytic background, measures of *self-concept* or *self-esteem* are derived primarily from phenomenological theories and therapy. According to a *phenomenological* perspective, actions are based on perceptions, and perceptions of the self constitute the self-concept. Because a person's behavior is the result of his or her view of the world and of the self, in order to change behavior, it is necessary to change those perceptions. Understanding another person and assisting him or her in attaining self-satisfaction and happiness requires seeing the world and the person from his or her own point of view.

A number of questionnaires have been designed to assess the self-concept and the level of self-esteem of a person, among which are the Offer Self-Image Questionnaire, the Self-Description Questionnaire, and the Self-Esteem Questionnaire. All three of these instruments are designed for administration to adolescents, who are at a stage of life in which identity and self-concept problems are undergoing rapid changes and are most crucial. Of the three, the Offer is probably the most widely researched. Unfortunately, recent reviews of research with this questionnaire have faulted it for inattention to psychometric characteristics such as reliability and validity (Allen, 1995; Furlong & Karno, 1995).

General Health Questionnaire

Administered more often in England and other United Kingdom countries than in the United States is the General Health Questionnaire (GHQ). The GHQ is a fairly short (3 to 8 minutes), self-administered screening questionnaire for detecting nonpsychotic psychiatric disorders. Appropriate for adolescents and adults, there are four forms (60, 30, 28, and 12 items) of the GHQ, each yielding a single score. The popularity of the GHQ as a research instrument is, like the Eysenck Personality Questionnaire, due in some measure to its brevity.

Attributional Style Questionnaire

Next to the GHQ in the number of times it is cited in the psychological research literature for 1990 to 1996 is the Attributional Style Questionnaire (ASQ) (Peterson et al., 1982). The ASQ presents 12 situations, six with positive (good) outcomes and six with negative (bad) outcomes. An example of a negative outcome is: "You go to a party and do not meet new friends." The respondent is asked to provide a causal explanation and rate it on a seven-point scale in terms of three attributional dimensions: locus (internal-external), stability, and generality (global-specific). Responses are scored in terms of these three dimensions, which are based on Seligman's (1992) *learned helplessness* theory of depression. According to this theory, depressed persons attribute bad outcomes to internal, stable, and global causes, but they attribute good outcomes to external, unstable, and specific causes.

Depression Questionnaires

Many, more direct, questionnaires to assess depression have been constructed. Two examples are the Depressive Experiences Questionnaire (DEQ) and the Levine-Pilowsky Depression Questionnaire. Developed to differentiate between the anaclitic and introjective dimensions of depression,[1] the DEQ is scored on three variables: dependency, self-criticism, and efficacy. Although the results of factor analysis have provided support for the DEQ as a measure of at least two of these factors (Riley & McCranie, 1990; Zuroff, Quinlan & Blatt, 1990), evidence for its validity and the underlying theory on which it is based is not strong (Viglione, Clemmey & Camenzuli, 1990).

Other Psychodiagnostic Questionnaires

In addition to administering questionnaires such as the GHQ, psychological examinations for purposes of psychiatric diagnosis typically involve in-depth interviews in which the present symptoms and a life history are obtained. In addition, a mental status examination may be conducted and several other tests administered. Questionnaires have been designed to facilitate all phases of diagnostic interviewing and assessment.

Time permitting, instruments such as the Defense Style Questionnaire, the Stress Management Questionnaire, and the Ways of Coping Questionnaire for determining the characteristic manner in which the patient copes with stress can provide useful information for psychodiagnostic and treatment purposes. All three of these questionnaires have also been used extensively in research. Other questionnaires that may be helpful in understanding and counseling individuals under stress are the Neuroticism Scale Questionnaire, the Suicidal Ideation Questionnaire, the Eight State Questionnaire, and various measures of alcohol and drug abuse (e.g., Drug Use Questionnaire and the Situational Confidence Questionnaire). Finally, feedback on the client's satisfaction with the counseling or psychotherapy received for a particular condition can be obtained by administering the Client Satisfaction Questionnaire.

Multivariable/Multifactor Personality Questionnaires

Many of the questionnaires described in the preceding section provide more than one score, but the majority focus on a single psychological construct. In addition, they concentrate on disorders of behavior and cognition rather than on normal differences in personality. In contrast, the multivariable or multifactor instruments discussed in this section were designed primarily for research on normal personality. In some cases, that research has led into the domain of psychopathology, but the instruments were not originally intended for the diagnosis of behavioral or cognitive disorders.

The first personality questionnaire designed to measure several variables—the Bernreuter Personality Inventory—was published over a decade after the Woodworth Personal Data Sheet. During the 1930s and subsequently, many other questionnaires that could be scored on several variables appeared. Construction of these questionnaires usually began with a rational/theoretical conception of what variables were important to measure and the preparation of relevant items grouped into categories or scales. Next, various statistical procedures were applied to sharpen the distinctions among the variables measured by the scales and to improve their internal consistency and external validity. New factor-analytic methods were applied in the construction of the Guilford-Zimmerman Temperament Survey and the Thurstone Temperament Schedule. Following the lead of J. P. Guilford and L. L. Thurstone, a number of psychologists in the United

States and Great Britain developed personality questionnaires based on factor analysis. Two of these products—the 16 Personality Factor Questionnaire and the Eysenck Personality Questionnaire—are among the most popular of all personality assessment instruments.

The 16 Personality Factor Questionnaire (16 PFQ) and Related Instruments

The current (fifth) edition of the 16 PFQ contains 185 items and can be administered in 35 to 50 minutes to an adult with at least fifth-grade reading ability. Sten (standard 10) scores are provided on the following 16 primary factors:

Warmth	Vigilance
Reasoning	Abstractness
Emotional Stability	Privateness
Dominance	Apprehension
Liveliness	Openness to Change
Rule Consciousness	Self-Reliance
Social Boldness	Perfectionism
Sensitivity	Tension

Scores may also be obtained on five second-order factors: Extraversion, Anxiety, Tough-Mindedness, Independence, and Self-Control. To provide a preliminary check on the validity of the responses, scores are determined on three response indices: Impression Management, Independence, and Acquiescence.

Scores on the fifth edition of the 16 PFQ, which was standardized in 1990, have fair reliabilities. This questionnaire has been used in a variety of research studies and applications concerned with such matters as employee and student selection and placement and with personality changes resulting from counseling, psychotherapy, and other treatments or interventions.

Four downward extensions of the 16 PFQ are the High School Personality Questionnaire (ages 12 to 18), the Children's Personality Questionnaire (ages 8 to 12), the Early School Personality Questionnaires (ages 6 to 8), and the Preschool Personality Questionnaire (ages 4 to 6). These instruments are not as popular as the 16 PFQ and have quite modest reliabilities, but they are well-constructed and can contribute to educational and research goals. Another instrument derived from the 16 PFQ is the Clinical Analysis Questionnaire (CAQ), which contains the 187 items from an earlier edition of the 16 PFQ and 144 clinical items. In addition to the factors measured by the 16 PFQ, the CAQ measures more clinically oriented variables such as hypochondriasis, agitated depression, guilt, energy level, and boredom.

Eysenck Personality Questionnaire, Revised (EPQ-R)

This is the most widely used of all personality assessment instruments with the word questionnaire in the title. It can be administered to adults, including those with lower educational attainments, in 10 to 15 minutes. More parsimonious than the 16 PFQ in the number of variables that it measures, and demonstrably shorter, the EPQ-R yields scores on three personality factors stemming from the research of H. J. Eysenck and others: Psychoticism or Tough-Mindedness (P), Extraversion (E), and Neuroticism or Emotionality (N). A Lie (L) score is also computed as a check on dissimulation or faking by the respondent.

The EPQ and its predecessors (Maudsley Personality Inventory, Eysenck Personality Inventory) have been used particularly in the research of Eysenck and his colleagues on the correlates and causes of the personality characteristics of introversion and extraversion. The brevity of the EPQ-R also makes it a favorite for inclusion with other measures in research on neuroticism, psychoticism, and other psychopathological conditions.

Personality Questionnaires in Other Countries

A number of questionnaires for measuring several personality variables have been constructed in Canada (e.g., Howarth Personality Questionnaire) and England (e.g, Rapid Personality Questionnaire). One of the most extensive series of instruments of this kind has been developed in South Africa. Among these questionnaires are the Intermediate Personality Questionnaire for Indian Pupils, the International Version of the Mental Status Questionnaire, the Interpersonal Relations Questionnaire, the Jung Personality Questionnaire, and the South African Personality Questionnaire. Many of these questionnaires were designed to determine whether students in different racial groups ("whites," Indians, "coloreds," etc.) meet particular standards established in the South African school system.

SUMMARY

Strictly speaking, a questionnaire constructed by experts and for which there are standard directions for administration and scoring is not standardized until norms have been obtained on a sample of people who are representative of the population for which the questionnaire is intended. By this definition, most *standard* questionnaires are not *standardized*.

Information on the construction, composition, applications, psychometric characteristics (reliability, validity, norms, etc.) of a standard questionnaire, as well as reports of research related to it, can be obtained from the manual and other technical information accompanying the questionnaire and from professional papers, chapters, and books concerned with its use.

Standard questionnaires in four areas—health and illness, home and school, jobs and organizations, personality traits and disorders— were discussed in this chapter. Two primary symptoms of health problems are pain and functional limitations, so questionnaires designed to measure these factors are common. A recent development in the health professions has been the focus on quality of life and instruments for measuring this construct. Two of the most widely used questionnaires in the health and illness category are the McGill Pain Questionnaire and the Menstrual Distress Questionnaire.

Areas of the home and school category in which questionnaires have been designed include ADHD and other developmental disorders, adjustment to school, individual differences in learning, and course and teacher evaluation. Questionnaires in the jobs and organizations category include those for measuring vocational interests; leadership and management skills; and for analyzing and evaluating jobs, positions, and entire organizations.

Questionnaires in the personality traits and disorders category may focus on a single construct (e.g., anxiety, attributional style, depression, self-concept, suicidal ideation, Type A personality) or on multiple characteristics of normal and mentally disordered persons. Among the most popular questionnaires in this category are the

Eysenck Personality Questionnaire, the General Health Questionnaire, and the 16 Personality Factor Questionnaire.

QUESTIONS AND ACTIVITIES

1. Define each of the following terms used in this chapter in a sentence or two. Consult the Glossary at the back of the book and a dictionary if you need help.

anaclitic depression	phenomenological perspective
assessment center	positive wellness
attention-deficit hyper-	quality of life
activity disorder	self-concept
(ADHD)	self-esteem
attributional style	situational management
health	standard questionnaire
introjective depression	standardized questionnaire
leadership	Type A personality
learned helplessness	visual analogue scale
menstrual distress	vocational interests

2. If you are a college student, complete the Questionnaire on Student Cheating and the Questionnaire on Student Interactions with Professors in programs I3 and I4 on the computer program diskette. Comment on these questionnaires and the kinds of information they provide.

3. Take and score the Altruism Questionnaire in program I6 of the computer diskette.

4. Which standard questionnaires or psychological inventories have you taken during the past few years? What did you understand to be the purposes of those instruments, and how did taking them affect your life?

5. For what purposes are questionnaires and inventories administered in each of the following contexts: consumer/sales, employment/occupational, health/medical, leisure/recreational, military/government, police/investigatory, school/academic?

6. What are some of the uses of questionnaires and interviews that you disapprove of and think should be banned? Why?

7. List and describe at least two standard questionnaires in each of the following areas: health care, learning and instruction, employment and other personnel services, diagnosis and treatment of behavior disorders.

SUGGESTED READING

Chapman, S. L. (1991). Chronic pain: Psychological assessment and treatment. In J. J. Sweet, R. H. Rozensky, & S. M. Tovian (Eds.), *Handbook of clinical psychology in medical settings* (pp. 401–442). New York: Plenum Press.

John, O. P. (1990). The "Big Five" factor taxonomy: Dimensions of personality in the natural language and in questionnaires. In L. A. Pervin (Ed.), *Handbook of personality theory and research* (pp. 67–100). New York: Guilford Press.

McDowell, I., & Newell, C. (1996). *Measuring health: A guide to rating scales and questionnaires* (2nd ed.). New York: Oxford University Press.

Sashkin, M., & Burke, W. W. (1990). Understanding and assessing organizational leadership. In K. E. Clark & M. B. Clark (Eds.), *Measures of leadership* (pp. 297–325). West Orange, NJ: Leadership Library of America.

Slabach, E. H., Morrow, J., & Wachs, T. D. (1991). Questionnaire measurement of infant and child temperament: Current status and future directions. In J. Strelau & A. Angleitner (Eds.), *Explorations in temperament: International perspectives on theory and measurement* (pp. 205–234). New York: Plenum Press.

Stewart, A. L., & Ware, J. E. (1992). *Measuring functioning and well-being: The Medical Outcomes Study.* Durham, NC: Duke University Press.

Thompson, C. (1992). Research questionnaires in routine clinical practice: Are they useful? In K. Hawton & P. J. Cowen (Eds.), *Practical problems in clinical psychiatry* (pp. 231–241). Oxford, England: Oxford University Press.

NOTE

1. *Anaclitic depression* is characterized by discomfort with interpersonal separation, whereas *introjective depression* is characterized by negative self-evaluation with respect to self-imposed standards.

8

Standard Inventories

The separation of questionnaires from inventories in this chapter and the preceding one, and indeed throughout the book, would seem to imply a substantive difference between these two types of instruments. Despite the overlap in the way in which the two labels are applied, questionnaires tend to be more open-ended or broader in scope than inventories. In fact, the term *questionnaire* is broader or more inclusive than *inventory*: All psychological inventories are questionnaires, but not all questionnaires are inventories. The items on a questionnaire designed for a survey research project, for example, are more heterogeneous and usually not grouped into categories or scales for scoring purposes. Unlike most questionnaires, inventories are designed to measure specific variables by means of subsets of items; the responses to a particular subset of items yields a score. A subset of items on an inventory that presumably measure the same variable are frequently referred to as a *scale*, although sometimes the instrument as a whole is called a scale rather than an inventory.

The names of a sample of commercially available scales that might just as well be called inventories are listed in Table 8.1. Scales are paper-and-pencil measures of cognitive, affective, behavioral, or physical characteristics of individuals or structural and functional features of groups. These variables are expressed in a wide range of interpersonal situations—domestic, school, clinical, vocational, avocational, and others. Several intelligence tests and many other instruments for

TABLE 8.1.   A Representative List of Noncognitive Scales

AAMD Adaptive Behavior Scale
Adaptive Behavior Evaluation Scale
Attention Deficit Disorders Evaluation Scale
Attitudes Toward Mainstreaming Scale
Beck Hopelessness Scale
Behavior Disorders Identification Scale
Bricklin Perceptual Scales
Career Decision Scale
Dissociative Experiences Scale
Family Environment Scale
Gifted Evaluation Scale
Health Locus of Control Scale
IPAT Anxiety Scale
IPAT Depression Scale
Learning Disability Evaluation Scale
Light's Retention Scale
Miner Sentence Completion Scale
Multidimensional Self Concept Scale
Perceptions of Parental Role Scales
Positive and Negative Syndrome Scale
Reynolds Adolescent Depression Scale
Rogers Criminal Responsibility Scales
Scale for the Assessment of Negative Symptoms
Scale for the Assessment of Positive Symptoms
Scale for the Assessment of Thought, Language, and Communication
Scale for the Identification of School Phobia
Scale of Feelings and Behavior of Love: Revised
Scale of Marriage Problems: Revised
Scale of Social Development
A Scale to Measure Attitudes Toward Disabled Persons
Scales of Early Communication Skills for Hearing-Impaired Children
Sex-Role Egalitarianism Scale
Social Climate Scales
Social-Emotional Dimension Scale
Spiritual Well-Being Scale
Stress Impact Scale
Stress Response Scale
Teacher Evaluation Scale
Tennessee Self-Concept Scale
Transition Behavior Scale
Vineland Social Maturity Scale

measuring cognitive and behavioral variables are labeled scales, but those in Table 8.1 are measures of noncognitive (affective) variables. An inspection of these scales would reveal that their composition and uses are similar to those of the inventories listed in Appendix D.

Although the term *scale* originally had the connotation of a graded set of measures on a continuum, that meaning has become less relevant over time. In fact, there is essentially no difference between many commercially available questionnaires, surveys, scales, or inventories in what they purportedly measure. The differences in terminology are mostly a matter of preference or custom rather than substantive content. In any case, just as the discussion in Chapter 7 was limited to commercially available instruments with *questionnaire* in the title, the present chapter is restricted to a consideration of instruments entitled *inventories.* Readers who wish to increase their familiarity with psychometric instruments having other labels are encouraged to consult the *Mental Measurements Yearbooks* and other sources of information concerning the surveys and scales listed in Tables 7.1 and 8.1. *Rating Scales and Checklists* (Aiken, 1996b) and other books on psychological and educational measurement (e.g., Aiken, 1996a, 1997a, 1997b) are particularly recommended.

As the list of addresses in Appendix E indicates, there are dozens of publishers of questionnaires and inventories throughout the world. The majority are located in the United States, but many commercial organizations in Australia, Canada, England, the Netherlands, and South Africa in particular also distribute large numbers of psychological tests and inventories. Appendix D provides a large, representative list of more than 180 commercially available inventories of normal personality characteristics, behavioral problems or disorders, vocational interests, values, attitudes, and human relationships, as well as inventories designed specifically for measuring and predicting development, educational attainment, job success, marital harmony, and other life consequences. Identifying information, a brief description, and a listing of review sources are provided for each of the instruments.

The remainder of this chapter provides detailed descriptions of selected instruments from Appendix D. We begin with inventories for assessing personality characteristics, proceed to inventories for evaluating stress and problem behaviors, inventories for analyzing marriage and other human relationships, and inventories for improving learning and instruction. Finally, inventories of interests, attitudes, values, leadership, and other important matters in the world of

TABLE 8.2.   The Most Frequently Cited Inventories in the Psychological
Research Literature, 1990–1996

Name of Questionnaire	Number of Articles Citing Questionnaire	Citation Rank
Beck Anxiety Inventory	46	14
Beck Depression Inventory	1337	1
Bem Sex-Role Inventory	214	6
Brief Symptom Inventory	151	8½
California Psychological Inventory	134	11
Children's Depression Inventories	196	7
Coopersmith Self-Esteem Inventories	66	13
Coping Inventory	56	15½
Eating Disorder Inventory	128	12
Eysenck Personality Inventory	394	4
Maslach Burnout Inventory	151	8½
Maudsley Personality Inventory	56	15½
Millon Clinical Multiaxial Inventory (I, II, III)	287	5
Minnesota Multiphasic Personality Inventory-2	772	3
NEO Personality Inventory	142	10
Personal Orientation Inventory	50	17
Personality Inventory for Children	41	20
The Problem-Solving Inventory	47	18
State-Trait Anxiety Inventory	869	2
Strong Interest Inventory	62	14

The second column is the number of articles in PsycLit during the period 1/90–6/96.

work are considered. The inventories in Appendix D that are most frequently used in research investigations are listed in Table 8.2.

PERSONALITY INVENTORIES

The first personality inventories were designed for psychiatric screening and diagnostic purposes, applications which remain dominant even
today. However, a number of inventories published during the 1930s
and subsequently were constructed for the purpose of describing and
analyzing normal personality. A rational/theoretical approach based
on common sense and personality theory guided the development of
the majority of these instruments. The trait/type conceptions of personality, on which several of the most prominent inventories were
based, were also hospitable to factor analysis and other procedures
stemming from correlational methodological. Rational/theoretical and

factor-analytic approaches have continued to play important roles in the design of personality inventories, but several widely used instruments, such as the MMPI, are based on criterion-keying methods.

Depression and Anxiety

The centrality of anxiety and depression in mental disorders and theories of psychopathology has led to the development and popularity of several questionnaires and inventories for measuring these constructs. Examples are the Beck Depression Inventory and the State-Trait Anxiety Inventory, which are ranked 1 and 2 among inventories in terms of frequency of usage in research investigations (see Table 8.2).

The Beck Depression Inventory-II (BDI-II) is based on clinical observations of attitudes, behavior, and other symptoms shown more frequently by depressed psychiatric patients than by nondepressed patients. It consists of 21 items for measuring cognitive, affective, somatic, and performance-related symptoms of depression; each item contains four statements reflecting increasing levels of a particular symptom of depression. Respondents indicate which of the four statements best expresses their feelings, and the responses are weighted on a scale ranging from 0 (no complaint) to 3 (severe complaint). The weights assigned to the respondent's selections are added to yield a total score and subscores on cognitive-affective and somatic-performance scales. A total score of 0–9 is considered "normal," 10–18 indicates "mild to moderate depression," 19–29 is indicative of "moderate to severe depression," and 30 or above indicates "extremely severe depression."

The State-Trait Anxiety Inventory (STAI) differentiates between temporary or "state" anxiety and more general, long-standing "trait" anxiety in adults. Feelings of apprehension, tension, nervousness, and worry, which occur in response to physical danger and psychological stress, are evaluated by the STAI. Each of the two scales—State and Trait—consists of 20 items containing four descriptive statements each. The respondent selects the description that best indicates how he or she feels.

Both the BDI and the STAI have good psychometric characteristics and have received favorable reviews (Dreger, 1978; Sundberg, 1992). The BDI has been employed extensively in clinical studies, especially those based on cognitive psychotherapies. The STAI has been used for screening students and military recruits and for evaluating the results of psychological counseling and other treatment procedures.

Self-Concept and Self-Esteem

Another psychological construct that has received a great deal of attention from theorists, researchers, and mental health workers is that of the *self.* The dictionary defines self as the perceived identity, individuality, or ego, the center of knowing and experiencing. The way in which a person perceives that self is known as the *self-concept,* while the evaluation placed on the self is known as *self-esteem.* In general, having a positive self-concept and high self-esteem are congruent with mental health.

Numerous measures of self-concept, self-esteem, self-actualization, self-perception, and the like have been published, several of which are listed in Appendixes C and D. Among these instruments are the Coopersmith Self-Esteem Inventories (CSEI), the Culture-Free Self-Esteem Inventories, and the Self-Worth Inventory. Only the first of these instruments has been used in an appreciable number of research investigations, so we will limit ourselves to a description of it.

The Coopersmith Self-Esteem Inventories—School Form, School Short Form, and Adult Form—consist of a series of 58, 50, and 25 dichotomous (Like Me, Unlike Me) items, respectively. The School Form, which is the most popular, is scored on General Self, Social Self-Peers, Home-Parents, School Academic, Total Self, and Lie Scale. Specific suggestions for counselors and teachers for improving the self-esteem of students are given in the manual. Unfortunately, the reliability, validity, and standardization data contained in the manual and in other publications concerned with this inventory are inadequate. Consequently, Peterson and Austin (1985) and Sewell (1985) concluded that the CSEI is appropriate for research but not for clinical purposes.

Personal Orientations

Related to self-concept and self-esteem is the construct of *self-actualization,* the extent to which people are able to realize their aspirations and potentials and become all that they are capable of being. Self-actualization may be characterized as a *personal orientation,* in that some people are oriented more than others toward striving to fulfill their potential. Another personal orientation is *sex role* or gender role; that is, adopting behaviors, attitudes, and cognitions that are more characteristic of one sex than the other.

The most widely used inventory of self-actualization is the Personal Orientation Inventory (POI), which was designed to measure the significant values and behaviors of self-actualizing people. This inventory consists of 150 forced-choice items and yields scores on two major orientation ratios: Time Ratio and Support Ratio. The former indicates whether the respondent is oriented primarily toward the past or the future, while the latter indicates whether the respondent's reactions are basically toward the self or toward other people. The POI is also scored on the following 10 scales: Self-Actualizing Value, Existentiality, Feeling Receptivity, Spontaneity, Self-Regard, Self-Acceptance, Nature of Man, Synergy, Acceptance of Aggression, and Capacity for Intimate Contact. The reliabilities of scores on these scales are quite modest, and the POI norms are based on fairly small samples of college freshman in the West and Midwest.

The Bem Sex-Role Inventory (BSRI) is the most extensively researched of all instruments designed to classify individuals according to the gender role they have adopted. The short version of the BSRI consists of 60 words or phrases to be rated on a seven-point scale (1 = "never or almost never true" through 7 = "always or almost always true"). Twenty items are designated as masculine, 20 as feminine, and 20 as sex-neutral. Scores on Masculinity (M), Femininity (F), and Androgyny (A) are determined first. Then the respondent is classified as Masculine (M above median and F below median), Feminine (F above median and M below median), Androgynous (both F and M above median), or Undifferentiated (both F and M below median). Payne's (1985) review of the BSRI is fairly positive, but he points out that the validity data are meager and the norms are unrepresentative of college students in general.

The MMPI and the CPI

The grandparent of all criterion-keyed personality inventories and the most widely used objective measure of personality in the United States and abroad is the Minnesota Multiphasic Personality Inventory (MMPI). Clinical psychologists in hospitals, clinics, counseling programs, and private practice have used the MMPI extensively for assisting in the diagnosis of mental disorders and selecting appropriate treatment methods. The second edition of this inventory, published in 1989, includes an adult form (MMPI-2) and an adolescent form (MMPI-A).

The MMPI-2 consists of 567 true-false items. The first 370 items are scored on four validity scales (L, F, K, ?) and 10 clinical scales; the remaining items are scored on numerous supplementary content and research scales. A sample profile of T scores on three validity scales, the 10 basic clinical scales, and three additional scales is shown in Figure 8.1. Traditionally, the shape of such a profile has been interpreted according to clinical experience and judgment, but computer-based interpretation of MMPI-2 scores has become quite common. The profile in Figure 8.1 is that of a 40-year-old divorced man with 11 years of education. He was diagnosed as having a *dysthymic disorder*, a nonpsychotic mood disorder also known as depressive neurosis. A secondary diagnosis was *dependent personality disorder*, the symptoms of which are a lack of self-confidence and a feeling of discomfort at having to be alone (Butcher, 1993).

In contrast to the psychopathology orientation of the MMPI-2, the California Psychological Inventory (CPI) was designed to emphasize the positive, normal aspects of personality. The revised CPI, third edition, consists of 434 true-false items, which can be scored on three conceptual categories: (1) 20 folk scales (Dominance, Empathy, Responsibility, Social Presence, Socialization, Tolerance, etc.); (2) 13 special scales (Anxiety, Creative Temperament, Managerial Potential, Work Orientation, etc.); and (3) three vector scales defining a theoretical model of personality structure. The first vector scale measures the interpersonal orientation theme (from internality to externality); the second measures the character or normative perspective theme (from norm-favoring to norm-questioning); the third vector scale measures the competence or realization theme (dispirited to self-fulfilled) of the respondent. Combinations of the three vector scales yield four personality types: alpha (authoritarian through steadfast), beta (dysphoric through humane), gamma (sociopathic through creative), and delta (disintegrative through visionary).

As with its parent instrument, the MMPI, reviews of the original and revised versions of the CPI have been mostly positive (e.g., Bolton, 1992; Engelhard, 1992). The CPI is an effective instrument for research and instructional purposes, and it can provide helpful information in counseling situations. Among its various uses are the identification of potential leadership qualities, the prediction of achievement, and the selection and development of employees to match jobs.

Other Personality Inventories

Like the MMPI, the Millon Clinical Multiaxial Inventory was designed primarily to assess personality disorders and clinical syndromes. The

MMPI-2 CLINICAL SCALES PROFILE

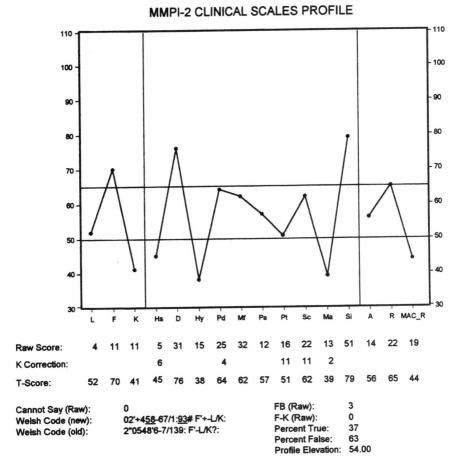

	L	F	K	Hs	D	Hy	Pd	Mf	Pa	Pt	Sc	Ma	Si	A	R	MAC_R
Raw Score:	4	11	11	5	31	15	25	32	12	16	22	13	51	14	22	19
K Correction:				6			4			11	11	2				
T-Score:	52	70	41	45	76	38	64	62	57	51	62	39	79	56	65	44

Cannot Say (Raw):	0	FB (Raw):	3
Welsh Code (new):	02'+458-67/1:93# F'+-L/K:	F-K (Raw):	0
Welsh Code (old):	2"0548'6-7/139: F'-L/K?:	Percent True:	37
		Percent False:	63
		Profile Elevation:	54.00

The names of the three validity scales in the left panel are: L = Lie, F = Infrequency, K = Defensiveness. The names of the 10 clinical scales in the middle panel are: Hs = Hypochondriasis, D = Depression, Hy = Conversion Hysteria, Pd = Psychopathic Deviate, Mf = Masculinity-Femininity, Pa = Paranoia, Pt = Psychasthenia, Sc = Schizophrenia, Ma = Hypomania, and Si = Social Introversion. The names of the three scales in the right panel are A = Anxiety, R = Repression, and Mac-R = MacAndrew Alcoholism-Revised.

Figure 8.1. Sample Profile of Scores on the MMPI-2. (*Source:* The Minnesota Report™, Adult Clinical System. Copyright © 1989 by the Regents of the University of Minnesota. All rights reserved.)

third edition of this inventory, MCMI-III, is coordinated with Theodore Millon's theory of personality and the fourth edition of the *Diagnostic and Statistical Manual* (DSM-IV) (American Psychiatric Association, 1994). The 175 items on the MCMI-III can be scored on 27 diagnostic scales, including 3 modifying indices, 11 clinical personality pattern scales, 3 severe personality pathology scales, 7 clinical syndrome scales, and 3 severe syndrome scales. A unique feature in scoring the MCMI-III is the computation of *base rate scores.* These scores take into account the frequency of particular characteristics or disorders in the general population, thereby maximizing the ratio of correct classifications *(valid positives)* to incorrect classifications *(false positives).* In general, the standardization and reliability of the MCMI-III are comparable with those of other well-designed inventories, but Butcher and Rouse (1996) warn of the danger of false positive errors in clinical applications of the instrument.

Another carefully designed and popular personality inventory, which assesses both normal and pathological personalities, is the NEO Personality Inventory. This inventory is based on a *five-factor model* of personality (The Big Five), including neuroticism, extraversion, openness to experience, agreeableness, and conscientiousness. The revised version of the inventory (NEO PI-R) breaks down each of these five factors, or *domains,* into six *facets:*

> *Neuroticism:* Anxiety, Angry Hostility, Depression, Self-Consciousness, Impulsiveness, Vulnerability
>
> *Extraversion:* Warmth, Gregariousness, Assertiveness, Activity, Excitement Seeking, Positive Emotions
>
> *Openness to Experience:* Fantasy, Aesthetics, Feelings, Actions, Ideas, Values
>
> *Agreeableness:* Trust, Straightforwardness, Altruism, Compliance, Modesty, Tender-Mindedness
>
> *Conscientiousness:* Competence, Order, Dutifulness, Achievement Striving, Self-Discipline, Deliberation

Thus, responses to the NEO PI-R are scored on five domains and 30 facets.

The NEO PI-R has received fairly positive reviews, but it is limited as a clinical instrument. In particular, the absence of validity scales and the utility of the analysis of domain scores as a clinical diagnostic technique have been criticized (Ben-Porath & Waller, 1992;

Butcher & Rouse, 1996). Even more fundamental is the criticism that the five-factor model of personality, on which the NEO PI-R is based, is an inadequate conceptualization of personality (e.g., Block, 1995; Butcher & Rouse, 1996).

STRESS AND BEHAVIOR PROBLEMS

The term *stress* is used somewhat ambiguously as either a stimulus that places physical and/or mental demands on the body or as the bodily changes produced by these demands. Hans Selye (1993) employed the term *stressor* for the stimulus and *stress* for the response, though in everyday English the stimulus is labeled "stress" and the response "strain." In Selye's conceptualization, stressors produce stress and hence lead to the mobilization of bodily resources and the expenditure of greater than normal energy. Stressors include physical conditions such as injuries, sleep deprivation, and inadequate nourishment, as well as psychological conditions such as frustration and conflict. Even relatively minor stressors such as the hassle of getting tied up in traffic or trying to get to school or work on time can produce physical and mental symptoms of stress. Several inventories and questionnaires have been designed to measure the number of minor stressors to which a person is subjected and their relative impacts; an example is the Daily Stress Inventory. Although everyday hassles can usually be dealt with fairly easily, major life events such as the death of a relative or a friend, the loss of a job, or a personal failure can lead to more intense, enduring stress. Furthermore, stress can be produced simultaneously in many people by a serious accident or a disaster.

The extent to which people are able to cope with stress depends on both the individual and the situation. In general, coping is more effective when the occurrence of the stressor is predictable and one can, as a result of ability and experience, control or prepare for it. Personality is a significant determiner of reactions to stressful situations, but it can be a deceptive predictor. Remaining cool, calm, and collected may be the best response to one type of stressful situation, whereas becoming aroused, angry, and adventurous may be more effective in another.

Coping Inventories

A number of inventories have been designed to assess an individual's resources and ways of coping with stress. Examples are the Coping

Inventory, the Coping Inventory for Stressful Situations, the Coping Resources Inventory, and the Coping Resources Inventory for Stress. Of these, the most widely used is the Coping Inventory. It consists of an observation form for children ages 3 to 16 years and a self-rating form for individuals 15 years and over. An observation instrument for children aged 4 to 36 months—the Early Coping Inventory—is also available in this set.

Burnout

Reactions to stress may be expressed in syndromes such as burnout, eating disorders, alcohol and drug abuse, grief, *posttraumatic stress disorder (PTSD)*, and a variety of physical conditions (migraine, headaches, skin disorders, chronic backache, bronchial asthma, etc.). Symptoms of *burnout*, a condition precipitated by the stress of over-work, include emotional exhaustion, negative attitudes, headaches, backaches, reduced productivity, feelings of depersonalization, and social withdrawal. One inventory designed to identify and counsel victims of burnout is the Maslach Burnout Inventory.

Eating Disorders

Many physical conditions (anorexia, bulimia, recurring headaches, es-sential hypertension, peptic ulcer, alcoholism, etc.) have been linked with stress and personality. *Anorexia nervosa,* characterized by ex-treme weight loss, a belief that one is too fat, and an intense fear of gain-ing weight, has stimulated a great deal of research. More receptive to treatment than anorexia is *bulimia,* the principal symptom of which is uncontrollable binge eating and purging. Two instruments designed to identify and assess eating disorders are the Eating Disorder Inventory-2 (EDI-2) and the Eating Inventory. The EDI-2 is appropriate for individu-als aged 12 years and over and has received very good reviews as a clin-ical tool (Ash, 1995; Schenke, 1995). The Eating Inventory is designed for older adolescents and adults.

Alcoholism and Drug Abuse

Like eating disorders, alcoholism and drug abuse are habit patterns that may be precipitated and exacerbated by stress. Illustrative of the various instruments designed to identify alcohol and drug problems for purposes of referral and treatment are the Alcohol Use Inventory and the Substance Abuse Subtle Screening Test. The Alcohol Use Inventory has received favorable reviews (Drummond, 1995; McNeely, 1995) for its psychometric properties in Caucasian populations. Because information concerning its use in other populations is lacking, it should be used cautiously with non-Caucasians. As indicated by its name, the Substance Abuse Subtle Screening Test is a screening test for chemical abusers. Skill and sensitivity to the legal issues associated with the use of this inventory are required, but it too has received fairly positive reviews (Kerr, 1995; Vacc, 1995). However, it is not anticipated that it will replace the less expensive breathalyzer test.

Suicide

Continuing stress and an inability to cope with it can lead to chronic anger and depression. The feelings of personal worthlessness and despair that accompany profound depression may, in turn, precipitate suicidal thoughts and attempts. Because people who are thinking about suicide often fail to realize that they need help, family members, friends, and others who interact with the individual should be alert to signs of suicidal thoughts and behavior. These signs include suicide threats, statements revealing a desire to die, previous suicide attempts, sudden changes in behavior (withdrawal, apathy, moodiness), depression (crying, sleeplessness, loss of appetite, hopelessness), and "final arrangements" such as giving away one's possessions (Beck, Brown & Steer, 1989).

Two instruments that may be useful in identifying and dealing with suicidal individuals are the Inventory of Suicide Orientation-30 and the Suicide Intervention Response Inventory. The former is an identification/screening inventory, while the latter assesses the ability of paraprofessionals to respond appropriately to self-destructive clients.

INTERPERSONAL RELATIONSHIPS

Human beings are social animals. For the most part, they live and work in groups, they feel more comfortable and secure when they are around other people, and they depend on social interactions and social reinforcement to learn, satisfy their needs, and grow. Dependence on other people is, however, a doubled-edged sword. People are the sources of both our greatest happiness and our greatest sadness, our joys and our sorrows.

Childhood is where social relationships begin, usually but not always in a family unit. The actions and interactions of the members of a family serve as a model or template of the wider society, and the responses learned in the smaller world tend to generalize to the larger one. Although first lessons, those learned in the primary family group, are extremely important, the acquisition of norms, roles, and other social behavior patterns is not limited to the family setting. Social skills and attitudes are also acquired in schools, peer groups, church groups, work groups, clubs, and other organizations.

Social Psychology

The field of social psychology is devoted to the study of the structure and functioning of groups, and in particular the dynamic interactions of people in those groups. Social psychologists have developed numerous questionnaires, inventories, and scales to study variables such as attitudes, communication patterns, group cohesiveness, group morale, and leadership. In addition, at the interface of social and personality psychology, many self-report measures of the behavior of individuals in groups have been developed. Examples of published instruments for assessing interpersonal communication are A Parent-Adolescent Communication Inventory and the Interpersonal Communication Inventory. The former inventory, including adolescent and parent forms, measures the perceptions of individuals aged 13 years and over of the patterns of their current communication with their parents. The latter inventory assesses the interpersonal communication skills and problems of individuals in grades 9 and above in situations outside the family setting. Three other self-report inventories for evaluating interpersonal relations are the Personal Relations Inventory, the Social Behavior Assessment Inventory, and the Situational Preference Inventory. The first of these assesses the construct of social "assertiveness" in individuals at the high school level and above. The second inventory was designed to measure the social skills of elementary and junior high school students, and the third measures the social interaction styles of individuals in grades 9 and above.

Marital Relations

In describing the behaviors that are crucial to human happiness, Sigmund Freud placed the ability to love above the ability to work. An indolent person might question the latter but certainly not the former ability. As documented by innumerable observational studies, surveys, and experiments, what Freud implied by "love," namely sexual gratification, is extremely important to most people. Self-report instruments such as the Derogatis Sexual Functioning Inventory and The Golombok Rust Inventory of Sexual Satisfaction also provide valuable information for counseling married or cohabiting sexual partners.

Despite the frequency of connubial arguments concerning sex and money, there is obviously more to marriage than these two matters. Marital compatibility involves a host of physical, mental, and affective concerns, and problems in any of these areas can create marital difficulties. The increased incidence of marital discord, separation, and divorce during the past few decades has led to an accelerated growth in the marriage and family counseling and education professions. Associated with that growth has been the development of numerous inventories, such as the:

Caring Relationship Inventory

Couple's Pre-Counseling Inventory, Revised Edition

The Golombok Rust Inventory of Marital State

A Marital Communication Inventory

Marital Satisfaction Inventory

Marriage Expectation Inventories

Marriage Role Expectation Inventory

Partner Relationship Inventory (Research Edition)

Personal Relationship Inventory

Unfortunately, all of these inventories can be faulted to some degree for the inadequacy of their psychometric characteristics. The most widely researched of them, and arguably the best self-report inventory of marital satisfaction currently available, is the Marital Satisfaction Inventory. This self-report measure of marital interaction and marital distress is designed for administration to couples who are beginning marriage counseling. The 11 areas on which it can be scored provide a fairly comprehensive list of the sources of marital discord: Conventionalism, Global Distress, Affective Communication, Problem-Solving Communication, Time Together, Disagreement about Finances, Sexual Dissatisfaction, Role Orientation, Family History of Distress, Dissatisfaction with Children, and Conflict over Childrearing.

LEARNING AND INSTRUCTION

Learning, defined as any change in behavior resulting from experience, starts even before birth. Formal learning begins at home and continues and expands at school. Many parents teach their children the rudiments of reading and arithmetic before the first day of school, but much is left for teachers to do.

School attendance makes people more aware of and knowledgeable about the world in which they live and better equipped to meet its challenges. But every child is different: Some children are bright, receptive students, while for others school learning is an unrewarding struggle. On the instructional side, some gifted teachers seem to work wonders with all children who come under their tutelage, whereas other teachers appear only to be marking time until they can go home and forget about students, parents, and school administrators.

Styles of Learning and Instruction

The recognition that different children learn in different ways and are receptive to different kinds of teachers and teaching methods has prompted a great deal of research in educational psychology. Individual differences among children are assessed even during the preschool years, as witnessed in the administration of reading readiness tests and screening instruments such as the Kindergarten Screening Inventory and the Teacher's School Readiness Inventory. The last two inventories were designed to help teachers identify differences among preschool children that are relevant to their success and failure in school. A parallel instrument to the Teacher's School Readiness Inventory, the Caregiver's School Readiness Inventory, must be completed by parents rather than teachers to identify preschool children "at risk" for later academic problems.

As in all research projects, methods of measuring the independent, dependent, and concomitant variables in studies of learner characteristics and how these variables interact with instructional methods are necessary. A number of inventories for assessing learning styles have been published, among which are the Canfield Learning Styles Inventory, the Learning Preference Inventory, the Learning-Style Inventory, the Learning Style Inventory, and the Learning Styles Inventory. The first of these, the Canfield Learning Styles Inventory, was designed to measure the learning preferences of students from junior high through college and adulthood. It consists of 30 items that provide information on preferred conditions for learning, areas of interest, mode of learning, and course grade expectations. The respondent's scores are classified into one of nine learning style categories: social, applied, social/applied, independent, independent/applied, conceptual, independent/conceptual, social/conceptual, and neutral preference. Students who have similar learning styles may then be placed in the same instructional group, presumably facilitating instruction.

In reviewing the Canfield Learning Styles Inventory, Benton (1992) criticized it for a lack of sound validity and reliability information. He concluded that, despite the apparent widespread use of learning styles inventories, it is unclear what they measure and whether taking responses to them into account improves learning. According to Benton, student knowledge and interest are probably more important than concerns about style in regulating instruction.

A similar picture emerges from a consideration of a companion instrument to the Canfield Learning Styles Inventory—the Canfield Instructional Styles Inventory. Based on the premise that matching instructional style to learning style improves learning, this inventory attempts to measure which teaching methods instructors prefer and which they would like to avoid. The inventory consists of 25 questions that are read and then ranked in order of preference. The results are scored on teacher preferences in four areas: conditions for instruction (peer, instructor, organization, detail, goal setting, independence, competition, authority), areas of interest (numeric, inanimate, qualitative, people), modes of instruction (lecturing, iconics, reading, direct experience), and influence (strength of belief that method of instruction affects learning).

Andrews (1992) criticized the Canfield Instructional Styles Inventory for lack of data relating the preferences expressed on it to actual classroom behavior. Although she found the idea of an instructional style and a corresponding inventory that might be used as a self-assessment and training tool appealing, Andrews concluded that, despite its intuitive appeal, the Canfield Instructional Styles Inventory could not be recommended.

Teacher Attitudes and Opinions

Recognition that the classroom teacher is one of the most important factors in student learning and that both the abilities and attitudes of the teacher can affect the extent to which students learn, many other self-report measures have been designed for administration to teachers. Among these are the Educational Leadership Practices Inventory, the Teacher Opinion Inventory, and the Teacher Stress Inventory. Brief descriptions of these inventories are given in Appendix D.

Creative Behavior

Similar to learning styles inventories, but focusing on creativity instead of learning, are the Creative Behavior Inventory, The Creative Styles Inventory, and The Creatix Inventory. These inventories, which were designed to measure certain variables that are presumably related to creativity (intuitive versus logical style, risk taking, etc.), are not widely used and are subject to some of the same criticisms as inventories of learning styles. Two "creativity" inventories designed specifically as screening instruments are the Group Inventory for Finding Creative Talent and the Group Inventory of Finding Interests. The former, taken by elementary schoolchildren, provides scores on imagination, independence, and many interests. The latter, designed for junior and senior high school students, yields five scores presumably indicative of creativity. An analysis of self-report inventories of creativity underscores that reliable measures of creativity can be constructed, but that validating these measures against an acceptable criterion of creative performance or behavior is difficult. This is particularly true when there is little or no consensus on what constitutes "creative" behavior.

Adaptive Behavior

On the other side of the ability continuum from the highly creative or gifted child is the child of limited ability who is faced with the task of simply adapting to the environment in which he or she finds him- or herself. Measures of *adaptive behavior* are often administered along with tests of intelligence to gauge the abilities of mentally retarded or learning-disabled individuals to adapt to home, school, work, and other environments. One measure of adaptive behavior, the Adaptive Behavior: Street Survival Skills Questionnaire, was mentioned in Chapter 7. Another measure of this kind, the Career Adaptive Behavior Inventory, was designed to assist teachers in improving the adaptability of developmentally disabled students aged 5 to 15. It consists of items to be rated by parents, teachers, or other professionals in 10 areas. Two other, somewhat more popular, measures of adaptive behavior are the Adaptive Behavior Inventory and the Adaptive Behavior Inventory for Children.

As with similar inventories, the Adaptive Behavior Inventory was designed to evaluate functional daily living skills and to identify children who are suspected of being mentally retarded or emotionally disturbed. This inventory consists of five scales (Self-Care Skills, Communication Skills, Social Skills, Academic Skills, Occupational Skills) containing 30 items each. In addition to scores on these scales, an overall adaptive behavior quotient can be obtained. The adaptive behavior quotient, standard score, and percentile rank norms are based on relatively small, but presumably representative, samples of disabled or mentally retarded students. The internal consistency reliabilities of the Adaptive Behavior Inventory are satisfactory, though evidence for other types of reliability and validity is skimpy.

VOCATIONAL INTERESTS AND OTHER WORK-RELATED VARIABLES

Preparation for entry into the world of work is an important developmental task for young people. Finding a job or entering a profession with which one is satisfied and can earn an acceptable living is a major step in attaining security and happiness. Despite the old saying that "money can't buy happiness," wealthier people tend to be healthier and happier than their poorer contemporaries. A high-paying job is not necessarily yours for life, but it does make you feel safer and freer to pursue other activities.

For most people, job satisfaction is related not only to job security but also to interests. People like to do things they are interested in and perceive as valuable. Interests are related to capability in that one promotes the other, but they are by no means identical. Furthermore, one may harbor a misperception as to what a particular occupation entails, only to discover upon beginning work that it is uninteresting, too easy, or too difficult.

Until the 1930s, industrial managers showed relatively little concern with whether workers were happy, satisfied, or interested in what they were doing. The main goal of business and industry was viewed as efficient production and service. Workers were selected for their ability to do the job and were seen as motivated by money and other external reinforcements rather than internal feelings of security, achievement, interest, and social acceptance. Subsequently, due in some measure to the research of industrial psychologists and sociologists, executives and managers became more aware of the role of human factors in job productivity and satisfaction. It became clear that taking human factors into account could lead to better prediction, not only of short-term productivity but also of events such as turnover, accidents, recruitment, and less objective or less tangible criteria.

Vocational Interests

The first standardized inventory of vocational interests, the Strong Vocational Interest Blank for Men, was developed by E. K. Strong, Jr. during the late 1920s. Research on this inventory, which was designed primarily as a tool for the vocational counseling of high school and college students, and revisions of it have continued to the present day. The current edition—the Strong Interest Inventory (SII)—consists of 317 items in eight parts: Occupations, School Subjects, Activities, Leisure Activities, Types of People, Preference between Two Activities, Your Characteristics, and Preference for the World of Work. Responses are scored on five groups of measures: Administrative Indexes, General Occupational Themes, Basic Interest Scales, Occupational Scales, and Personal Style Scales. In interpreting the results, scores on the Administrative Indexes are checked first to determine whether the examinee understood the directions and answered conscientiously. Then the T scores on six General Occupational Themes (Realistic, Investigative, Artistic, Social, Enterprising, Conventional) and the 25 Basic Interest Scales are examined to reveal the general areas or categories in which the examinee's vocational interests fall. Finally, T scores on the Occupational Scales are inspected for high and low scores in each of 109 different occupations. These scores are based on numerical weights obtained from the criterion-keying procedure of comparing the examinee's item responses with those of norm groups of individuals in specific occupations. In career counseling with the SII, it should be emphasized that success (or failure) in a particular occupation depends not only on interests but also on specific abilities, time devoted to training and performance, and unpredictable contingency factors.

The SII is directed principally at young people of average or above average mental ability who are planning to enter professional occupations. Other interest inventories, such as the Career Assessment Inventory, have been developed for counseling individuals for entrance into nonprofessional occupations, but they are not as widely used as the SII. Even less frequently administered, and also less valid, are nonverbal instruments such as the Geist Picture Interest Inventory and the Reading-Free Vocational Interest Inventory.

Because a person's vocational interests tend to be somewhat unrealistic before senior high school, most interest inventories are designed for individuals who are at least 15 years old. However, several inventories (Career Beliefs Inventory, Career Development Inventory, Career Directions Inventory, Career Interest Inventory) can be administered as early as the eighth grade. Reaching down even further are the Career Maturity Inventory, which has a floor of sixth grade, and the Vocational Interest Inventory, with a third-grade floor. Although the results obtained from administering an interest inventory to students in late elementary or junior high school would not be expected to be very stable, taking such an inventory and discussing their scores with a teacher or other knowledgeable person may serve to introduce students to specific occupations and what they entail.

The fact that vocational interests are related to personality is expressed in several inventories. For example, the Vocational Interest Inventory—Revised (VII) is based on Anne Roe's two-dimensional (person-oriented versus nonperson-oriented, orientation to purposeful communication versus orientation to resource utilization) theory linking interests to personality. Designed for students in grade 3 and above, the VII consists of 112 forced-choice items focusing on eight occupational areas: Service, Business Contact, Organization, Technical, Outdoor, Science, General Culture, and Arts and Entertainment.

More popular than the VII is the Vocational Preference Inventory (VPI), which is based on J. L. Holland's theory that occupations are describable in terms of personality characteristics. The format of the VPI is the soul of simplicity: 160 different occupations to which older adolescent or adult examinees respond with "like" or "dislike." Responses are scored on 11 scales: Realistic, Investigative, Artistic, Scientific, Enterprising, Conventional, Self-Control, Status, Masculinity-Femininity, Infrequency, and Acquiescence. Note that scores on the first six variables, the *RIASEC themes,* are also obtained in scoring the Strong Interest Inventory. An examinee's RIASEC scores on the VPI may be referred to an occupations finder (SDS Occu-Find) for career exploration and guidance purposes.

Attitudes, Values, and Leadership

Attitudes, defined as learned predispositions to respond positively or negatively to certain objects, situations, institutions, or persons, are discussed in detail in Chapter 8 of *Rating Scales and Checklists.* Both attitudes and *values*—the usefulness, importance, or worth associated with particular activities or objects—play a role in job acquisition and satisfaction. Although most measures of attitudes and values are non-standardized questionnaires, inventories, or scales constructed for specific research or informational purpose, many instruments of this kind are also commercially available. Examples are the Work Values Inventory and the Work Adjustment Inventory, which can be administered to individuals as early as the seventh grade. Others, such as the Employment Values Inventory and the Employee Attitude Inventory, are appropriate only for adults.

Most attitude inventories used in business and industrial organizations are administered to on-the-job employees. Some inventories of attitudes and other characteristics, however, are used as preemployment selection devices. Examples are the Employability Inventory and the Employee Reliability Inventory.

Attitudes are of special importance on jobs requiring a great deal of interpersonal contact, for example, sales and management. A multitude of questionnaires and inventories for assessing the skills, practices, and attitudes of applicants for sales, managerial, and other leadership positions are commercially available. One of the most extensively researched management development inventories is the Leadership Practices Inventory. This inventory has received fairly positive reviews and, unlike many other instruments with a similar purpose, it is more than an attractively packaged inventory with poor psychometric qualities.

Two other organization-oriented inventories that deserve mention are the Motivational Patterns Inventory and the Organizational Culture Inventory. The former was designed to assist members of organizations in exploring their motivations, so that their contributions to the success of the organization might be enhanced. The latter inventory goes beyond the individual member to measure the norms and expectations of the members of an organization as a whole.

SUMMARY

The most widely administered of all psychological inventories are those that focus on normal variations in personality traits or psychopathology. Illustrative of carefully designed inventories of a single psychological characteristic are the Coopersmith Self-Esteem Inventories, the Personal Orientation Inventory, the Beck Depression Inventory, and the State-Trait Anxiety Inventory. Popular inventories of multiple characteristics are the Minnesota Multiphasic Personality Inventory (MMPI), the California Psychological Inventory, the Millon Clinical Multiaxial Inventory, and the Revised NEO Personality Inventory.

Stress reactions and problem behaviors can be assessed to some degree by personality inventories such as the MMPI, but a number of inventories designed for the identification and analysis of specific behavioral syndromes related to stress are also available. Examples are the Maslach Burnout Inventory, the Eating Disorder Inventory-2, the Alcohol Use Inventory, and the Inventory of Suicide Orientation-30.

Because of the central importance of maintaining harmonious relationships with other people for effective personal functioning, numerous self-report inventories have been constructed. Illustrative of instruments of this type are the Personal Relations Inventory, the Derogatis Sexual Functioning Inventory, and the Marital Satisfaction Inventory.

Human development is evaluated not only by physical growth and functioning but also by the acquisition of required knowledge and skills for adjusting and coping with the everyday and exceptional tasks of living. Efforts to improve the value of formal educational experiences in meeting the needs of the individual and society can be improved by educational research and assessment. Inventories of styles of learning and instruction have been devised in an attempt to match the ways in which students learn with different modes of instruction and different kinds of teachers, but so far with quite modest success. Measures of teachers' attitudes and opinions, as well as the creative and adaptive behaviors of students, may also prove helpful in improving the conditions under which learning takes place, and hence the effectiveness of efforts to enhance it.

Next to personality inventories, vocational interest inventories such as the Strong Interest Inventory are the most widely used self-report measures for practical counseling purposes. Measures of interests, attitudes, and values are useful in a variety of academic and organizational contexts for assessing motivations, beliefs, and other affective variables and for introducing adolescents and young adults to the world of work. Instruments of these kinds can also contribute to the prediction of individual effectiveness in interpersonal-contact occupations such as sales and management.

QUESTIONS AND ACTIVITIES

1. Define each of the following terms in a sentence or two. Consult the Glossary and a dictionary if you need help.

adaptive behavior
alcoholism
anorexia nervosa
anxiety
attitude
base rate scores
bulimia
burnout
coping inventory
creative behavior
dependent personality
   disorder
depression
domains
dysthymic disorder
facets

false positives
five-factor model
human factors
personal orientation
posttraumatic stress disorder
   (PTSD)
RIASEC themes
scale
self-actualization
self-concept
self-esteem
sex role
stress
stressor
valid positives
values

2. Complete and score the Personal Identity Inventory in program I9 on the computer diskette.

3. Complete and score the Personality Inventory in Figure 3.2. Allow one point for circled responses corresponding to the scoring key given in the caption for Figure 3.2. Construct a psychograph (psychological profile) of your scores on the five factors by plotting each score (0 to 3) on the vertical axis against its factor designation on the horizontal axis. What can you conclude from inspecting the psychograph of your scores?

4. For what purposes would a single-construct inventory be most appropriate? A multiple-construct inventory? How might the two kinds of inventories be used in conjunction in a specific situation for a particular purpose?

5. Why do you think that it is important for the variables measured by an empirically validated (criterion-keyed) inventory to have low correlations with each other but have high correlations with an external criterion?

6. Discuss and evaluate the ways in which inventories of personality characteristics, interests, attitudes, and values might be used in counseling situations.

7. Complete and score the following inventory:

Inventory of Opinions Concerning Personality Assessment

Directions: Each of the following numbered statements expresses an opinion concerning personality assessment. Indicate the extent of your agreement with the opinion expressed in the statement by writing the letter(s) corresponding to your response next to the number of the statement: sa = strongly agree, a = agree, u = uncertain, d = disagree, sd = strongly disagree.

_____ 1. Many personality inventories are reliable and valid measures of temperament and other stylistic aspects of behavior.

_____ 2. It is appropriate to use scores on personality inventories for diagnostic purposes in clinical, counseling, and educational contexts.

_____ 3. Personality inventories are valid measures of personality characteristics in adults but not in children.

_____ 4. Personality inventories are equally fair measures of affective characteristics in people of all ethnic and socioeconomic groups.

_____ 5. Personality inventories are not valid predictors of a person's performance in school or on the job.

_____ 6. Personality inventories are useful in the diagnosis of mental disorders in children and adults.

_____ 7. Scores on personality inventories should not be used for purposes of selection and promotion in employment contexts.

_____ 8. Personality inventories should not be administered because they upset people and make them wonder about themselves.

_____ 9. It is fair to use scores on personality inventories in selecting students for admission to colleges, universities, and professional schools.

_____ 10. It is inappropriate to use personality inventories for academic and/or vocational counseling purposes.

Scoring: Assign points to your response to each item according to the following scale: sd = 0, d = 1, u = 2, a = 3, sa = 4. Then determine your total score by the formula: Total score = Item(1) + Item(2) - Item(3) + Item(4) - Item(5) + Item(6) - Item(7) - Item(8) + Item(9) - Item(10) + 20. Determine the percentage of the maximum score by multiplying your score by 2.5. Interpret the result.

SUGGESTED READING

Eyberg, S. (1992). Parent and teacher behavior inventories for the assessment of conduct problem behaviors in children. In L. D. VandeCreek, S. Knapp, & T. L. Jackson (Eds.), *Innovations in clinical practice: A source book* (Vol. 11, pp. 261–270). Sarasota, FL: Professional Resource Press/Professional Resource Exchange.

Finn, S. E., & Butcher, J. N. (1991). Clinical objective personality assessment. In M. Hersen, A. E. Kasdin, & A. S. Bellack (Eds.), *The clinical psychology handbook* (2nd ed., pp. 362–373). New York: Pergamon.

Hansen, J. C. (1994). The measurement of vocational interests. In M. G. Rumsey, C. B. Walker, & J. H. Harris (Eds.), *Personnel selection and classification* (pp. 293–316). Hillsdale, NJ: Lawrence Erlbaum.

Keller, L. S., Butcher, J. N., & Slutske, W. S. (1990). Objective personality assessment. In G. Goldstein & M. Hersen (Eds.), *Handbook of psychological assessment* (2nd ed., pp. 345–386). New York: Pergamon Press.

Lachar, D. (1993). Symptom checklists and personality inventories. In T. R. Kratochwill & R. J. Morris (Eds.), *Handbook of psychotherapy with children and adolescents* (pp. 38–57). Boston: Allyn & Bacon.

Miller, T. W. (1996). Current measures in the assessment of stressful life events. In T. W. Miller (Ed.), *Theory and assessment of stressful life events* (pp. 209–233). Madison, CT: International Universities Press.

Appendix A

Computer Programs for Questionnaires and Inventories

INTRODUCTION

The programs on this diskette will run on "qbasic" or "basica." Qbasic is provided on the diskette. You can run the programs off the floppy diskette or from your computer's hard drive. The programs will run faster from your hard drive. To copy the files from the diskette to your hard drive follow the instructions given below.

MINIMUM SYSTEM REQUIREMENTS

- IBM-PC or compatible computer with DOS 3.3 or higher
- 3.5" floppy disk drive

HOW TO INSTALL THE FILES ONTO YOUR COMPUTER

We recommend that you copy the files from the diskette to your hard drive by running the installation program. To install files do the following:

1. Insert the diskette into the floppy disk drive of your computer.
2. At the DOS prompt, type **A:\INSTALL** and press Enter. The opening screen of the installation program will appear. Press Enter to continue.
3. The default destination directory is **C:\QUESTION**. If you wish to change the default destination, you may do so now. Follow the instructions on the screen.
4. The installation program will copy all files including the qbasic program to your hard drive in the **C:\QUESTION** or user-designated directory.

USING THE PROGRAMS

If you are running the programs off the floppy disk drive do the following:

1. Insert the diskette into your floppy disk drive.
2. In DOS, type **A:** at the DOS prompt.
3. Type **menu** or **prog** at the A:\> prompt and press Enter. The command "menu" will get you into the program menu, from which you can make a choice of programs to run. The command "prog" is followed by the query "Category and number of program?," at which you must specify the category (A through I) and the number of the program you wish to run (e.g., prog.a1).

You can also run this program when you are in Windows. From the File Menu in Program Manager or from the Start Menu, choose the Run command. Type **a:menu** or **a:prog** in the command box. Click on the OK button.

If you installed the program to your hard drive do the following:

1. In DOS, type **cd C:\QUESTION** (or the user designated directory) and press Enter.
2. Type **menu** or **prog** at the C:\QUESTION> prompt and press Enter. The command "menu" will get you into the program menu, from which you can make a choice of programs to run. The command "prog" is followed by the query "Category and number of program?," at which you must specify the category (A through I) and the number of the program you wish to run (e.g., prog.a1).

You can also run this program when you are in Windows. From the File Menu in Program Manager or from the Start Menu, choose the Run command. Type **C:\QUESTION\MENU** or **C:\QUESTION\PROG** in the command box. (If you installed the program to another directory replace C:\QUESTION with the name of directory you designated.) Click on the OK button.

You can escape from a running program by pressing the function key F1.

The output for some of the programs is displayed on the screen and/or in a disk output file named *results.* Follow the directions for each program carefully and you should have few problems. All the programs display in color, but work on a black-and-white monitor as well. Keep in mind that the questionnaires and inventories administered by the programs in Category I are illustrative rather than serious efforts at assessment. Consequently, you should view the results as suggestive rather than definitive and advise other users to do likewise.

USER ASSISTANCE

If you need basic assistance with installation, or need to replace a damaged disk, please call our product support number at (212) 850-6194 weekdays between 9 A.M. and 4 P.M. Eastern Standard Time.

To place additional orders or to request information about other Wiley products, please call (800) 225-5945.

QBASIC © copyright 1996–1997 Microsoft Corporation.

ABOUT THE PROGRAMS

The following brief descriptions should suffice to acquaint you with the programs.

CATEGORY A. CONSTRUCTING, ADMINISTERING, AND SCORING QUESTIONNAIRES AND INVENTORIES

1. *Constructing a Questionnaire or Inventory.* This program enables you to construct a questionnaire or an inventory, review and revise the constructed instrument, then print it. Many different questionnaires and inventories, depending on their lengths, may be stored in appropriately coded files on the same diskette as the program or on a companion diskette. The title, directions, and questions for a specific questionnaire or inventory may be edited or changed after the instrument has been administered. The program also permits you to change the password and to enter a series of respondent identification numbers. The initial password is *question.*

2. *Administering a Questionnaire Constructed by Program A1.* This program administers a questionnaire or inventory constructed by program A1. The options enable the user to (1) complete or administer a questionnaire or inventory, (2) review the items and answers to the instrument, and (3) print a table of item responses and response times. The respondent must enter the password (*answer* to begin), the number of the instrument, and his or her identification number. The printout from option 3 includes the instrument number, the respondent's identification number, and a six-column table. The first two columns of the table list the part and item numbers; the third column lists the respondent's first responses to the items; the fourth column lists the times (in seconds) for the first responses to the items; the fifth column lists the respondent's last (second, third, etc.) responses to the items; the sixth column lists the times (in seconds) for the changed responses to the items.

3. *Storing a Questionnaire or Inventory in a Designated File.* This program stores any single- or multipart questionnaire or inventory in a file designated by the user and in the file named *results* as well. The number of parts in the instrument, the number of items in each part, the general directions, and the specific directions and items for each part are entered from a computer keyboard. The number of parts and the number of items in each part are recorded at the top of the results file and the output file designated by the user; they should be deleted from the file if a clean copy of the questionnaire is needed.

4. *Administering a Questionnaire Stored by Program A3.* This program administers any questionnaire or inventory stored in a designated ASCII file by program A3 and stores the respondent's answers in the *results* file. The number of parts and the number of items in each part must appear at the top of the input file, one number per line. This happens automatically if the questionnaire has been constructed by program A3, but these numbers must be added manually to the file if the questionnaire has been stored in another fashion. Single spacing must be used within the directions and within items, and double-spacing between the directions and between items. The respondent's answers may be printed, by part and item number, immediately after completing the questionnaire or at any other convenient time.

5. *Scoring and Storing Responses to Questionnaires and Inventories.* This program scores and stores the responses to any questionnaire, inventory, or scale. The responses and the scoring key may be entered from a computer keyboard or transferred from a designated file where they are stored in ASCII format. Different numerical weights may be assigned to the responses to items in different sections of the questionnaire. Separate scores on each part or section and total scores are computed for each respondent. The results are printed on the screen and in the *results* file.

6. *Constructing a Questionnaire to Measure Group Cohesiveness.* This program generates and prints a questionnaire from the designated names of the members of any kind of group. Group members fill out the printed questionnaires by evaluating each named person on a 2 to 7 category scale. The respondent indicates how much he or she would like or dislike to engage in some activity with the person, how close the respondent feels toward the person, how willing the respondent is to cooperate with the person, how important the respondent considers the person to the successful functioning of the group, or any other interpersonal perception or attitude. The questionnaire can be administered at the beginning and again at the end of a course or other regularly scheduled meeting to determine changes in intragroup perceptions and attitudes.

7. *Scoring Responses to a Questionnaire for Measuring Group Cohesiveness.* This program scores the responses obtained from the questionnaires generated by program A6 and computes several indexes of intragroup perceptions or attitudes. The measures include: (1) a coefficient for each respondent indicating how he or she feels toward the other members of the group; (2) a coefficient for each respondent revealing how the rest of the group feels toward him or her; and (3) a coefficient reflecting how the entire group feels about the group as a whole.

8. *Estimating Responses Using the Randomized Response Technique.* This program estimates the number of respondents likely to answer yes to a sensitive question by the randomized response technique and application of a conditional probability formula. The user enters: (1) the total number of respondents; (2) the number of respondents receiving the sensitive question); (3) the number of respondents answering yes to either the sensitive or the innocuous question; and (4) the probability that a randomly selected person will answer yes to the innocuous question. The printout consists of the estimated number and percentage of respondents receiving the sensitive question who answered yes to it.

9. *Programs on Alternative Voting Systems.* From an n by c matrix of the ranks assigned by n voters to c candidates, this set of five programs determines: (1) the frequency distributions, means, medians, and Borda counts for the candidates; (2) the Condorcet candidate; (3) the elected candidates by using the Hare system of single transferable vote (STV); (4) agreement indexes across voters for each candidate, an overall agreement index, and the z value for determining the statistical significance of the overall agreement index; (5) the number of votes distributed among the c candidates by the n voters, as determined by the cumulative or approval voting procedures. The ranked data must be entered from a data file.

CATEGORY B. SELECTING AND ASSIGNING SAMPLES

1. *Selecting Simple Random Samples.* This program selects a sample of m integers at random, with or without replacement, from a population of n successive

integers. When $m = n$, the numbers are selected without replacement and the result is a random permutation of the numbers.

2. *Selecting Random Samples from a Multivariable Data File.* This program selects a sequential or random sample of cases from a designated data file and stores it in a second designated file. Any number of cases and variables up to the maximum number in the original file may be selected.

3. *Selecting Systematic Samples.* This program selects a systematic sample of m integers from a population containing n successive integers. In the first (traditional) procedure, the first integer, s, is selected at random as an integer between 1 and n/m. The ith integer in the sample is then determined by adding to s the value of $n(i - 1)/m$ and rounding the result to the nearest integer. In the second (interval) procedure, n is divided into m intervals, and an integer within each interval is selected at random.

4. *Selecting Stratified Random Samples.* A sample of n integers is randomly selected from or assigned to b strata, levels, or blocks, each consisting of g groups. The number of integers selected from or assigned to each stratum is proportional to the total number of integers within the stratum in the population of interest. Within a given stratum, the sampled integers are assigned at random to groups.

5. *Selecting Multistage Cluster Samples.* In this program, a specified number of clusters is randomly selected at each stage from clusters randomly selected at the preceding stage. Up to five sampling stages are possible. At the final stage, all observational elements, or a random sample selected by program B1, may be examined.

CATEGORY C. ESTIMATING SAMPLE SIZE AND POWER

1. *Computing Required Sample Size for One-Sample Tests on Population Proportions.* The program computes the required sample size for z tests on population proportions. The user specifies the population size, the hypothesized population proportion, the desired confidence level, and the degree of accuracy expressed as a proportion. Procedures for both finite and infinite populations are provided.

2. *Estimating Power and Minimum Sample Sizes for Binomial or Sign Tests.* This program estimates power and minimum sample size for binomial or sign tests. The user enters the value of alpha, whether a one- or a two-tailed test is desired, and the proportion of positive signs under the alternative hypothesis. The binomial probability and power are computed. The program prints out the critical number of positive signs needed to reject the null hypothesis, the power of the test, and the probability of a Type II error.

3. *Estimating Power and Minimum Sample Size for One- and Two-Sample z Tests.* This program estimates the power and required sample size for one- and two-sample z tests on means. The user specifies a one- or two-sample case and whether a one- or two-tailed test is desired. Next, the value of alpha must be indicated, and whether Cohen's (1988) rule of thumb for effect size is to be applied. If Cohen's rule is to be applied, the magnitude of the effect (on a scale of 0 to 1) that it is desirable to detect must be specified. If Cohen's rule is not applied, the arithmetic mean(s) under the null and alternative hypotheses (one-sample case) or the arithmetic means of populations 1 and 2 (two-sample case) and the standard deviation(s) of the population(s) must be supplied. Whether or not

Cohen's rule is applied, the user has the option of computing either (a) the power of rejecting the null hypothesis (for a specified sample size); or (b) the required sample size (for a specified power).

4. *Two-Sample Test of Significance of Difference in Proportions & Minimum Size of Second Sample.* This program conducts either (a) a z test of the significance of the difference between the proportions of individuals in two independent samples endorsing an item; or (b) determines the minimum number of individuals in a second sample required for the difference between the specified proportions in a first sample of a given size and the second sample endorsing an item to be statistically significant.

5. *Sample Sizes for Randomized Groups Analysis of Variance.* This program is based on the tables and approach described by Bratcher et al. (1970). The user enters the power of the test (.7, .8, .9, or .95), the effect size (1.0, 1.25, 1.75, 2.0, 2.5, or 3.0), the alpha level (.20, .10, .05, or .01) and the number of treatment levels or blocks (1, 2, 3, 4, 5, 6, 7, 8, 9, 10, 11, 13, 16, 21, 25, or 31). Although the required sample sizes for the various numbers of levels or blocks are computed only for completely randomized designs, the resulting values are also very close to those for randomized blocks designs.

CATEGORY D. CHECKING, TRANSFORMING, AND DESCRIBING DATA

1. *Detecting and Correcting Errors in a Questionnaire/Inventory Data Bank.* This program (a) stores the responses of individuals to questions in several categories or parts of a questionnaire that are entered from a computer keyboard; (b) outputs the responses to a line printer; (c) checks the responses for errors; (d) corrects the errors; (e) prints a table of response errors; and (f) prints the matrix of corrected responses. Input data are in alphanumeric format. Errors in recording the responses may be identified and corrected in two ways: (1) by finding recorded responses to questions in a particular part that are not among the permissible options for that part; (2) by reentering the data to determine its correspondence with the originally entered data.

2. *Transforming and Recoding Item Responses.* This program recodes alphabetically coded responses as numerical responses, or vice versa, or performs any recoding of responses to designated categories. It also transforms raw numerical responses or scores to percentile ranks, normalized and nonnormalized standard scores, square roots, arc sines, and logarithms.

3. *Frequency Distributions and Descriptive Statistics.* This program constructs frequency distributions and associated descriptive statistics (category percentages, mean, median, standard deviation) from responses to questions or items on a questionnaire or inventory. The frequency distributions and descriptive statistics for all the variables or any subset of variables in a specified data file may be determined.

CATEGORY E. COMPUTING MEASURES OF ASSOCIATION

1. *Measures of Association for Nominal-Level Data.* Four measures of association or relationship between data on a nominal-level measurement scale (lambda, phi,

contingency coefficient, and Cramer's V) may be computed with this program. The frequencies in the respective cells of the contingency table may be entered from the keyboard, or raw data may be entered from a data file.

2. *Measures of Association for Ordinal-Level Data.* Four measures of association or relationship between data on an ordinal-level measurement scale may be computed with this program: gamma, Spearman's rho, Somer's *d*, Kendall's *tau-b*. The *z* value for a test of significance of gamma in large samples and the *t* value for a test of significance of Spearman's rho are also computed. For gamma, Somers' *d*, and Kendall's *tau-b*, the frequencies in the respective cells of the contingency table may be entered from the keyboard, or raw data may be entered from a data file.

3. *Pearson Correlation and Linear Regression Equation.* This program computes the product-moment correlation coefficient between two variables and the associated two-tailed probability, the linear regression equation for predicting Y from X, and the means and standard deviations of X and Y for 3 to 100 pairs of values. The number of false positive and false negative errors, hits, and correct rejections for a specified criterion cutoff score (minimum acceptable performance) can also be determined.

4. *Biserial, Point-Biserial, and Rank-Biserial Correlations.* This program computes biserial, point-biserial, and rank-biserial correlation coefficients for a set of items on a questionnaire. To compute biserial and point-biserial coefficients, the user has two options: (1) enter the raw data in the form **item number-group number (0 or 1)-criterion score,** for example **1 0 10,** from a data file; or (2) enter the number of respondents in each of the dichotomous groups, the mean criterion scores of the groups, and the standard deviation of both groups combined. The resulting coefficients are stored, by item number, in the results file and can be viewed on a computer monitor or printed. To compute the rank-biserial coefficient between a dichotomous variable and a ranked variable, the user enters the criterion scores of each of the two groups. The resulting rank-biserial coefficient is displayed on the monitor but is not stored in a file.

5. *Multiple Regression Analysis.* This program computes the standardized and unstandardized regression weights, the multiple correlation coefficient *(R)*, the standard errors of the regression weights, and *t* values for tests of significance of the regression weights for a linear regression analysis with one, two, or three independent variables. Input data are the means, standard deviations, and intercorrelations of the variables.

CATEGORY F. COMPUTING SCORE LIMITS AND CONFIDENCE INTERVALS

1. *Determining Minimum and Maximum Values of Population Proportions or Means.* This program is designed to compute minimum and maximum values of population proportions or means from a given sample. The program is based on a procedure described by Aiken (1988). With either dichotomous or multipoint items, the user indicates the number of elements in the responding sample, the number in the population, and whether the items are dichotomous or multipoint. When the items are dichotomous, the user indicates the sample proportion of respondents who endorsed the item. In this case, the printout consists

of the minimum and maximum proportions of respondents in the population. When the items are multipoint, the user indicates the minimum and maximum scores in the population and the mean score of the sample. The program then computes and prints the minimum and maximum values of the population means.

2. *Estimating Confidence Intervals When There Are Nonrespondents.* This program, which is based on a procedure described by Aiken (1988), estimates the upper and lower confidence limits for population proportions (of those who would endorse an item) when there are nonrespondents in a survey research study. The user enters the desired confidence level, the sample size, the proportion of respondents in the sample who endorsed the item, whether the proportion of respondents in the population is known (and if so, what it is), and the proportion of the sample who responded. The upper and lower confidence limits for the proportion of the population who would endorse the item are printed.

3. *Estimating Confidence Intervals for Population Proportions and Means.* This program determines confidence intervals for population proportions and means for one- or two-tailed z tests. The user indicates the number of samples (1 or 2); whether the statistics are proportions or means; the desired confidence level; the sample size; whether the population is finite or infinite, and if finite, how large it is. The values of the sample proportion(s) or mean(s), and the estimated population standard deviation(s) are also entered. The lower and upper confidence limits for a population proportion or mean, or for the difference between two population proportions or means, in addition to the results of a z test of significance, are printed.

CATEGORY G. CONDUCTING STATISTICAL TESTS OF HYPOTHESES

1. *Chi Square Tests of Goodness of Fit and Independence.* This program performs a chi square test of goodness of fit (one basis of classification) or independence (two bases of classification). When there is only one degree of freedom, the user has the option of employing Yates's correction. The data may be entered as cell frequencies from the keyboard or raw data from a data file. For the goodness-of-fit test, the value of chi square, the degrees of freedom, the associated probability, and the observed and expected frequencies are printed. For the test of independence, in addition to the value of chi square, the degrees of freedom, and the associated probability, the observed and expected frequencies in each cell are printed.

2. *t Test for Independent Groups.* This program conducts a t test of the significance of the difference between the means of two independent (unrelated) samples. Scores may be entered from the keyboard or from a separate data file.

3. *t Test for Dependent Groups.* This program performs a t test of the statistical significance of the mean of the differences between the scores in two dependent (related) samples. Scores may be entered from the keyboard or from a separate data file.

4. *Oneway Between-Subjects Analysis of Variance.* This program conducts an analysis of variance with one between-subjects factor. An overall F test and post hoc multiple-comparisons (Scheffé) tests between group means are made. The data may be entered from the keyboard or a file.

5. *Oneway Within-Subjects Analysis of Variance.* This program computes a oneway repeated measures within-subjects analysis of variance. Scores may be entered from the keyboard or from a data file.

6. *Twoway Between-Subjects Analysis of Variance.* This program conducts an analysis of variance with two between-subjects factors. Scores may be entered from the keyboard or from a data file.

7. *Twoway Within-Subjects Analysis of Variance.* This program computes a twoway repeated measures within-subjects analysis of variance. Scores may be entered from the keyboard or from a data file.

8. *Twoway Mixed-Design Analysis of Variance.* This program computes a mixed-design analysis of variance for one between-subjects factor and one within-subjects factor. The input data must be entered from a file.

CATEGORY H. COMPUTING NORMS, RELIABILITY, AND VALIDITY

1. *Normal Deviates and Probabilities.* This program may be used to compute the normal probability for a given z value, or the z value corresponding to a given cumulative normal probability.

2. *Percentile and Standard Score Norms.* From a frequency distribution, this program computes the standard z and T scores, and the normalized z (z_n) and T (T_n) corresponding to the interval midpoints of the raw score distribution. The user specifies the number of score intervals, the midpoint of the first interval, and the interval width. Then, for each interval, the user specifies the frequency on the interval. The output, which appears on the screen, is a table listing the midpoint, the frequency, the midpoint percentile rank, and the values of z, T, z_n, and T_n for each interval.

3. *Kuder-Richardson Reliability.* This program computes the internal consistency reliability of a test by using Kuder-Richardson formulas 20 and 21. The user enters the number of items, the number of respondents, and the score (0 or 1) of each respondent on each item. Scores may be entered from the keyboard or from a data file. Kuder-Richardson 20 and Kuder-Richardson 21 coefficients are displayed on the computer screen.

4. *Coefficient Alpha.* This program computes coefficient alpha, a measure of the internal consistency reliability of a psychometric instrument. The user begins by entering the number of items and the number of respondents. Next, the item scores of the respondents on a multipoint scale are entered, either from the keyboard or from a data file. Coefficient alpha for the data is displayed on the monitor screen.

5. *Coefficient Kappa and Index of Agreement.* This program computes a weighted or unweighted value of coefficient kappa *(kap)* and the coefficient of agreement (p_o), maximum values of *kap* and p_o, 95% and 99% confidence limits, approximated right-tail normal curve probabilities of *kap* and p_o in large samples ($n > 29$), and exact right-tail hypergeometric probabilities of *kap* and p_o in small samples ($n < 30$). The number of rows or columns in the $k \times k$ matrix of observed frequencies may range from 2 to 5. For observed frequencies on the major diagonal, disagreement weights are set equal to 0. For unweighted kappa, disagreement weights in off-diagonal frequencies are set equal to 1. For

weighted kappa, the user specifies the weights assigned to the off-diagonal frequencies.

6. *Indexes of Content Validity and Reliability.* This set of programs computes three numerical indexes (*V*, *R*, and *H*): the content validity *(V)* of a questionnaire or inventory, and the test-retest *(R)* and internal consistency *(H)* reliabilities of the ratings of the content validity of the instrument. The indexes range from 0 to 1; they are computed as the ratio of the sum of the absolute values of differences between obtained ratings of content validity to the maximum sum of differences in ratings of content validity, or as 1 minus that ratio. Included in the program are subprograms for calculating the indexes, their associated discrete and cumulative right-tail probabilities, and the population mean and standard deviation of each index. Discrete and right-tail probabilities for specified values of the three indexes can be generated for any number of evaluation categories, evaluators, and items. When the number of items or evaluators is large (n>25), the right-tail probability associated with any value of a particular index may be estimated by a z-score procedure.

CATEGORY I. COMPLETING ILLUSTRATIVE QUESTIONNAIRES AND INVENTORIES

1. *Questionnaire Concerning Success in Sports.* This program administers a questionnaire concerning the determinants of success in sports. It measures the degree of agreement or disagreement with the proposition that success in sports activities is attained more by individual effort than by cooperative group effort.

2. *Inventories on Aging and Death.* This program administers and scores four inventories concerned with death anxiety, life expectancy, attitude toward capital punishment, and attitude toward war. Total scores are computed on each inventory.

3. *Questionnaire on Student Cheating.* This program administers a 35-item questionnaire on student cheating. Responses to each item, true (t) or false (f), are recorded by item number in the results file and can be displayed on the monitor and/or printed.

4. *Questionnaire on Student Interactions with Professors.* This program administers a 10-item questionnaire on various aspects of student interactions with professors. Responses, yes (y) or no (n), are recorded, by item number, in the results file and can be printed at runtime or later.

5. *Sensation-Seeking Scale.* This program administers and scores Form V of the Sensation-Seeking Scale, which was designed to measure thrill-seeking behavior, a desire for new experiences, or a willingness to take risks. Individuals who make high total scores on the scale tend to seek out new, varied, and exciting experiences. The 40 items on the scale are in paired (forced-choice) format. The respondent is asked to select the statement (a or b) that best describes his or her true feeling. In addition to total scores, part scores on Thrill and Adventure Seeking (TAS), Experience Seeking (ES), Disinhibition (Dis), and Boredom Susceptibility (BS) are computed. Raw scores on the four subscales and the total scale are converted to *T* scores (reproduced with permission from Zuckerman, 1994).

6. *Altruism Inventory.* The inventory administered and scored by this program is designed to measure the personality characteristic of altruism. Eight items of the 15-item inventory are worded in the positive direction, and the remaining seven items in the negative direction. The respondent enters sa (strongly agree), a (agree), u (undecided), d (disagree), or sd (strongly disagree) in response to each of the randomly arranged statements. Total score ranges from 0 to 60.

7. *Sociability, Activity, and Emotionality Inventory.* This 15-item inventory is designed to measure the personality variables of sociability, activity level, and emotionality. Responses are made on a scale ranging from 0 (Not at all) to 4 (Very much), depending on how true the respondent considers the statement to be of him or her. Score ranges on the three variables are interpreted as above average, average, or below average, depending on the gender of the respondent (reproduced with permission from Willerman, 1975).

8. *Vocational Interests, Personality, and Careers.* This program, based on Holland's RIASEC theory of vocational personalities, consists of three screens. On the first screen are brief descriptions of the six RIASEC interest themes: The respondent is asked to select the theme that best fits him or her. On the second screen, six descriptions of personality characteristics corresponding to the six RIASEC themes are presented: The respondent is asked to select the description that best fits him or her. On the last screen, two clusters of career possibilities, one cluster corresponding to the interest group selected and a second cluster corresponding to the personality description selected by the respondent, are presented.

9. *Personal Identity Inventory.* This inventory was devised by Ochse and Plug (1986) to assess the degree to which a person has developed a sense of identity, as defined by Erik Erikson. For each of the 19 items, the respondent indicates whether the statement never applies, occasionally or seldom applies, applies fairly often, or applies very often to him or her. The respondent's total raw score on the inventory, the corresponding T score, and a brief interpretation are displayed on the monitor.

Appendix B

Descriptions of Variables in File gss.dat and List of Data Definition Statements in File gss.sys

1. ABANY: Do you think it should be possible for a pregnant woman to obtain a *legal* abortion if the woman wants it for any reason?

0 = Not applicable, 1 = Yes, 2 = No, 8 = Don't know

2. AGE: Age of respondent.

18–89

3. ALIKE1: In what way are an orange and a banana alike?

0 = Incorrect, 1 = Partly correct, 2 = Correct, 8 = Don't know

4. ALIKE2: In what way are a dog and a lion alike?

0 = Incorrect, 1 = Partly correct, 2 = Correct, 8 = Don't know

5. ALIKE3: In what way are an eye and an ear alike?

0 = Incorrect, 1 = Partly correct, 2 = Correct, 8 = Don't know

6. ALIKE4: In what way are an egg and a seed alike?

0 = Incorrect, 1 = Partly correct, 2 = Correct, 8 = Don't know

7. ALIKE5: In what way are a table and a chair alike?

0 = Incorrect, 1 = Partly correct, 2 = Correct, 8 = Don't know

8. ALIKE6: In what way are work and play alike?

0 = Incorrect, 1 = Partly correct, 2 = Correct, 8 = Don't know

9. ALIKE7: In what way are a fly and a tree alike?

0 = Incorrect, 1 = Partly correct, 2 = Correct, 8 = Don't know

10. ALIKE8: In what way are praise and punishment alike?

0 = Incorrect, 1 = Partly correct, 2 = Correct, 8 = Don't know

11. ATTEND: How often do you attend religious services?

0 = Never, 1 = Less than once a year, 2 = About once or twice a year, 3 = Several times a year, 4 = About once a month, 5 = 2-3 times a month, 6 = Nearly every week, 7 = Every week, 8 = Several times a week, 9 = Don't know or no answer

12. CAPPUN: Do you favor or oppose the death penalty for persons convicted of murder?

1 = Favor, 2 = Oppose, 8 = Don't know

13. COURTS: In general, do you think the courts in this area deal too harshly or not harshly enough with criminals?

0 = Not applicable, 1 = Too harshly, 2 = Not harshly enough, 3 = About right, 8 = Don't know

14. EDUC: What is the highest grade in elementary school, high school, or college that you completed?

6 = 6th grade, 7 = 7th grade, 8 = 8th grade, 9 = 9th grade, 10 = 10th grade, 11 = 11th grade, 12 = 12th grade, 13 = 1 year of college, 14 = 2 years of college, 15 = 3 years of college, 16 = 4 years of college, 17 = 5 years of college, 18 = 6 years of college, 19 = 7 years of college, 20 = 8 years of college

15. GOD: Which statement comes closest to expressing what you believe about God?

0 = Not applicable, 1 = I don't believe in a God, 2 = I don't know whether there is a God and I don't believe there is any way to find out, 3 = I don't believe in a personal God, but I do believe in a Higher power of some kind, 4 = I find myself believing in God some of the time, but not at others, 5 = While I have doubts, I feel that I do believe in God, 6 = I know God really exists and I have no doubts about it, 8 = Don't know

16. GRASS: Do you think the use of marijuana should be made legal or not?

0 = Not applicable, 1 = Should, 2 = Should not, 8 = Don't know

17. GUNLAW: Would you favor or oppose a law that would require a person to obtain a police permit before he or she could buy a gun?

0 = Not applicable, 1 = Favor, 2 = Oppose, 8 = Don't know

18. HAPPY: Taken all together, how would you say things are these days; would you say that you are very happy, pretty happy, or not too happy?

0 = Not applicable, 1 = Very happy, 2 = Pretty happy, 3 = Not too happy, 8 = Don't know

19. HEALTH: Would you say your own health, in general, is excellent, good, fair, or poor?

0 = Not applicable, 1 = Excellent, 2 = Good, 3 = Fair, 4 = Poor, 8 = Don't know

20. HOMOSEX: What about sexual relations between two adults of the same sex; do you think it is always wrong, almost always wrong, wrong only sometimes, or not wrong at all?

0 = Not applicable, 1 = Always wrong, 2 = Almost always wrong, 3 = Wrong only sometimes, 4 = Not wrong at all, 5 = Other, 8 = Don't know

21. INCOME: In which of these groups did your total *family* income, from *all* sources, fall last year before taxes?

00 = Not applicable, 01 = Under $1,000, 02 = $1,000–$2,999, 03 = $3,000–$3,999, 04 = $4,000–$4,999, 05 = $5,000–$5,999, 06 = $6,000–$6,999, 07 = $7,000–$7,999, 08 = $8,000–$9,999, 09 = $10,000–$14,999, 10 = $15,000–$19,999, 11 = $20,000–$24,999, 12 = $25,000 or over, 13 = Refused, 98 = Don't know

22. LETDIE1: When a person has a disease that cannot be cured, do you think doctors should be allowed by law to end the patient's life by some painless means if the patient and his or her family request it?

0 = Not applicable, 1 = Yes, 2 = No, 8 = Don't know

23. MARITAL: Are you currently married, widowed, divorced, separated, or have you never been married?

1 = Married, 2 = Widowed, 3 = Divorced, 4 = Separated, 5 = Never married

24. MELTPOT: Some people say that it is better for America if different racial and ethnic groups maintain their distinct cultures. Others say that it is better if groups change so they blend into the larger society as in the idea of a melting pot. What score between 1 and 7 comes closest to the way you feel?

0 = Not applicable, 1 = Racial and ethnic groups should maintain their distinct cultures, 2 =   , 3 =   , 4 =   , 5 =   ,

6 =   , 7 = Groups should change so that they blend into the larger society, 8 = Don't know

25. PARTYID: Generally speaking, do you usually think of yourself as a Republican, Democrat, Independent, or what?

0 = Strong Democrat, 1 = Not very strong Democrat,
2 = Independent, close to Democrat, 3 = Independent (Neither, No response), 4 = Independent, close to Republican,
5 = Not very strong Republican, 6 = Strong Republican,
7 = Other party, refused to say, 9 = No answer

26. PRAYER: The United States Supreme Court has ruled that no state or local government may *require* the reading of the Lord's Prayer or Bible verses in public schools. What are your views on this; do you approve or disapprove of the court ruling?

0 = Not applicable, 1 = Approve, 2 = Disapprove, 8 = No opinion

27. RACE: What race do you consider yourself?

1 = White, 2 = Black, 3 = Other

28. REGION: Region of interview.

1 = New England, 2 = Middle Atlantic, 3 = East North Central,
4 = West North Central, 5 = South Atlantic, 6 = East South Central, 7 = West South Central, 8 = Mountain, 9 = Pacific

29. RELIG: What is your religious preference? Is it Protestant, Catholic, Jewish, some other religion, or no religion?

1 = Protestant, 2 = Catholic, 3 = Jewish, 4 = None, 5 = Other,
9 = No answer

30. SEI: Respondent's socioeconomic index.

17.10–92.80

31. SEX: Respondent's sex.

1 = Male, 2 = Female

32. SIBS: How many brothers and sisters do you have? Please count those born alive, but no longer living, as well as those alive now. Also include stepbrothers and stepsisters, and children adopted by your parents.

0–25, 99 = No answer

33. TAX: Do you consider the amount of federal income tax which you have to pay as too high, about right, or too low?

0 = Not applicable, 1 = Too high, 2 = About right, 3 = Too low, 4 = Respondent pays no income tax, 8 = Don't know

```
SET LISTING='A:RESULTS'.
DATA LIST FILE='A:GSS.DAT' FREE/ABANY AGE ALIKE1 ALIKE2 ALIKE3
ALIKE4 ALIKE5 ALIKE6 ALIKE7 ALIKE8 ATTEND CAPPUN COURTS EDUC GOD
GRASS GUNLAW HAPPY HEALTH HOMOSEX INCOME LETDIE1 MARITAL MELTPOT
PARTYID PRAYER RACE REGION RELIG SEI SEX SIBS TAX.
VARIABLE LABELS ABANY 'ABORTION IF WOMAN WANTS FOR ANY REASON'
/AGE 'AGE OF RESPONDENT'
/ALIKE1 'HOW ALIKE: ORANGE & BANANA'
/ALIKE2 'HOW ALIKE: DOG & LION'
/ALIKE3 'HOW ALIKE: EYE & EAR'
/ALIKE4 'HOW ALIKE: EGG & SEED'
/ALIKE5 'HOW ALIKE: TABLE & CHAIR'
/ALIKE6 'HOW ALIKE: WORK & PLAY'
/ALIKE7 'HOW ALIKE: FLY & TREE'
/ALIKE8 'HOW ALIKE: PRAISE & PUNISHMENT'
/ATTEND 'HOW OFTEN R ATTENDS RELIGIOUS SERVICES'
/CAPPUN 'FAVOR OR OPPOSE DEATH PENALTY FOR MURDER'
/COURTS 'COURTS DEALING WITH CRIMINALS'
/EDUC 'HIGHEST YEAR OF SCHOOL COMPLETED'
/GOD "RESPONDENT'S CONFIDENCE IN THE EXISTENCE OF GOD"
/GRASS 'SHOULD MARIJUANA BE MADE LEGAL'
/GUNLAW 'FAVOR OR OPPOSE GUN PERMITS'
/HAPPY 'GENERAL HAPPINESS'
/HEALTH 'CONDITION OF HEALTH'
/HOMOSEX 'HOMOSEXUAL SEX RELATIONS'
/INCOME 'TOTAL FAMILY INCOME'
/LETDIE1 'ALLOW INCURABLE PATIENTS TO DIE'
/MARITAL 'MARITAL STATUS'
/MELTPOT "RESPONDENT'S ATTITUDE TOWARD MIXING CULTURES IN US"
/PARTYID 'POLITICAL PARTY AFFILIATION'
/PRAYER "APPROVE OF COURT'S PRAYER RULING?"
/RACE 'RACE OF RESPONDENT'
/REGION 'REGION OF INTERVIEW'
/RELIG "RESPONDENT'S RELIGIOUS PREFERENCE"
/SEI "RESPONDENT'S SOCIOECONOMIC INDEX"
/SEX "RESPONDENT'S SEX"
/SIBS 'NUMBER OF BROTHERS AND SISTERS'
/TAX "RESPONDENT'S FEDERAL INCOME TAX."
VALUE LABELS ABANY 0 'Not applicable' 1 'Yes' 2 'No' 8 'Dont know'
/ALIKE1 0 'Incorrect' 1 'Partly correct' 2 'Correct' 8 'Dont know'
/ALIKE2 0 'Incorrect' 1 'Partly correct' 2 'Correct' 8 'Dont know'
/ALIKE3 0 'Incorrect' 1 'Partly correct' 2 'Correct' 8 'Dont know'
/ALIKE4 0 'Incorrect' 1 'Partly correct' 2 'Correct' 8 'Dont know'
/ALIKE5 0 'Incorrect' 1 'Partly correct' 2 'Correct' 8 'Dont know'
/ALIKE6 0 'Incorrect' 1 'Partly correct' 2 'Correct' 8 'Dont know'
/ALIKE7 0 'Incorrect' 1 'Partly correct' 2 'Correct' 8 'Dont know'
/ALIKE8 0 'Incorrect' 1 'Partly correct' 2 'Correct' 8 'Dont know'
```

```
/ATTEND 0 'Never' 1 'Less than once a year'
2 'About once or twice a year' 3 'Several times a year'
4 'About once a month' 5 '2-3 times a month'
6 'Nearly every week' 7 'Every week' 8 'Several times a week'
9 'Dont know or No answer'
/CAPPUN 1 'Favor' 2 'Oppose' 8 'Dont know' 9 'No answer'
/COURTS 1 'Too harshly' 2 'Not harshly enough' 3 'About right'
8 'Dont know'
/EDUC 6 '6th grade' 7 '7th grade' 8 '8th grade' 9 '9th grade'
10 '10th grade' 11 '11th grade' 12 '12th grade'
13 '1 year of college' 14 '2 years of college'
15 '3 years of college' 16 '4 years of college'
17 '5 years of college' 18 '6 years of college'
19 '7 years of college' 20 '8 years of college'
/GOD 0 'Not applicable' 1 'Dont believe in God'
2 'Dont know & cant find out' 3 'Believe in higher power'
4 'Believe in God some of the time' 5 'Have doubts but believe'
6 'No doubts that God exists' 8 'Dont know'
/GRASS 0 'Not applicable' 1 'Should' 2 'Should not' 8 'Dont know'
/GUNLAW 0 'Not applicable' 1 'Favor' 2 'Oppose' 8 'Dont know'
/HAPPY 0 'Not applicable' 1 'Very happy' 2 'Pretty happy'
3 'Not too happy' 8 'Dont know'
/HEALTH 0 'Not applicable' 1 'Excellent' 2 'Good' 3 'Fair'
4 'Poor' 8 'Dont know'
/HOMOSEX 0 'Not applicable' 1 'Always wrong'
2 'Almost always wrong' 3 'Wrong only sometimes'
4 'Not wrong at all' 5 'Other'
8 'Dont know'
/INCOME 00 'Not applicable' 01 'Under $1,000' 02 '$1,000-$2,999'
03 '$3,000-$3,999' 04 '$4,000-$4,999' 05 '$5,000-$5,999'
06 '$6,000-$6,999' 07 '$7,000-$7,999' 08 '$8,000-$9,999'
09 '$10,000-$14,999' 10 '$15,000-$19,999' 11 '$20,000-$24,999'
12 '$25,000 or over' 13 'Refused' 98 'Dont know'
/LETDIE1 0 'Not applicable' 1 'Yes' 2 'No' 8 'Dont know'
/MARITAL 1 'Married' 2 'Widowed' 3 'Divorced' 4 'Separated'
5 'Never married'
/MELTPOT 0 'Not applicable' 1 'Should maintain distinct cultures'
7 'Should blend into society' 8 'Dont know'
/PARTYID 0 'Strong Democrat' 1 'Not very strong Democrat'
2 'Independent, close to Democrat'
3 'Independent (Neither, No response)'
4 'Independent, close to Republican'
5 'Not very strong Republican'
6 'Strong Republican' 7 'Other party, refused to say'
/PRAYER 0 'Not applicable' 1 'Approve' 2 'Disapprove'
8 'No opinion'
/RACE 1 'White' 2 'Black' 3 'Other'
```

/REGION 1 'New England' 2 'Middle Atlantic' 3 'East North Central'
4 'West North Central' 5 'South Atlantic' 6 'East South Central'
7 'West South Central' 8 'Mountain' 9 'Pacific'
/RELIG 1 'Protestant' 2 'Catholic' 3 'Jewish' 4 'None' 5 'Other'
9 'No answer'
/SEX 1 'Male' 2 'Female'
/SIBS 99 'No answer'
/TAX 1 'Too high' 2 'About right' 3 'Too low'
4 'Respondent pays no income tax' 8 'Dont know'.

Appendix C

Commercially Available Questionnaires

Adaptive Behavior: Street Survival Skills Questionnaire (Assesses functional impairment, independent living skills, and appropriate vocational and residential placement for children, adolescents, and adults with physical, mental, or developmental disabilities; children, adolescents, & adults; D. Linkenhoker & L. McCarron; The Psychological Corporation; review MMYB 11:6)

Adult Neuropsychological Questionnaire (Identifies complaints, symptoms, and signs suggesting underlying brain impairment; 59 items; 10 minutes; F. Melendez; Psychological Assessment Resources; review MMYB 12:19)

Adult Suicidal Ideation Questionnaire (Designed to evaluate the presence and frequency of suicidal thoughts in adults; 10 minutes; total score; M. Reynolds; Psychological Assessment Resources: Sigma Assessment Systems; review MMYB 12:21)

Alleman Leadership Development Questionnaire (For measuring mentoring activity between people or in an organization or work unit; 12 scores (Teach the Job, Teach Politics, Assign Challenging Tasks, Career Counseling; General Counseling, Career Help, Demonstrated Trust, Endorse Acts/Views, Sponsor, Protect, Associate Socially, Friendship); E. Alleman; Leadership Development Corporation)

Attitude Toward School Questionnaire (Measures attitudes toward school in primary school students; grades K–3; G. P. Strickland, R. Hoepfner, & S. P. Klein; Monitor)

Attributional Style Questionnaire (For determining the locus (internal-external), stability, and generality (global-specific) of attributed causes for 12 hypothetical situations—6 with positive and 6 with negative outcomes; adolescents and adults; Peterson et al., 1982)

Behavioral Assessment of Pain Questionnaire (Used for gaining a better understanding of factors that may be maintaining the subacute and chronic noncancerous pain experience; 34 scores; M. J. Lewandowski & B. H. Tearnam; Pendrake, Inc.; 60 minutes; 34 scores; review MMYB 12:49)

Change Agent Questionnaire (Assesses the underlying assumptions and practical strategies employed by agents of change as they seek to influence others; adults; 20 scores (Client-Centered Change (Philosophy, Strategy, Evaluation, Total), Charismatic Change (Philosophy, Strategy, Evaluation, Total), Custodial Change (Philosophy, Strategy, Evaluation, Total), Compliance Change (Philosophy, Strategy, Evaluation, Total), Credibility Change (Philosophy, Strategy, Evaluation, Total); J. Hall & M. S. Williams; Teleometrics Int'l)

Child Neuropsychological Questionnaire (For evaluating children suspected of having brain dysfunctions; children; 1 score, overall evaluation of neuropsychological impairment; F. Melendez; Psychological Assessment Resources; review MMYB 12:72)

Children's Personality Questionnaire, 1985 Edition (For measuring personality traits to predict and evaluate the course of personal, social, and academic development; ages 8–12; 14–18 primary factors (e.g., outgoing, emotionally stable, shy, conscientious, assertive, shrewd, circumspect); R. B. Porter & R. B. Cattell; Institute for Personality & Ability Testing; review MMYB 9:222)

Class Activities Questionnaire (To measure students' perceptions of the classroom situation as compared to the teacher's intended and predicted classroom situation; grades 6–12; 21 factors in 5 dimensions; J. M. Steele; Creative Learning Press, Inc.; review MMYB 9:226)

Classroom Atmosphere Questionnaire (To assess classroom atmosphere through ratings of teachers by students; grades 4–9; 2 scores (Acceptance-Understanding, Problem-Solving Skills); J. F. Hoffmeister; Test Analysis & Development Corporation; review MMYB 8:366)

Clinical Analysis Questionnaire (Designed to assess both deviant behavior and normal coping skills; ages 16 and over; 21 normal personality traits and 16 clinical factors; S. E. Krug; Institute for Personality & Ability Testing; reviews MMYB 9:232 & TC I:202)

Clinical Analysis Questionnaire (Short Form). (Multidimensional personality test that combines the diagnostic assessment of deviant behavior with the measurement of an individual's normal coping skills; 16 years and older; R. B. Cattell; NCS Systems)

Conners' Abbreviated Symptom Questionnaire (Evaluates and monitors hyperactive behavior; ages 3–17; C. K. Conners; Psychological Assessment Resources)

Conners-March Developmental Questionnaire (Designed for completion by parents of children and adolescents referred for ADHD; collects information on description of problem(s), home environment, treatment history, birth history, motor development, medical and psychiatric history of family and child, school behavior and performance, temperament, and medical history; children and adolescents; C. K. Conners & J. March; Psychological Assessment Resources)

Course Evaluation Questionnaire (Designed to provide information about how students regard some of their educational experiences; high school and college; 5 scores (Openness to Students and Ideas, Contextual Approach to Learning, Dynamism Enthusiasm, Organization Clarity, Quality Meaningfulness); J. K. Hoffmeister; Test Analysis & Development Corporation; review MMYB 8:368)

Depressive Experiences Questionnaire (Designed to assess depressive experiences in adolescents and adults (patients and normals) in terms of three variables: scores—dependency, self-criticism, efficacy; S. J. Blatt, J. P. D'Afflitti, & D. M. Quinlan; Sidney J. Blatt; review MMYB 9:316)

Drug Use Questionnaire (Assesses potential involvement with drugs; clients of addictive treatment; total score only; available in French; 5–10 minutes; H. A. Skinner; Addiction Research Foundation (Canada))

Early School Personality Questionnaire (Measures 13 personality characteristics; ages 6–8; R. W. Coan & R. B. Cattell; Western Psychological Services; review MMYB 8:540)

Edinburgh Questionnaires, The (Constructed to measure personal interests and organizational climate; adults; scores—3 sections—Quality of Work Life (Working Conditions, Type of Work Wanted, Relationships, General); Important Activities, Consequences (Compatibilities, Perceptions of Task and Personal Reactions, Reactions of Superiors, Reactions of Colleagues and Workmates, Benefits and Disbenefits to Others, Competencies Engaged; J. Raven; NFER Nelson Pub. Co.; review MMYB 10:102)

Educational Process Questionnaire (Designed to aid teachers in their own development by providing objective information about the processes used in the teacher's own actual classroom; grades 4–12; 5-scale scores (Reinforcement of Self-Concept, Academic Learning Time, Feedback, Expectations, Development of Multiple Talents; Institute for Behavioral Research in Creativity); review MMYB 11:125)

Eight State Questionnaire (To assess 8 specific emotional states and needs; age 17 and over; 8 scores (Anxiety, Stress, Depression, Regression, Fatigue, Guilt, Extraversion, Arousal); 25–35 minutes; J. P. Curran & R. B. Cattell; Institute for Personality & Ability Testing; review MMYB 8:547)

EMO Questionnaire (Designed to assess an individual's personal-emotional adjustment; adults; 10 diagnostic dimensions; G. O. Baehr & M. E. Baehr; SRA/London House; review MMYB 9:383)

Eysenck Personality Questionnaire (Revised). (Provides 5 personality scores in adults (Psychoticism or Tough-Mindedness, Extraversion, Neuroticism or Emotionality, Lie, Addiction; ages 7–15, 16 and over; H. J. Eysenck & S. B. G. Eysenck; Educational & Industrial Testing Service; review MMYB 8:554, earlier edition review TC I:27)

Functional Time Estimation Questionnaire (Provides an overview of children's abilities to estimate time correctly; ages 7–11; 30–35 minutes; J. M. Dodd, L. Burd, & J. R. Cook; Academic Therapy Publications; review MMYB 12:157)

General Health Questionnaire (Designed to screen for nonpsychotic psychiatric disorders; adolescents to adults; total scores; D. Goldberg & P. Williams; NFER-Nelson; review MMYB 9:434)

Group Process Questionnaire (Designed to assess the effectiveness of groups; adults; 29–145 scores; R. Hill, D. J. Fisher, T. Webber, & K. A. Fisher; Aviat; review MMYB 11:151)

High School Interest Questionnaire (For measuring occupational interests; Standards 7–10 in South African schools; 8 scores; J. B. Wolfaardt; Human Sciences Research Council (South Africa))

High School Personality Questionnaire (Focuses on 14 personality characteristics for understanding adolescents; R. B. Cattell, M. D. Cattell, & E. Johns; Institute for Personality & Ability Testing; reviews MMYB 9:559 & MMYB 11:188)

Home Environment Questionnaire (Measures "dimensions of the child's psychological environment that exert specific types of pressure on the child"; grades 5–6; 10 scores; J. O. Sines; Psychological Assessment and Services; review MMYB 10:141)

Home Screening Questionnaire (For screening the home environment for factors related to the child's growth and development; birth to age 3, ages 3–6; 3 scores (Questions, Toy Checklist, Total); C. E. Coons, E. C. Gay, A. W. Fandal, C. Ker, & W. K. Frankenburg; Denver Developmental Materials, Inc.; review MMYB 9:482)

Howarth Personality Questionnaire (For measuring personality and affect dimensions; college and adults; 10 scores; Edgar Howarth (Canada); review MMYB 9:486)

Illinois Course Evaluation Questionnaire (Measures college course effectiveness; college; 30 scores; ratings by students; R. E. Spencer, L. M. Aleamoni, & D. C. Brandenburg; Measurement & Research Division, University of Illinois at Urbana-Champaign; review MMYB 8:373)

Illness Behaviour Questionnaire, Second Edition (For recording aspects of illness behavior, particularly those attitudes that suggest inappropriate or maladaptive modes of responding to one's state of health; pain clinic, psychiatric, and general practice patients; 8 scores; I. Pilowsky & N. D. Spence; I. Pilowsky (South Africa))

Individualised Classroom Environment Questionnaire (For measuring perceptions of the classroom environment among secondary school students or their teachers; junior and senior high school students and teachers; 5 scores; B. J. Fraser; Australian Council for Educational Research; review MMYB 11:176)

Inquiry Mode Questionnaire: A Measure of How You Think and Make Decisions (Developed to measure individual preferences in the way people think; business and industry; 5 scores—Synthesist, Idealist, Pragamatist, Analyst, Realistic; A. F. Harrison & R. M. Bramson; INQ Educational Materials Inc.; review MMYB 12:189)

Intermediate Personality Questionnaire for Indian Pupils (For determining the structural aspects of personality; Standards 6–8 in South African schools; 10 scores; S. Oosthuizen; Human Sciences Research Council (South Africa))

International Version of the Mental Status Questionnaire (Standards 6 to 8) (For determining the structural aspects of personality; Standards 6–8 in South African schools; 10 scores; S. Oosthuizen; Human Science Research Council (South Africa))

Interpersonal Relations Questionnaire (To identify specific problems in connection with interpersonal relations and identify formation; "white pupils" in Standards 5–7 in South African schools; 13 scores; M. Joubert & D. Schlebusch; Human Sciences Research Counsel (South Africa); review MMYB 11:181)

Intrex Questionnaire (Designed to measure the patient's perception of self and others, based on trait × state × situational philosophy and Structural Analysis of Social Behavior; psychiatric patients and normals; L. S. Benjamin; Intrex Interpersonal Institute, Inc.; reviews MMYB 9:522 & MMYB 12:192)

IPAT Anxiety Scale Questionnaire (Measure of anxiety; ages 14 and over; total score plus 7 optional scores; R. B. Cattell, S. E. Krug, and I. H. Scheir; Institute for Personality & Ability Testing; review MMYB 8:582)

Job Activity Preference Questionnaire (To obtain a measure of job interests or preferences; adults; 16 scores; R. C. Meacham; A. F. Harris, E. J. McCormick, & P. R. Jeaneret; PAQ Services, Inc.; review MMYB 9:547)

Jung Personality Questionnaire (To assist pupils in choosing a career; Standards 7, 8 and 10 in South African school system; 4 scores (Extraversion vs. Introversion, Thinking vs.

Feeling, Sensation vs. Intuition, Judgment vs. Perception); L. B. H. duToit; Human Sciences Research Council (South Africa))

Katz-Zalk Opinion Questionnaire (Measures "racial attitudes in children"; grades 1–6; 3 scores (Negative, Positive, Total); P. A. Katz & S. R. Zalk; Sue R. Zalk)

Law Enforcement Perception Questionnaire (Developed to assess attitudes toward law enforcement and law enforcement personnel; law enforcement personnel; F. Lee; Psychometric Affiliates)

Leader Behavior Description Questionnaire (Developed to obtain supervisees' descriptions of supervisors; revision of Leader Behavior Description Questionnaire; employee ratings of supervisors, 12 scores; Business Research Support Services, Ohio State University; review MMYB 8:1175)

Leadership Opinion Questionnaire (To measure supervisory leadership dimensions; supervisors and prospective supervisors; 2 scores (Structure, Consideration); E. A. Fleishman; Science Research Associates/London House; review MMYB 7:1149)

Learning Process Questionnaire (Identifies motives and strategies for learning in secondary school students, leading to the formulation of four approaches to learning—surface, deep, achieving, deep-achieving; J. Biggs; Australian Council for Educational Research; secondary students; review MMYB 11:202)

Leatherman Leadership Questionnaire, Revised (To aid in selecting leaders, providing specific feedback to participants on their leadership knowledge for career counseling, conducting accurate needs analysis, and screening for assessment centers or giving pre-/postassessment feedback; managers, supervisors, team leaders, and potential leaders; 28 scores; R. W. Leatherman; International Training Consultants, Inc.; review MMYB 12:219, earlier edition review MMYB 11:205)

Levine-Pilowsky Depression Questionnaire (Questionnaire for classifying depression; adults; 8 subscales; I. Pilowsky; I. Pilowsky (Australia))

Management Styles Questionnaire (To understand the concept of situational management, recognize the advantages and disadvantages of various styles of management, recognize which style(s) of management are appropriate for a particular work situation, identify one's on-the-job management style, and develop a plan for modifying one's management style; managers and employees; D. Michalak; Michalak Training Associates; review MMYB 10:184)

Managerial Style Questionnaire (Measures individuals' perceptions of how they manage based on the assessment of 6 managerial styles; persona in managerial situations; 6 scores (Coercive, Authoritative, Affiliative, Democratic, Pacesetting, Coaching); McBer and Company; review MMYB 10:185)

Menstrual Distress Questionnaire (Designed as a self-report inventory for use in the diagnosis and treatment of premenstrual and menstrual distress; women who experience strong to severe premenstrual or menstrual distress; 8 scores; R. H. Moos; Western Psychological Services; review MMYB 12:230)

Minnesota Importance Questionnaire (Designed to measure 20 psychological needs and 6 underlying values that have been found to be relevant to work adjustment, specifically to satisfaction with work; ages 16 and over; 21 scores; J. B. Rounds, Jr. et al.; Vocational Psychology Research; review MMYB 11:243)

Minnesota Job Description Questionnaire (Designed to measure the reinforcer characteristics of jobs; employees and supervisors; 21 reinforcer dimensions; F. H. Borgen et al.; Vocational Psychology Research; review MMYB 8:1051)

Minnesota Satisfaction Questionnaire (Designed to measure an employee's satisfaction with his/her job; business and industry; 21 scores (long form), 3 scores (short form); D. J. Weiss et al.; Vocational Psychology Research; review MMYB 8:1052)

Motivated Strategies for Learning Questionnaire (To assess college students' motivational orientations and their use of different learning strategies for a college course; grades 13–16; 15 scores; P. R. Pintrick et al.; National Center for Research to Improve Postsecondary Teaching and Learning)

Multifactor Leadership Questionnaire (Designed to capture the broadest range of leadership behaviors while differentiating ineffective from effective leaders; managers; 10 factors; B. M. Bass & B. J. Avolio; Consulting Psychologists Press; review MMYB 12:247)

Multimodal Life History Questionnaire (to provide therapists with an in-depth assessment tool for adult counseling; adult counseling clients; A. A. Lazarus; Research Press)

The Neuroticism Scale Questionnaire (Brief measure of neurotic trends in the normal or abnormal adult and adolescent; ages 13 and over; 5 scores (Depressiveness, Submissiveness, Overprotection, Anxiety, Total); I. H. Scheier & R. B. Cattell; Institute for Personality & Ability Testing; reviews MMYB 6:148 & TC V:283)

Nisonger Questionnaire for Parents, The (Constructed to establish the parameters of a child's problems as perceived by the parents; handicapped children ages 2–8; No scores, 10 inquiry areas; W. E. Loadman, F. A. Benson, & D. McElwain; Ohio State University)

Occupational Personality Questionnaire (Self-report measure of personality and motivational characteristics particularly relevant to the world of work; business and industry; 31 scores in 4 areas (Relationships with People, Thinking Style, Feelings and Emotions, Social Desirability; Saville & Holdsworth Ltd.; review MMYB 11:267)

Offer Self-Image Questionnaire, Revised (Designed to measure the self-image of adolescents; ages 13–19; 13 scores; D. Offer, E. Ostrov, K. I. Howard, & S. Dolan; Western Psychological Services; reviews MMYB 9:855 & MMYB 12:268)

Oliver Organization Description Questionnaire (To describe occupational organizations along 4 dimensions; adults; 4 scores; J. E. Oliver, Jr.; Organizational Measurement Systems Press; review MMYB 11:271)

Personal Experience Screening Questionnaire (Designed as a brief screening tool to aid . . . in the identification of teenagers likely to need a drug abuse assessment referral; adolescents; 3 scores (Infrequency, Defensiveness, Problem Severity); K. C. Winters; Western Psychological Services; review MMYB 12:286)

Personal Questionnaire (Designed as an aid to the interviewer in educational or career counselling and in selection; adolescents, adults; Educational & Industrial Test Services, Ltd.; review MMYB 9:944)

Personal Questionnaire Rapid Scaling Technique (Developed to monitor fluctuations in the intensity of personal experiences such as feelings, beliefs, symptoms, etc.; psychiatric patients; total score only; D. J. Mulhall; NFER-Nelson Publishing Co., Ltd.; review MMYB 9:945)

Personal Resource Questionnaire (Provides information about adults' social networks and perceived levels of social support; ages 18–80; 3 scores for Part I (Size of Network, Number of Problems Experienced, Degree of Satisfaction with Help Received); Part II (total score only); P. Brandt & C. Weinert; Patricia Brandt and Clarann Weinert; review MMYB 11:286)

Personal Values Questionnaire (Measures individual values related to achievement, affiliation, power; adults; 3 scores (Achievement, Affiliation, Power); J. J. Fink & R. Mansfield; McBer and Company)

Philadelphia Head Injury Questionnaire (Developed for use in gathering the history of individuals with head injuries; head trauma patients; no scores; L. M. Curry, R. G. Ivins, & T. L. Gowen; Western Psychological Services; review MMYB 12:293)

PHSF Relations Questionnaire (Constructed to measure the personal, home, social and formal relations of high school students and adults, in order to determine their level of adjustment; Standards 6–10 in South African school system, college, and adults; 12 scores; F. A. Fouche & P. E. Brobbelaar; Human Sciences Research Council (South Africa))

Picture Vocational Interest Questionnaire for Adults (To measure interests in certain occupational activities; long-term South African prisoners who have passed Standard 5; J. J. Taljaard & J. S. Gericke; Human Sciences Research Council (South Africa))

Position Analysis Questionnaire (Constructed to analyze jobs in terms of work activities and work-situation variables; business and industrial jobs; 45 score dimensions in 7 divisions; E. J. McCormick, P. R. Jeanneret, & R. C. Meacham; Consulting Psychologists Press; review MMYB 12:299)

Preliminary Diagnostic Questionnaire (To assess the functional capacities of persons with disabilities in relation to employability; persons involved with vocational rehabilitation agencies or facilities and workers' compensation claimants; 8 subscales; B. Moriarty; West Virginia Research and Training Center; review MMYB 11:297)

Preschool Behavior Questionnaire, The (Designed as a screening tool to identify emotional/behavioral problems in children; ages 3–6; 4 scores (Hostile-Aggressive, Anxious-Fearful, Hyperactive-Distractible, Total); L. Behar & S. Stringfield; Lenore Behar; review MMYB 9:978)

Professional and Managerial Position Questionnaire (For evaluating professional positions according to elements such as communicating, planning, and exercising judgment, personal characteristics necessary to succeed on the job, and other factors such as the number of people supervised or the amount of supervision needed; J. L. Mitchell & E. J. McCormick; Consulting Psychologists Press; reviews MMYB 9:993 & MMYB 12:311)

Purdue Interest Questionnaire (To help students identify an appropriate specialization within or outside of engineering; freshmen engineering students; 18 scale scores; W. K. LeBold & K. D. Shell; Purdue Research Foundation)

Quality of Life Questionnaire (Developed to assess the quality of an individual's life across a broad range of specific areas; ages 18 and over; 17 scores; D. R. Evans & W. E. Cope; Multi-Health Systems, Inc.; review MMYB 11:318)

Questionnaire Measure of Trait Arousability (Designed to measure individual differences to positive and/or negative emotionality, emotional sensitivity, or emotional reactivity; ages 15 and older; total score only; A. Mehrabian; Albert Mehrabian; review MMYB 9:1025)

Questionnaire on Resources and Stress (Measures stress in families who are caring for ill or disabled relatives; families with children who have developmental disabilities, psychiatric problems, renal disease, cystic fibrosis, neuromuscular disease, or cerebral palsy; 15 scores; J. Holroyd; Clinical Psychological Publishing Co., Inc; review MMYB 11:319)

Rapid Personality Questionnaire (Designed to measure the big 5 personality dimensions to provide (easily scored) assessment of individuals; ages 16 years and over; 5 bipolar trait scales (Extroversion/Introversion, Confidence/Anxiety, Conscientiousness/Expediency, Tough-Mindedness/Benevolence, Conformity/Inquisitiveness); J. Rusk; The Test Agency Ltd. (England))

Relating to Each Other: A Questionnaire for Students (To provide information about students' perceptions and experiences concerning the other sex; college students; no scores; Project on the Status and Education of Women, Association of American Colleges; Center for Women Policy Studies)

Relating with Colleagues: A Questionnaire for Faculty Members (Designed to examine some aspects of the day-to-day campus environment with respect to sex-based discrimination; college faculty; no scores; Project on the Status and Education of Women, Association of American Colleges; Center for Women Policy Studies)

Revised Denver Prescreening Developmental Questionnaire (To facilitate earlier identification of children whose development may be delayed; ages 0–9 months, 9–24 months, 2–4 years, 4–6 years; item scores only; ratings by parents; W. K. Frankenburg; Denver Developmental Materials, Inc.)

Sales Personality Questionnaire (Developed to assess personality characteristics necessary for sales success; sales applicants; 12 scores; Saville & Holdsworth Ltd.; review MMYB 12:337)

SAQ—Adult Probation (Substance Abuse Questionnaire) (Designed specifically for adult probation department and corrections use as a risk and needs assessment instrument; adult probationers; Behavior Data Systems, Ltd.; adult probationers; behaviors/characteristics relevant to probation risk and needs assessment in 6 areas; Behavior Data Systems; review MMYB 12:338)

Self-Administered Dependency Questionnaire (To identify dependency in mother/child relationships; ages 8–15; 4 scores (Affection, Assistance, Communication, Travel); I. Berg; Ian Berg (England))

Self-Description Questionnaire—I, II, III (To measure aspects of self-concept; ages 5–12, 13–17, 16–adult; H. W. Marsh; SDQ Instruments, Publication Unit (Australia))

Self-Esteem Questionnaire (Measures self-esteem and satisfaction with self-esteem; ages 9 and over; 2 scores (Self-Esteem, Self-Other Satisfaction); J. K. Hoffmeister; Test Analysis & Development Corporation)

Situation Diagnosis Questionnaire (To understand the concept of situational management, recognize situations in which various management styles are most appropriate, identify the management style(s) most appropriate for the individual's situation, and develop a plan to use a more appropriate management style on the job; managers and employees; D. Michalak; Michalak Training Associates, Inc.; review MMYB 10:335)

Situational Confidence Questionnaire (Designed to help clients identify high-risk drinking relapse situations; adult alcoholics; 9 scores; H. M. Annios & J. M. Graham; Addiction Research Foundation (Canada))

16 Personality Factor Questionnaire, 5th edition (Designed as a comprehensive measure of personality traits; ages 16 and over; 24 scores; R. B. Cattell, A. K. Cattell, & H. E. P. Cattell; Institute for Personality & Ability Testing; review MMYB 12:354)

South African Personality Questionnaire (Designed to assess personality traits relevant to the functioning of individuals in a wide variety of everyday situations; grades 12 and over; 5 scores; D. W. Steyn; National Institute for Personnel Research (South Africa); review MMYB 9:1155)

Stress Management Questionnaire (Identifies how one responds to life stressors and copes with stress; adults and adolescents; 11 scores; J. C. Petersen; The Assessment Centre; review MMYB 10:348)

Student Adaptation to College Questionnaire (Designed to assess how well a student is adapting to the demands of the college experience; college freshmen; 5 scores; R. W. Baker & B. Siryk; Western Psychological Services; review MMYB 11:383)

Student Styles Questionnaire (Measures styles of learning, relating and working of students; grades 3–12; 4 scales—Extraverted/Introverted, Thinking/Feeling, Practical/Imaginative, and Organized/Flexible; T. Oakland, J. Glutting, & C. Horton; The Psychological Corporation)

Study Process Questionnaire (To assess the extent to which a tertiary student at college or university endorses different approaches to learning and the more important motives and strategies comprising those approaches; college students; 10 scores; J. Biggs; Australian Council for Educational Research; review MMYB 11:389)

Suicidal Ideation Questionnaire (For screening adolescents for suicidal ideation, one aspect of suicidal behavior that may point to suicidal intentions; grades 7–9, 1–12; Total Suicidal Ideation score; W. M. Reynolds; Psychological Assessment Resources; review MMYB 11:393)

Time Questionnaire: Assessing Suicide Potential (Semiprojective personalty technique using time perspective as an index of suicide potential for research use only; adults; 8 scores; R. Yufit & B. Benzies; Consulting Psychologists Press; review MMYB 9:1294)

Ways of Coping Questionnaire (To identify the thoughts and actions an individual has used to cope with a specific stressful encounter; adults; 8 scores; S. Folkman & R. S. Lazarus; Consulting Psychologists Press; review MMYB 11:462)

Work Attitudes Questionnaire (Designed to differentiate the "workaholic" or the Type A personality from the highly committed worker; managers; 3 scores (Work Commitment, Psychological Health, Total); M. S. Doty & N. E. Betz; Marathon Consulting & Press; review MMYB 9:1395)

Appendix D

Commercially Available Psychological Inventories

ACT Study Power Assessment and Inventory (For assessing study skills in senior high school students; grades 10–12; 7 scores; American College Testing; review MMYB 12:11)

ACT Study Skills Assessment and Inventory (College Edition) (For assessing study skills in college students; 6 scores; American College Testing; review MMYB 12:12)

Adaptive Behavior Inventory (Evaluates functional daily living skills of school-age children and helps identify students believed to be mentally retarded or emotionally disturbed; ages 5–18; scored on self-care skills, communication skills, social skills, academic skills, and occupational skills; L. Brown & J. E. Leigh; ages 5–18; pro•ed)

Adaptive Behavior Inventory for Children (A component of the *System of Multicultural Pluralistic Assessment,* this inventory is a measure of a child's performance in social roles within the family, peer group, and community; six scales—family, community peer relations, nonacademic school roles, earner/consumer, and self-maintenance; J. R. Mercer & J. F. Lewis; 5–11 years; The Psychological Corporation)

Adult Career Concerns Inventory (To measure career planning and concerns with the career development tasks during various stages of life; ages 24 and over; 13 scores; D. E. Super, A. S. Thompson, & R. H. Lindeman; Consulting Psychologists Press; review MMYB 12:18)

Adult Personality Inventory (Designed as a tool for analyzing and reporting individual differences in personality, interpersonal styles, and career-style preferences; ages 16–adult; 25 scores; S. E. Krug; MetriTech; review MMYB 9:54, 12:20, & TC VI:21)

Alcohol Use Inventory (To assess a person's pattern of alcohol consumption and problems associated with it; adults suspected of problem drinking; J. L. Horn, K. W. Wanberg, & F. M. Foster; NCS Assessments; review MMYB 12:25)

The APT Inventory (Designed to measure an individual's relative strength on 10 personality traits; adults; 10 traits; Training House, Inc.)

254

ASPIRE (A Sales Potential Inventory for Real Estate) (Selection system developed to aid in selection of residential real estate sales associates; real estate sales candidates; 1 overall rating plus 5 life history dimensions; Life Insurance Marketing and Research Association; review MMYB 12:32)

Association Adjustment Inventory (Designed for use as a screening instrument for maladjustment and immaturity; normal and institutionalized adults; 13 scores; M. M. Bruce; reviews MMYB 6:201 & TC I:70)

Athletic Motivation Inventory (Measures personality and motivational factors of athletes participating in competitive sports; athletes aged 13 and over and coaches; 14 scores; T. A. Tutko, L. P. Lyon & B. C. Oglive; Institute of Athletic Motivation; review MMYB 12:37)

Basic Personality Inventory (Multiphasic measure of psychopathology; ages 12 and over; 12 scores; D. N. Jackson; Sigma Assessment Systems; reviews MMYB 12:42 & TC VIII:38)

Basic Reading Inventory, Fifth Edition (For assessing reading performance level in elementary and junior high school students by means graded word lists and reading passages; grades pre-primer to 8; 3 reading level scores for each of 3 subtests; J. L. Johns; Kendall/Hunt Publishing Co.; review MMYB 12:43)

Beck Anxiety Inventory (1993 Edition) (Measures the severity of anxiety in older adolescents and adults; A. T. Beck & R. A. Steer; The Psychological Corporation)

Beck Depression Inventory (1993 revised) (Designed to assess the severity of depression in older adolescents and adults; ages 13–80; A. T. Beck & R. A. Steer; The Psychological Corporation; previous edition review MMYB 11:31)

Bem Sex-Role Inventory (Assesses psychological femininity and masculinity; high school and college students and adults; 3 scores—femininity, masculinity, femininity-minus-masculinity difference; S. L. Bem; Consulting Psychologists Press; review MMYB 9:137)

Brief Symptom Inventory (Self-report inventory of psychological symptoms; 9 dimension scores plus 3 global indices; L. R. Derogatis & P. M. Spencer; Leonard R. Derogatis)

Burns/Roe Informal Reading Inventory: Preprimer to Twelfth Grade, Third Edition (To provide information concerning the reading skills, abilities, and needs of students to plan a program of reading instruction for individual students; beginning readers–grade 12; 2 scores—Word Recognition, Comprehension; 14 levels; B. D. Roe & P. C. Burns; Houghton Mifflin Co.; review MMYB 12:56)

California Psychological Inventory, Revised Edition (Designed to assess personality characteristics and to predict what people will say or do in specified contexts; ages 13 and over; H. G. Gough; Consulting Psychologists Press; reviews MMYB 11:54 & TC VII:66)

California Test of Personality (Designed to identify and reveal the status of certain factors in personality and social adjustment; children and adults; 15 scores; E. W. Tiegs, W. W. Clark & L. P. Thorpe; CTB/McGraw-Hill; review MMYB 9:183)

Canfield Instructional Styles Inventory (To identify instructional preferences among instructors; 21 scores; A. A. Canfield & J. S. Canfield; Western Psychological Services; review MMYB 11:56)

Canfield Learning Styles Inventory (To assess learning preferences among students; junior high, high school, college, and adults in business settings; 21 scores; A. A. Canfield; Western Psychological Services; review MMYB 11:57)

Career Adaptive Behavior Inventory (Designed to assist teachers in improving the developmentally disabled student in 10 areas; ages 5–15; ratings by parents, teachers, or other professionals in 10 major categories; T. P. Lombardi; Special Child Publications)

Career Assessment Inventories for the Learning Disabled (Designed to be used by counselors and other educators who work with learning-disabled children and adults; learning-disabled elementary school grades and over; 3 tests—Attributes Inventory, Ability Inventory, and Interest Inventory; C. Weller & M. Buchanan; Academic Therapy Publications; review MMYB 9:193)

Career Assessment Inventory—Enhanced Version (Interest inventory for comparing occupational interests and personality preferences with those of individuals in specific careers; adults and students 15 years or older; scored on 6 general occupational themes, 25 basic interest scales, 111 occupational scales, and 4 nonoccupational scales; C. B. Johansson; NCS Assessments)

Career Assessment Inventory, Second Edition (Vocational Version) (Vocational interest assessment tool for individuals planning to enter occupations requiring a four-year college degree or less; grade 10 through adult; 125 scores; C. B. Johansson; NCS Assessments; review MMYB 11:59)

Career Attitudes and Strategies Inventory (Assesses career attitudes and obstacles in employed and unemployed adults; J. L. Holland & G. D. Gottfredson; Psychological Assessment Resources)

Career Beliefs Inventory (To assist people in identifying career believes that may influence their career goals; junior high school and over; 26 scores; J. D. Krumboltz; Consulting Psychologists Press; review MMYB 12:64)

Career Development Inventory (Assesses components of career development and career maturity; grades 8–12 and college; 8 scores; D. E. Super et al., Consulting Psychologists Press; review MMYB 9:105)

Career Directions Inventory (To assess components of career development and career maturity; grades 8–12 and college; 8 scores; D. E. Super et al.; Consulting Psychologists Press; review MMYB 9:195)

Career Directions Inventory (For identifying the respondent's degree of interest in a large number of different occupations; high school and college students and adults; 15 basic interest scales; D. N. Jackson; Sigma Assessment Systems; review MMYB 10:44)

Career Interest Inventory (Provides information concerning individual's educational goals, interest in various school subjects and school-related activities, and interest in occupations; grades 7–12 and adults; The Psychological Corporation)

Career Maturity Inventory (grades 6–12; attitude scale—screening and counseling form, competence test yielding 5 scores; J. O. Crites; CTB/McGraw-Hill; review MMYB 8:997)

Caregiver's School Readiness Inventory (Ratings by parents to predict a preschool child's success in school; ages 3–11 to 5–10; total score only; M. L. Simner; Phylmar Associates; review MMYB 12:65)

Caring Relationship Inventory (For measuring the elements of love or caring in human relationships; premarital and marital counselees; 7 scores; E. L. Shostrom; Educational & Industrial Testing Service; review MMYB 8:333)

The Child Abuse Potential Inventory (To assist in screening suspected physical child abuse cases; male and female parents or primary caregivers suspected of physical child abuse; 12 scale scores; J. S. Miller; Psytec Inc.; review MMYB 10:50)

Child Care Inventory (For evaluating child care programs to determine the level of program implementation and to improve their effectiveness; child care programs; 11 performance area scores; M. S. Abbott-Shim & A. M. Sibley; Humanics Publishing Group; review MMYB 12:71)

Children's Depression Inventory (Self-report measure of depression in school-age children and adolescents; 7–17 years; total score and five subscores by age and sex; M. Kovacs; Western Psychiatric Institute and Clinic; review MMYB 11:66)

Children's Inventory of Self-Esteem (For measuring self-esteem in elementary school-age children from ratings by parents and teachers; ages 5–12; 15 scores; R. A. Campbell; Brougham Press; review MMYB 12:78)

College Major Interest Inventory (For identifying academic majors best suited to students' interests pattern; high school and college students; 135 scale scores; R. D. Whetstone & R. G. Taylor, Consulting Psychologists Press; review MMYB 12:84)

Comprehensive Personality Profile (Designed to identify individuals with personality traits that are compatible with occupational and organizational demands; adults; 17 scores; Wonderlic Personnel Test & L. L. Craft)

Coopersmith Self-Esteem Inventories (Measures the evaluation a person makes and customarily maintains with regard to him- or herself; ages 8–15; S. Coopersmith; Consulting Psychologists Press; review MMYB 9:267)

Coping Inventory (A measure of the behavior patterns and skills resources used by a person to meet personal needs and adapt to environmental demands; ages 3–adulthood; 9 scores; S. Zeitlin; Scholastic Testing Service)

Coping Inventory for Stressful Situations (A measure of three main coping styles–Task-Oriented Coping, Emotion-Oriented Coping, and Avoidance Coping; the last is broken into two components—Distraction and Social Diversion; adults; N. Endler & J. Parker; Psychological Publications)

Coping Resources Inventory (To assess a person's resources for coping with stress; high school and over; A. L. Mammer & M. S. Marting; Consulting Psychologists Press; reviews MMYB 12:95 & TC VIII:111)

Coping Resources Inventory for Stress (Designed to measure coping resources that help lessen the negative effects of stress; adults; 16 scores; W. L. Curlette et al.; Health Prisms)

COPS Interest Inventory (Provides job activity interest scores related to occupational clusters; 7th grade through high school, college and adults; R. R. Knapp & L. F. Knapp, Educational & Industrial Testing Service)

COPS Interest Inventory Form R (Provides for measurement of the 14 COPSystem Interest Clusters in terms of the simplified language and use of a single norms profile; 6th grade through high school; L. F. Knapp, R. R. Knapp, & L. Knapp-Lee; Educational & Industrial Testing Service)

COPS Picture Inventory of Careers (Provides job activity interest scores using pictures only; elementary through high school, and adults—nonverbal; L. Knapp-Lee; Educational & Industrial Testing Service)

COPS-P Interest Inventory (Measures interests at the professional level, providing job activity interests scores related to occupational clusters; L. Knapp-Lee, L. F. Knapp, & R. R. Knapp; Educational & Industrial Testing Service)

Couple's Pre-Counseling Inventory, Revised Edition (Designed to provide a comprehensive picture of the strengths and concerns of couples to serve as a basis for planning specific treatment strategies; married or cohabiting couples beginning counseling; 13 score areas; R. B. Stuart & B. Jacobson; Research Press; review MMYB 11:92)

Creative Behavior Inventory (Designed to measure behavioral characteristics associated with creativity; grades 1–6, 7–12; 5 scores; R. J. Kirschenbaum; Creative Learning Press; review MMYB 11:93)

Creative Styles Inventory (To identify a preference for assimilating information by means of an intuitive or logical style; high school (advanced); total score only; B. McCarthy & Excell, Inc.; McBer & Company)

The Creatix Inventory (To help people identify their levels of creativity as well as their orientations toward risk taking; members of organizations; Creativity and Risk Taking scores; R. E. Byrd; Pfeiffer & Company)

Culture-Free Self-Esteem Inventories, Second Edition (To measure self-esteem and monitor treatment progress; grades 2–9, ages 16–65; 6 scores; J. Battle; pro•ed; review MMYB 12:100)

Daily Stress Inventory (To measure the number and relative impact of minor stresses in a person's life; age 17 and older; P. J. Brantley & G. N. Jones; Sigma Assessment Systems; review MMYB 11:101)

Derogatis Sexual Functioning Inventory (Multiscaled inventory of a group of clinically relevant sexual and personality dimensions; adults; 12 scores; Leonard R. Derogatis; review MMYB 9:317)

Early Coping Inventory (Measure of adaptive behavior; ages 4–36 months; 4 scores—Sensorimotor Organization, Reactive Behavior, Self-Initiated Behavior, Total; S. Zeitlin & G. G. Williamson; Scholastic Testing Service; review MMYB 11:120)

Eating Disorder Inventory-2 (Self-report measure of psychological characteristics associated with anorexia nervosa and bulimia nervosa; ages 12 and over; 11 scores; D. M. Garner; Psychological Assessment Resources; review MMYB 12:130)

Eating Inventory (Assesses three dimensions of eating behavior found to be important in recognizing and treating eating-related disorders: cognitive control of eating, disinhibition, and hunger; age 17 and over; A. J. Stunkard & S. Messick; The Psychological Corporation).

Educational Leadership Practices Inventory (Measures ideal and actual attitudes for individual and group teacher styles; for teachers and administrators; 2 scores—ideal and actual; C. W. Nelson & J. J. Valenti; Management Research Associates)

Employability Inventory (Self-assessment instrument to assess job-seeking and job-keeping skills; prospective employees; item scores only; J. D. Hartz, M. Stephey, D. Steel, & S. Kosmo; Education Associates; review MMYB 12:135)

Employee Attitude Inventory (Designed to help identify an organization's potential exposure to employee theft and counterproductive behavior; London House)

Employee Reliability Inventory (Preemployment inventory for assessing various dimensions of reliable and productive work behavior; prospective employees; 7 scores; G. L. Borofsky; Bay State Psychological Associates; review MMYB 12:137)

Employment Values Inventory (Measures personal values associated with work and the working environment; adults; 14 scores)

Environmental Response Inventory (Measures differences in the ways in which people think about and relate to the physical environment; college and adults; 9 scores; G. E. McKechnie; Consulting Psychologists Press; review MMYB 8:550)

Eysenck Personality Inventory (Measures two independent dimensions of personality—extraversion-introversion and neuroticism-stability; adults; 3 scores; H. J. Eysenck & S. B. G. Eysenck; Educational & Industrial Testing Service; reviews MMYB 9:405 & TC II:258)

Family Relationship Inventory (Examines family relationships and clarifies individual feelings and interpersonal behavior; young children, adolescents, and adults; 2 scores—positive and negative for each family member; R. B. Michaelson et al.; Psychological Publications; review MMYB 10:112)

Food Choice Inventory (Assesses food choice behaviors; junior and senior high students and adults; 9 scores; National Dairy Council and University of Illinois at Chicago; National Dairy Council; review MMYB 10:118)

Geist Picture Interest Inventory (Used to identify vocational and avocational interests of culturally different and educationally deprived individuals; grade 8 through high school, college, and adulthood; H. Geist; Western Psychological Services)

The Golombok Rust Inventory of Marital State (For assessing the overall quality of the relationship between married or cohabiting heterosexual partners; married or unmarried heterosexual couples living together; total score only; J. Rust, I. Bennun, M. Crowe, & S. Golombok; NFER-Nelson; review MMYB 12:164)

The Golombok Rust Inventory of Sexual Satisfaction (Objectively assesses the quality of a sexual relationship and of a person's functioning within it; sex therapy clients; 13 scores; J. Rust & S. Golombok; NFER-Nelson; review MMYB 10:127)

The Grief Experience Inventory (Multidimensional measure of grief; bereaved adults; 15–18 scores; C. M. Sanders, P. A. Mauger, & P. N. Strong; Consulting Psychologists Press; review MMYB 12:168)

Group Inventory for Finding Creative Talent (Designed to screen elementary school students for programs for the creatively gifted by identifying students with attitudes and values related to creativity; grades K–2, 3–4, 5–6; overall score and 3 dimension scores—imagination, independence, many interests; S. B. Rimm; Educational Assessment Service; review MMYB 9:454)

Group Inventory of Finding Interests (For screening creatively gifted children; grades 6–9, 9–12; 5 dimension scores; S. B. Rimm & G. A. Davis; Educational Assessment Service)

Guilford-Zimmerman Interest Inventory (A measure of vocational interests; college and adults; 10 scores; J. S. Guilford & W. S. Zimmerman; Consulting Psychologists Press; review MMYB 12:174)

Hall Occupational Orientation Inventory (To help people understand their values, needs, interests, and preferred lifestyles as they are related to career goals and educational plans; grades 3–7, 8–16 and adults, low literate adults, junior high students–adults; 22 scores; L. G. Hall & R. B. Tarrier; Scholastic Testing Service; review MMYB 12:175)

Hogan Personality Inventory (Revised) (Measures of normal personality designed for use in personnel selection, individualized assessment, and career-related decision-making; college students and adults; 14 scores; R. Hogan & J. Hogan; Hogan Assessment Systems; earlier edition reviews MMYB 10:140 & TC VI:216)

Hutchins Behavior Inventory (Designed to assess the interaction of thoughts, feelings, and actions; high school and older; 8 scores; D. E. Hutchins & R. O. Mueller; Consulting Psychologists Press; review MMYB 12:184)

Interpersonal Communication Inventory (To assess a person's interpersonal communication to provide clues to communication problems outside of the family relationship; grade 9 to adult; 12 scores; Millard J. Bienvenu)

Interpersonal Style Inventory (Designed to describe personality in terms of 15 bipolar trait dimensions of self-report; high school and college students and adults; 15 scores; M. Lorr & R. P. Youniss; Maurice Lorr; review MMYB 10:151)

Inventory for Counseling and Development (Designed to identify strengths, assets, and coping skills of college students seeking assistance with vocational, educational, and personal problems; 23 scores; N. S. Giddan, F. R. Creech, & V. R. Lovell; NCS Assessments; review MMYB 11:182)

Inventory of Perceptual Skills (Assesses visual and auditory perceptual skills; ages 5–10; 11 scores; D. R. O'Dell; Stoelting; review MMYB 11:193)

Inventory of Suicide Orientation-30 (To identify adolescents at risk for suicide orientation; 2 scores—final raw score, final critical item score; J. D. King & B. Kowalchuk; NCS Assessments)

Inwald Personality Inventory—Revised (Developed to aid public safety/law enforcement and security agencies in selecting new officers; public safety, security, and law enforcement applications (police, correction, fire, security); R. Inwald; Hilson Research; 26 scores; review MMYB 11:183 & 12:194)

Jackson Personality Inventory—Revised (Provides a set of measures of personality reflecting a variety of interpersonal, cognitive, and value orientations; grades 9–16 and adults; 16 scores; D. N. Jackson; Sigma Assessment Systems; earlier edition reviews MMYB 8:593 & TC II:369)

Johnson Informal Reading Inventory (For assessing reading comprehension in junior and senior high school students; grades 7–12; 2 scores—Vocabulary Screening and Reading Comprehension; M. C. Johnston; Educational Publications; review MMYB 12:202)

Jr.–Sr. High School Personality Inventory (Designed as a tool for adolescents with behavior problems; measures 14 primary personality dimensions and other broader trait patterns; 12–18 years; R. B. Cattell, M. D. Cattell, E. Johns, & M. McConville; Institute for Personality & Ability Testing; review MMYB 11:188)

Junior Eysenck Personality Inventory (For measuring neuroticism or emotionality and extraversion-introversion in children; H. J. Eysenck & S. B. G. Eysenck; Educational & Industrial Testing Service; review MMYB 7:96)

Kindergarten Screening Inventory (To help teachers identify differences among entering kindergarten children that are relevant to their education; 16 subtests; M. N. Milone & V. H. Lucas; Zaner-Bloser; review MMYB 10:165)

Leadership Competency Inventory (Assesses the use of 4 competencies related to leadership; adults; 4 scores—information seeking, conceptual thinking, strategic orientation, service orientation; S. P. Kelner; McBer & Company)

Leadership Practices Inventory (For obtaining ratings on 5 leadership behaviors; managers; 5 scores; J. M. Kouzes & B. Z. Posner; Pfeiffer & Company International Publishers; review MMYB 12:213)

Leadership Skills Inventory (To assess strengths and weaknesses in the area of leadership; grades 4–12; 9 scores; F. A. Karnes & J. C. Chauvin; pro•ed; review MMYB 10:172)

Leadership Skills Inventory (To help individuals acquire the ability to handle the "people" side of enterprise; adults; 7 scores; T. D. Anderson; Consulting Resource Group International)

Learning Preference Inventory (For helping teachers identify student learning preferences or styles; elementary through adult students; 6 preference scores; H. F. Silver & J. R. Hanson; Hanson Silver Strong & Associates, Inc.; review MMYB 11:201)

Learning-Style Inventory (To help students assess their learning modes and styles; grade 6–adults; 8 scores; D. A. Kolb; McBer & Co.; review MMYB 10:173)

Learning Style Inventory (To identify elements that are critical to a person's learning style, and to serve as an aid in prescribing the type of environment, instructional activities, social grouping, and motivational factors that optimize group achievement; grades 3–12; 22 area scores; R. Dunn, K. Dunn, & G. E. Price; Price Systems)

Learning Styles Inventory (For identifying the learning needs of students; students and adults; scored on 9 subtopics in 2 areas—Learning and Working; Piney Mountain Press)

Leisure Interest Inventory (For assessing preferred leisure activities; college students; 5 scores; Edwina E. Hubert)

Lewis Counseling Inventory (For identifying pupils in need of guidance counseling; student adolescents; 8 scores; NFER-Nelson; review MMYB 9:614)

Life Styles Inventory (Designed to assess a person's thinking and behavioral styles; adults; 12 scores; J. C. Lafferty; Human Synergistics; review MMYB 12:222)

Maferr Inventory of Feminine Values (Designed to measure various perceptions of women's sex roles; college students and adults; scores on 5 tests labeled "forms"; A. G. Steinmann, D. J. Fox & M. Toro; Maferr Foundation; review MMYB 9:641)

Maferr Inventory of Masculine Values (Designed to provide self and ideal male sex role descriptions; high school & college students and adults; scores on 5 tests labeled "forms"; A. G. Steinmann, D. J. Fox & M. Toro; Maferr Foundation; review MMYB 9:642)

Management Inventory on Leadership, Motivation, and Decision-Making (For use in training and selecting managers; managers and manager trainees; total score only; Donald L. Kirkpatrick; review MMYB 12:226)

Management Styles Inventory (For assessing management style under a variety of conditions; adults; 5 scores; J. Hall, J. B. Harvey, & M. S. Williams; Teleometrics International; review MMYB 12:227)

A Marital Communication Inventory (Designed to assess communication in marriage; adults; total score only; M. J. Bienvenu; Family Life Publications; review MMYB 9:651)

Marital Satisfaction Inventory (Self-report inventory for broadly evaluating marital relationships; married couples beginning counseling; scores on 11 scales; D. K. Snyder; Western Psychological Services; review MMYB 9:652)

Marriage Expectation Inventories (A clinical tool for obtaining information from engaged and married couples; no scores; 9 areas—love, communication, freedom, sex, money, selfishness, religious expectations, relatives, expectations related to children; P. J. McDonald et al.; Family Life Publications; review MMYB 9:654)

Marriage Role Expectation Inventory (Designed to measure traditional and companionship expectations of marital relationships; adolescents and adults; 9 scores; M. S. Dunn & J. N. DeBonis; Family Life Publications; review MMYB 9:655)

Maslach Burnout Inventory (Designed to measure three components of the burnout syndrome—emotional exhaustion, development of negative attitudes toward service recipients, and development of a tendency to evaluate oneself negatively with regard to one's work; staff members in human service and educational institutions; C. Maslach & S. E. Jackson; Consulting Psychologists Press; review MMYB 9:659)

Maudsley Personality Inventory (Designed to measure two dimensions of personality as others—extraversion-introversion and neuroticism-stability; college students and adults; 2 scores—neuroticism and introversion-extraversion; H. J. Eysenck, & R. R. Knapp; Hodder & Stoughton; reviews MMYB 6:138 & TC IV:387)

Millon Adolescent Clinical Inventory (Assesses adolescent personality along with self-reported concerns and clinical syndromes; ages 13–19 years; scored on 3 modifying indices, 12 personality patterns, 8 expressed concerns, and 7 clinical syndromes; T. Millon, C. Millon, & R. Davis; NCS Assessments; review MMYB 12:236)

Millon Adolescent Personality Inventory (Designed to identify, predict, and understand a wide range of psychological attributes in adolescents; ages 13–19; 20 scales; C. J. Green & R. B. Meagher; NCS Assessment Systems; review MMYB 9:707)

Millon Behavioral Health Inventory (Brief self-report personality inventory designed to assess psychological coping factors related to the physical health care of adult medical patients; 18 years and older; 8 basic coping styles; 6 psychogenic attitudes, 3 psychosomatic correlates, and 3 prognostic indicators; T. Millon, C. J. Green, & R. B. Meagher; NCS Assessments)

Millon Clinical Multiaxial Inventory (I, II, III) (Provides a profile of the scale scores and a detailed analysis of personality and symptom management; adults 18 years and older; T. Millon; NCS Assessments; MCMI-II reviews MMYB 11:239 & TC VIII:457)

Minnesota Infant Development Inventory (Measures infant development from mother's observations; birth to 15 months; 5 developmental areas; H. Ireton & E. Thwing; Behavior Science Systems, Inc.)

Minnesota Multiphasic Personality Inventory-2 (Designed to assess a number of the major patterns of personality and emotional disorders; ages 18 and over; S. R. Hathaway, J. C.

McKinley, & J. N. Butcher; published by University of Minnesota, distributed by NCS Assessments; reviews MMYB 11:244, TC VIII:485, & TC X:424)

Minnesota Multiphasic Personality Inventory—Adolescent Version (Designed to assess major patterns of personality and emotional disorders in adolescents; ages 14–18; 16 Basic Scales; J. N. Butcher et al.; Published by University of Minnesota Press and distributed by NCS Assessments; review MMYB 12:238)

Motivational Patterns Inventory (To help members of an organization explore dominant motivations so they can affect their contributions to organizational success; organizational members; 3 scores—Farmer, Hunter, Shepherd; R. E. Byrd & W. R. Neher; Pfeiffer & Company; review MMYB 12:245)

The Multidimensional Self-Esteem Inventory (Provides measures of the components of self-esteem; college students; 11 scores; E. J. O'Brien & S. Epstein; Psychological Assessment Resources; review MMYB 11:250)

Multiscore Depression Inventory (To provide an objective measure of the severity of self-reported depression; ages 13 through adult; D. J. Berndt; Western Psychological Services; review MMYB 11:251)

NEO Personality Inventory—Revised (Analyzes personality using the "Five Factor" model; ages 17 and older; 35 scores; P. T. Costa, Jr. & R. R. McCrae; Psychological Assessment Resources; review MMYB 12:330; earlier edition review MMYB 11:258)

Occupational Stress Inventory (Research Version) (Measures 3 dimensions of occupational adjustment—occupational stress, psychological strain, and coping resources; adults; S. J. Osipow & A. R. Spokane; Sigma Assessment Systems; adults; reviews MMYB 11:269 & TC X:498)

Organizational Culture Inventory (For measuring organizational norms and expectations; 12 culture styles; R. A. Cook & J. C. Lafferty; Human Synergistics, Inc.)

Orientation and Motivation Inventory (Measures motivational variables that account for the behavior of people; grades 11, 12, and college freshmen and sophomores; 12 scales; M. Loor, R. P. Youniss, & E. C. Stefic; Maurice Lorr; review MMYB 9:911)

A Parent-Adolescent Communication Inventory (Designed to measure adolescents' perceptions of their current communication patterns with their parents; ages 13 and over; adolescent and parent forms; M. J. Bienvenu; Family Life Publications; review MMYB 9:916)

Partner Relationship Inventory (Research Edition) (For assessing interactional, emotional, and sexual needs in a relationship, and to point to areas of conflict; married couples; scored for Interactional Needs and Emotional Needs; C. N. Hoskins; Consulting Psychologists Press; review MMYB 12:281)

Personal Distress Inventory and Scales (Consists of 4 scales based on Foulds' and Bedford's hierarchical model of personal (psychiatric) illness—Delusions-Symptoms-States Inventory, Delusions-Symptoms-State Inventory/State of Anxiety and Depression, Delusions-Symptoms-States Inventory/Neurotic Symptoms, and Personality Deviance Scale; psychiatric patients and normal adults; A. Bedford & G. Foulds; NFER-Nelson Publishing Co.; review MMYB 9:940)

Personal Experience Inventory for Adults (Provides comprehensive information concerning substance abuse patterns in adults; used to identify alcohol and drug problems, make referrals, and plan treatment; adults; 11 problem severity scales and 11 psychosocial scales, validity indicators; K. C. Winters; Western Psychological Services)

A Personal Inventory (Designed to measure current concerns, emotional status, life stresses, and personal functioning; ages 16 and over; self-rating scale with no scores; H. Ireton; Behavior Science Systems)

Personal Inventory of Needs (Self-assessment tool for identifying the strengths of three basic needs; employees; 3 scores—Achievement, Affiliation, Power; Training House; review MMYB 12:287)

Personality Assessment Inventory (Designed to provide information relevant to clinical diagnosis, treatment planning, and screening for psychopathology; ages 18–adult; 54 scores; L. C. Morey; Psychological Assessment Resources; review MMYB 12:290)

Personality Inventory for Children—Revised Format (Designed to identify certain emotional and interpersonal problems in children, in addition to assessing the child's cognitive development and the psychological climate of the family; completed by person who knows the child and his or her behavior well; 33 scores; R. D. Wirt, D. Lachar, J. E. Klinedinst, P. D. Seat, & W. E. Broen; Western Psychological Services; previous edition review MMYB 9:949).

Personality Inventory for Youth (Self-report measure for assessing psychological problems in 9- to 18-year-olds; 24 subscales; D. Lachar & C. P. Gruber; Western Psychological Services).

Personal Orientation Inventory (Designed to measure values and behaviors that are important in the development of self-actualizing people; high school and college students and adults; scored on 2 major orientation ratios—Time Ratio and Support Ratio—and 10 scales; E. L. Shostrom; Educational & Industrial Testing Service; review; review MMYB 8:641)

Personal Relations Inventory (Self-report instrument designed to measure the construct of "assertiveness"; high school and over; 5 scale scores; M. Lorr & W. W. More; Maurice Lorr; review MMYB 9:947)

Personal Relationship Inventory (For assessing the capacity to love and engage in intimate interpersonal relationships; ages 15 and over; 13 scores; R. L. Mann; Behaviordyne; review MMYB 12:288)

Personal Styles Inventory (Assesses normal personality characteristics; adults; 24 style scores; J. T. Kunce, C. S. Cope, & R. M. Newton; Educational & Psychological Consultants)

Preschool Development Inventory (Designed to screen preschool children having developmental and other problems that may affect their ability to learn; ages 3–0 to 5–5; parental report of child's current functioning; H. Ireton; Behavior Science Systems; review MMYB 10:291)

Problem Behavior Inventory (For helping clinicians to structure and focus the diagnostic interview; adolescents and adults; no scores; L. Silverton; Western Psychological Services)

Problem-Solving Decision-Making Style Inventory (To provide feedback on an individual's perception of problem-solving and decision-making styles; high school and college students and adults in organizational settings; P. Hersey & W. E. Natemeyer; Pfeiffer & Company; review MMYB 10:295)

The Problem-Solving Inventory (To measure a person's perceptions of his or her own problem-solving behaviors and attitudes; ages 16 and above; 4 scores; P. P. Heppner; Consulting Psychologists Press; review MMYB 11:303)

Psychological Screening Inventory (Brief true-false mental health screening inventory designed to identify people who might benefit from more intensive examination and professional attention; adolescents through adults; 5 scores; R. I. Lanyon; Sigma Assessment Systems)

Quick Cognitive Inventory (To observe school-related skills in non-English-speaking students or those with language-delay deficits; grades 1–3; 5 scores; A. M. Markoff; Academic Therapy Publications)

Rahim Organizational Conflict Inventories. (For measuring 3 independent dimensions of organizational conflict and 5 independent styles of dealing with interpersonal conflict; M. A. Rahim; Consulting Psychologists Press; review MMYB 10:303)

Reading-Free Vocational Interest Inventory (For measuring vocational interests in individuals with limited reading ability or language problems; mentally retarded and learning-disabled; ages 13 to adult; 11 scores; R. L. Becker; Elbern Publications)

Revised BRIGANCE® Diagnostic Inventory of Early Development (For determining the developmental or performance level of the infant or child; birth to age 7; 11 area scores; A. H. Brigance; Curriculum Associates; review MMYB 12:326)

Risk-Taking Attitude-Values Inventory (For obtaining a general profile of the values and behaviors of individuals or group; ages 3 and over; numerous scores; R. E. Carney; Timao Foundation for Research and Development; review MMYB 8:659)

Self-Actualization Inventory (Designed to measure the degree to which physical, security, relationship, respect, independence, and actualization needs are unfulfilled; managers and students of administration; 6 scores; W. J. Reddin & K. Rowell; Organizational Tests Ltd.; review MMYB 9:1094)

Self-Description Inventory (Brief personality inventory that complements interest inventories and ability tests by identifying personality strengths relevant to the world of work; 15 years and older; scored on 11 Personality Scales, 6 General Occupational Themes, and 5 Administrative Indices; C. B. Johansson; NCS Assessments; review MMYB 9:1096)

Self-Perception Inventory: Nursing Forms (Designed primarily for research on student nurses and professional staff; 7 scales; A. T. Soares & L. M. Soares; SOARES Associates; review MMYB 11:356)

Self-Worth Inventory (To increase the understanding of respondents about their feelings of self-worth and how they develop; adults; 8 scores; E. Robinson; Consulting Resource Group International)

Singer-Loomis Inventory of Personality (For assessing personalty factors that may help in self-understanding and in utilizing skills, talents, and abilities to better deal with interactions between the self and the environment; high school and college students and adults; 8 scores; J. Singer & M. Loomis; Consulting Psychologists Press; review MMYB 10:334).

Situational Preference Inventory (For assessing individual styles of social interaction; grade 9–16 and adults; 3 scores—Cooperational, Instrumental, Analytic; author and publisher, Carl N. Edwards)

Social Behavior Assessment Inventory (For assessing social skills in elementary and junior high students; grades K–9; 30 scores; T. M. Stephens & K. D. Arnold; Psychological Assessment Resources; review MMYB 12:361)

Speech-Ease Screening Inventory (Designed to assess kindergarten and first-grade pupils for articulation and language development; grades K–1; item scores in 5 areas; T. Pigott et al.; pro•ed; review MMYB 12:368)

State-Trait Anger Expression Inventory, Research Edition (To measure the experience and expression of anger; ages 13 and over; C. D. Spielberger; Psychological Assessment Resources; reviews MMYB 11:379 & TC IX:510)

State-Trait Anxiety Inventory (Designed to differentiate between state and trait anxiety; adults; C. D. Spielberger; Psychological Assessment Resources; reviews MMYB 8:683 & TC I:626)

State-Trait Anxiety Inventory for Children (A research tool for studying anxiety in elementary school children; grades 4–6; 2 scores—state anxiety and trait anxiety; C. D. Spielberger et al.; Consulting Psychologists Press; review MMYB 8:684)

Strong Interest Inventory (Fourth Edition) (Designed to measure interests in a wide range of occupations; ages 16 and over; 264 scores; E. K. Strong, Jr. J. C. Hansen, & D. P. Campbell; Consulting Psychologists Press; review MMYB 12:374)

Student Adjustment Inventory (For identifying common affective-social problems; upper elementary through beginning college; 7 scores; J. R. Barclay; MetriTech; review MMYB 12:377)

Styles of Management Inventory (For assessing individual management style under a variety of conditions; adults; 5 scores; J. Hall, J. B. Harvey, & M. S. Williams; Teleometrics International; review MMYB 12:380)

Substance Abuse Subtle Screening Inventory (For identifying alcohol- and drug-dependent individuals and to differentiate them from social users and general psychiatric patients; ages 12–18, adults; 8 scores; G. A. Miller, The SASSI Institute; review MMYB 12:381)

Suicide Intervention Response Inventory (For assessing the ability of paraprofessionals to select appropriate responses to self-destructive clients; mental health paraprofessionals, total score only; author and publisher, Robert A. Neimeyer)

Teacher Opinion Inventory, Revised Edition (For assessing teachers' opinions concerning many facets of the school, to compile teachers' recommendations for improvement, and to provide data to guide the school professional staff in decision-making regarding program development; elementary and secondary school teachers; 7 subscale scores; National Study of School Evaluation)

Teacher Stress Inventory (Assesses degree of occupational stress in teachers; American public school teachers; 11 scores; M. J. Fimian; Clinical Psychology Publishing Co.; review MMYB 11:415)

Teacher's School Readiness Inventory (Screening instrument for children who are at risk for school failure; prekindergarten to kindergarten children; total score only; M. L. Simner; Phylmar Associates; review MMYB 12:387)

Temperament and Values Inventory (Designed to measure individual differences that may affect contentment in work situations; ages 15 and over; 14 scores; C. B. Johansson & P. L. Webber; NCS Assessments; reviews MMYB 11:423 & TC I:660)

Temperament Inventory (Designed to measure a set of 4 genetically determined temperaments; college and adults; 4 scores; R. J. Cruise, W. P. Blitchington, & W. G. A. Futcher; Andrews University Press; review MMYB 9:1235)

Time Problems Inventory (For identifying reasons why people waste time; management and administrative personnel; 4 scores—Priorities, Planning, Delegation, Discipline; A. A. Canfield; Western Psychological Services; review MMYB 9:190)

Vocational Interest Inventory and Exploration Survey (For assessing a student's interest in school-based training programs and to provide information about the training area; vocational education students; 15 vocational training interest areas; N. L. Scott & C. Gilbreath; Piney Mountain Press)

Vocational Interest Inventory—Revised (Measures students' interests in Anne Roe's 8 occupational areas; high school students; P. W. Lunneborg; Western Psychological Services)

Vocational Preference Inventory (Brief personality inventory consisting entirely of job titles and designed to assess career interests; older adolescents and adults; 11 scores; J. L. Holland; Psychological Assessment Resources)

Vocational Research Interest Inventory (For measuring the occupational interests of students and clients in vocational counseling, and rehabilitation and job training program participants; high school students and adults; 12 scores; H. Dansky, J. A. Harris, & T. W. Gannaway; Vocational Research Institute; review MMYB 11:458)

The Western Personality Inventory (Designed to identify the potential alcoholic personality and to measure the extent of addiction in alcoholics; M. P. Manson; Western Psychological Services)

Wisconsin Personality Disorder Inventory (Self-report questionnaire derived from an interpersonal perspective on DSM-III-R personality disorders; adults; M. H. Klein, L. S. Benjamin, R. Rosenfeld, C. Treece, & J. H. Greist, 1993)

Work Adjustment Inventory (For evaluating adolescents' and young adults' temperament toward work activities, work environments, other employees, and other aspects of work; adolescents and young adults; 7 scores; J. E. Gilliam, pro•ed)

Work Values Inventory (Measures the relative importance of work values in grades 7–12; provides guidance counselors, teachers, and administrators with profiles of student values for counseling them in occupational choices and course selections; grades 7–12; 15 values scores; D. Super; Riverside Publishing Company)

Appendix E

Publishers and Distributors of Standardized Questionnaires and Psychological Inventories

Academic Therapy Publications
20 Commercial Boulevard
Novata, CA 94949–6191

Addiction Research Foundation
Marketing Services
Dept. Cat. 86
33 Russell St.
Toronto, Ontario M5S 2SI, Canada

American College Testing
2201 N. Dodge St.
P.O. Box 168
Iowa City, IA 52243

Andrews University Press
Berrien Springs, MI 49104

Association of American Colleges
1818 R St., N.W.
Washington, DC 20009

Australian Council for Educational
    Research Ltd.
19 Prospect Hill Road
Private Bag 55
Camberwell, Victoria 3124, Australia

Aviat
555 Briarwood Circle, Suite 104
Ann Arbor, MI 48108

Bay State Psychological Associates, Inc.
225 Friend St., 8th Fl., Box 401
Boston, MA 02114

Lenore Behar
State of North Carolina, Department of
    Human Resources
Albemarle Building, 323 No. Salisbury St.
Raleigh, NC 27611

Behavior Data Systems, Ltd.
P.O. Box 32938
Phoenix, AZ 85064

Behavior Science Systems, Inc.
P.O. Box 580274
Minneapolis, MN 55458

Behaviordyne, Inc.
994 San Antonio Ave.
P.O. Box 10994
Palo Alto, CA 94303–0992

268

Ian Berg
Leeds Western Health Authority
The General Infirmary at Leeds
Belmont Grove, Leeds, L52 9NS, England

Millard J. Bienvenu, Sr.
Northwest Publications
710 Watson Dr.
Natchitoches, LA 71457

Sidney J. Blatt
Yale University School of Medicine,
    Department of Psychiatry
25 Park St.
New Haven, CT 96519

Patricia Brandt
Parent Child Nursing, School of Nursing
University of Washington
Seattle, WA 98195

Brougham Press
Dept. C., P.O. Box 2702
Olathe, KS 66062

Martin M. Bruce, Ph.D.
Publishers
50 Larchwood Road
Larchmont, NY 10538

Business Research Support Services
Ohio State University, College of Business
1775 College Road
Columbus, OH 43210–1309

California Test Bureau (CTB)
20 Ryan Ranch Road
Monterey, CA 93940–5703
(800) 538–9547

Clinical Psychology Publishing Co., Inc.
    (CPPC)
4 Conant Square
Brandon, VT 95733

Consulting Psychologists Press, Inc.
3803 East Bayshore Road, P.O. Box 10096
Palo Alto, CA 94303
(800) 624–1765

Consulting Resource Group
    International, Inc.
200 West 3rd St.
Sumas, WA 98295–8000

Creative Learning Press, Inc.
P.O. Box 320
Mansfield Center, CT 06250

CTB/McGraw-Hill
20 Ryan Ranch Rd.
Monterey, CA 93940–5703

Curriculum Associates, Inc.
5 Esquire Road
North Bilerica, MA 01862–2589

Denver Developmental Materials, Inc.
P.O. Box 6919
Denver, CO 80206–0919

Leonard R. Derogatis
1228 Wine Spring Ln.
Towson, MD 21204–3631

EdITS/Educational and Industrial
    Testing Service
P.O. Box 7234
San Diego, CA 92167
(619) 226–1666

Education Associates, Inc.
8 Crab Orchard Road, P.O. Box Y
Frankfort, KY 40602

Educational and Industrial Test
    Services Ltd.
83 High St. Hemel
Hempstead, Hertfordshire HP1 3AH,
    England

Educational & Psychological
    Consultants, Inc.
601 East Broadway, Suite 101
Columbia, MO 65201

Educational Assessment Service, Inc.
Apple Publishing Company
W6050 Apple Road
Watertown, WI 53094

Educational Publications
532 E. Blacklidge
Tucson, AZ 85705

Carl N. Edwards
P.O. Box 279
Dover, MA 02030

Elbern Publications
P.O. Box 09497
Columbus, OH 43209

Hanson Silver Strong & Associates, Inc.
34 Washington Rd.
Princeton Junction, NY 08550

Hawthorne Educational Services, Inc.
800 Gray Oak Drive
Columbia, MO 65201
(800) 542–1673

Health Prisms, Inc.
130 Pleasant Pointe Way
Fayetteville, GA 30214

Hilson Research, Inc.
P.O. Box 239
82-28 Abingdon Road
Kew Gardens, NY 11415

Hodder & Stoughton Educational
Hodder Headline PLC
338 Euston Rd.
London NW1 3BH, England

Houghton Mifflin Co.
222 Berkeley St.
Boston, MA 02116–3764

Edwina E. Hubert
313 Wellesley S.E.
Albuquerque, NM 87106

Human Sciences Research Council
P.O. Box 32410
Braamfontein 2917, South Africa

Human Synergistics
39819 Plymouth Rd.
Plymouth, MI 48170

Humanics Publishing Group
1482 Mecaslin St., N.W.
P.O. Box 7400
Atlanta, GA 30357–0400

Institute for Behavioral Research in
  Creativity
1570 South 1100th East
Salt Lake City, UT 84105

Institute for Personality and Ability
  Testing (IPAT)
P.O. Box 1188
Champaign, IL 61824–1188
(800) 225–4728

Institute for Social Research
The University of Michigan
P.O. Box 1248
Ann Arbor, MI 48106–1248

Institute of Athletic Motivation
1 Lagoon Drive, Suite 141
Redwood Shores, CA 94065

International Training Consultants, Inc.
P.O. Box 35613
Richmond, VA 23235–0613

Intrex Interpersonal Institute, Inc.
677 Cortex St.
Salt Lake City, UT 84103

Jastak Associates
P.O. Box 3410
Wilmington, DE 19804–0250
(800) 221-WRAT

Kendall/Hunt Publishing Co.
4050 Westmark Dr.
P.O. Box 1840
Dubuque, IA 52004–1840

Donald L. Kirkpatrick
1920 Hawthorne Dr.
Elm Grove, WI 53122

Leadership Development Consulting Co.
5819 South Shandle
Mentor, OH 44060

London House
9701 West Higgins Road
Rosemont, IL 60018
(800) 221–8378

Maurice Lorr
Dept. of Psychology
The Catholic University of America
Washington, DC 20064

Maferr Foundation, Inc.
9 East 81 St.
New York, NY 10028

Management Research Associates
5970 S. Amo Court
Terre Haute, IN 47802

Marathon Consulting and Press
P.O. Box 09189
Columbus, OH 43209–0189

McBer and Company
116 Huntington Ave.
Boston, MA 02116

Measurement & Research Division
University of Illinois at Urbana-
Champaign
307 Engineering Hall, 1308 West Green
Urbana, IL 61801

Albert Mehrabian
1130 Alta Mesa Road
Monterey, CA 93940

MetriTech, Inc.
4106 Fieldstone Road
P.O. Box 6479
Champaign, IL 61826–6479
(217) 398–4868

Michalak Training Associates, Inc.
8041 E. Chancey
Tucson, AZ 85715–5566

Multi-Health Systems, Inc.
908 Niagara Falls Blvd.
North Tonawanda, NY 14120–2060

National Center for Research to Improve
Postsecondary Teaching and Learning
2400 School of Education Building
The University of Michigan
Ann Arbor, MI 48109–1259

National Dairy Council
6300 North River Road
Rosemont, IL 60018–4233

National Institute for Personnel
Research of the Human Sciences
Research Council
P.O. Box 32410
Braamfontein 2017, South Africa

National Study of School Evaluation
5201 Leesburg Pike
Falls Church, VA 22041

NCS Assessments
5605 Green Circle Drive
P.O. Box 1416
Minneapolis, MN 55440
(800) 627–7271

Robert A. Neimeyer
Department of Psychology
Memphis State University
Memphis, TN 38152

NFER-Nelson Publishing Co., Ltd.
Darville House, 2 Oxford Road East
Windsor, Berkshire SL4 1DF England

Organizational Measurement Systems
Press
P.O. Box 1656
Buffalo, NY 14221

Organizational Tests Ltd.
P.O. Box 324
Fredericton, N.B. E3B 4Y9, Canada

PAQ Services, Inc.
Data Processing Division
1635 North 1000 East
Logan, UT 84321

Pendrake, Inc.
2270 Southampton Dr.
Reno, NV 89509

Pfeiffer & Company International
Publishers
8517 Production Ave.
San Diego, CA 92121–2280

Phylmar Associates
Educational Publishers and Consultants
191 Iroquois Ave.
London, Ontario N6C 2K9, Canada

I. Pilowsky
University of Adelaide
Department of Psychiatry, Royal Adelaide
Hospital
Adelaide 001, South Australia

Piney Mountain Press, Inc.
P.O. Box 333
Cleveland, GA 30528

Price Systems, Inc.
Box 1818
Lawrence, KS 66044

pro•ed
8700 Shoal Creek Boulevard
Austin, TX 78757–6897
(512) 451–3246

Psychological and Educational
Publications, Inc.
1477 Rollins Road
Burlingame, CA 94010-2316
(800) 523-5775

Psychological Assessment and
Services, Inc.
P.O. Box 1031
Iowa City, IA 52244

Psychological Assessment Resources, Inc.
(PAR)
P.O. Box 998
Odessa, FL 33556
(800) 331-TEST

The Psychological Corporation
555 Academic Court
San Antonio, TX 78204-2498
(800) 228-0752

Psychological Publications, Inc.
290 Conejo Ridge Avenue, Suite 100
Thousand Oaks, CA 91361
(800) 345-TEST

Psychometric Affiliates
P.O. Box 807
Murfreesboro, TN 37133

Psytec Inc.
P.O. Box 564
Dekalb, IL 60115

Purdue Research Foundation
Attn: William K. LeBold, Educational
Research and Information Systems
Engineering and Administration Bldg.,
Purdue University
West Lafayette, IN 47907

Research Press
Dept. G, P.O. Box 9177
Champaign, IL 61826

The Riverside Publishing Co.
8420 Bryn Mawr Ave.
Chicago, IL 60631

Saville & Holdsworth Ltd.
The Old Post House
81 High St.
Esher, Surrey KT 10 9QA, England

Scholastic Testing Service, Inc. (STS)
480 Meyer Road
Bensenville, IL 60106-1617
(708) 766-7150

SDQ Instruments
Publication Unit
Faculty of Education, University of
Western Sydney, Macarthur
P.O. Box 555
Campbelltown, N.S.W. 2560, Australia

Sigma Assessment Systems, Inc.
P.O. Box 610984
Port Huron, MI 48061-0984
(800) 265-1285

SOARES Associates
111 Teeter Rock Road
Trumbull, CT 06611

SOI Systems
P.O. Box D
45755 Goodpasture Rd.
Vida, OR 97488
(503) 896-3936

Special Child Publications
P.O. Box 33548
Seattle, WA 98133

SRA Product Group
London House
9701 West Higgins Road
Rosemont, IL 60018
(800) 237-7685

Stoelting Co.
Oakwood Center
620 Wheat Lane
Wood Dale, IL 60191

Teleometrics International
1755 Woodstead Court
The Woodlands, TX 77380

The Test Agency Ltd.
Cournswood House
North Dean, High Wycombe
Bucks HP 14 4NW, England

Test Analysis & Development Corporation
2400 Park Lake Dr.
Boulder, CO 80301

Timao Foundation for Research and
Development
2828B Alta View Drive
San Diego, CA 92139

Training House
P.O. Box 3090
Princeton, NJ 08543

Vocational Psychology Research
N620 Elliott Hall
University of Minnesota—Twin Cities
75 East River Road
Minneapolis, MN 55455–0344

Vocational Research Institute
2100 Arch St., Suite 6104
Philadelphia, PA 19103

West Virginia Research and Training
Center
5800 Washington St., West
Cross Lanes, WV 25313

Western Psychiatric Institute and Clinic
3811 O'Hara St.
Pittsburgh, PA 15213–2593

Western Psychological Services (WPS)
12031 Wilshire Boulevard
Los Angeles, CA 90025–1251
(800) 648–8857

Wonderlic Personnel Test, Inc.
1509 N. Milwaukee Ave.
Libertyville, IL 60048–1380

Sue R. Zalk
Hunter College of the City University of
New York
695 Park Ave.
New York, NY 10021

Zaner-Bloser Co.
Educational Publishers
P.O. Box 16764
Columbus, OH 43216–6764

Appendix F

University-Based Survey Research Centers

Arizona State University
Survey Research Laboratory
Sociology Dept./Box 872101
SS 317
Tempe, AZ 85287–2101
(602) 965–5000

Kennesaw State College
Hewlett-Packard Telephone Survey
    Research Laboratory
P.O. Box 444
Marietta, GA 30061
(404) 423–6464

Northwestern University
Survey Laboratory
625 Haven
Evanston, IL 60208
(708) 491–8759

Oregon State University
Survey Research Center
Statistics Department
Corvallis, OR 97331
(503) 737–3366

Sam Houston State University
Survey Research Program
Criminal Justice Center
Huntsville, TX 77341
(409) 294–1660

San Diego State University
Center for Survey Research
San Diego, CA 92182–0350
(619) 594–5407

Sangamon State University
Institute for Public Affairs
Springfield, IL 62794–9243
(217) 786–6576

Temple University
Institute for Survey Research
1601 N. Broad Street
Philadelphia, PA 19122
(215) 204–8355

Texas A&M University
Survey Research Center
Dept. of Rural Sociology
Special Services Building
College Station, TX 77843–2125
(409) 845–5332

University of Akron
Survey Research Center
Olin Hall, 275–276
Akron, OH 44325–1911
(216) 972–5111

University of Alabama
Capstone Poll
P.O. Box 870216
Tuscaloosa, AL 35487–0216
(205) 348–3820

274

University of Arizona
Survey Research Center
1230 N. Part, Ste. 207
Tucson, AZ 85721
(602) 621–3898

University of California at Berkeley
Survey Research Center
2538 Channing Way
Berkeley, CA 94720
(510) 642–6578

University of Delaware
Center for Applied Demography and
    Survey Research
College of Urban Affairs & Public Policy
Graham Hall
Newark, DE 19716
(302) 831–8406

University of Georgia
Survey Research Center
114 Barrow Hall
Athens, GA 30602
(706) 542–6110

University of Illinois at Chicago
Survey Research Laboratory
910 W. Van Buren St., Ste. 500
Chicago, IL 60607
(312) 996–5300

University of Kentucky
Survey Research Center
403 Breckinridge Hall
Lexington, KY 40506
(606) 257–4684

University of Louisville
Center for Urban and Economic Research
Survey and Evaluation Research Unit
Louisville, KY 40292
(502) 852–6626

University of Maryland
Survey Research Center
1103 Art-Sociology Building
College Park, MD 20742
(301) 314–7831

University of Massachusetts
Center for Survey Research
100 Morrissey Boulevard
Boston, MA 92125
(617) 287–7200

University of Michigan
Survey Research Center
P.O. Box 1248
Ann Arbor, MI 48106
(313) 764–8365

University of Minnesota
Minnesota Center for Survey Research
2331 University Ave., SE, No. 141
Minneapolis, MN 55414–3067
(612) 627–4288

University of Missouri—St. Louis
Public Polling Research Center
8001 Natural Bridge Rd.
St. Louis, MO 63121
(314) 553–5273

University of Nevada, Las Vegas
Center for Survey Research
Department of Sociology
4505 Maryland Pkwy., Box 455033
Las Vegas, NV 80154
(702) 895–3322

University of New Orleans
Survey Research Center
Department of Political Science
New Orleans, LA 70122–9989
(504) 286–6459

University of North Carolina at Charlotte
Urban Institute, Survey Service
Charlotte, NC 28223
(704) 547–2307

University of Regina
Sample Survey and Data Bank Unit
3737 Wascana Pkwy.
Regina, SD, Canada S43 9A2
(306) 585–4764

University of Utah
Survey Research Center
2120 Annex Building
Salt Lake City, UT 84112
(801) 581–6491

University of Wisconsin
Wisconsin Survey Research Laboratory
Lowell Hall
1930 Monroe Street
Madison, WI 53711
(608) 262–3122

University of Wisconsin—Parkside
Center for Survey & Marketing Research
MOLN 216/218
900 Wood Road
Kenosha, WI 53141–2000
(414) 595–2008

University of Wyoming
Survey Research Center
Box 3925, University Station
Laramie, WY 82071–3925
(307) 766–2930

Glossary

Acquiescence response set. Tendency to answer affirmatively (yes or true) to questions or items on questionnaires and inventories and in other alternative response situations.

Adaptive behavior. The extent to which an individual can interact effectively and appropriately with his or her environment.

ADHD. Attention deficit hyperactive disorder.

Adjustment. Ability to cope and to satisfy one's needs.

Affective assessment. Measurement of noncognitive or nonintellective variables or characteristics, such as personality traits, interests, attitudes, opinions, and values.

Age norm. Median score on a test made by children of a given chronological age.

Alpha. The probability of a Type I error (rejecting a true null hypothesis); the level of significance selected in a research investigation.

Alternate-forms reliability. An index of reliability determined by correlating the scores of individuals on one form of a psychometric instrument with their scores on another form.

Alternative hypothesis. Research (statistical) hypothesis that the null hypothesis is false.

Anecdotal record. A written record of behavioral observations of a specified individual. Care must be taken to differentiate between observation and interpretation if the record is to be objective.

Anonymous questionnaire. Coding or marking the return envelope of a questionnaire that is ostensibly completed anonymously in order to identify the respondent.

Archival research. Using public or private documents to investigate events that occurred in the past.

Area sampling. Sampling in which a geographical area such as a city is divided into areas or blocks, and a certain number of dwelling units within each block is selected at random.

Assessment. Appraising the presence or magnitude of abilities, personality traits, and other characteristics of an individual by means of observations, interviews, tests, questionnaires, inventories, and projective techniques.

Assessment center. Technique for assessing the characteristics and behaviors of a group of candidates for executive positions while they are performing a variety of tasks.

Attitude. Tendency to react positively or negatively to some object, person, or situation.

Attitude scale. A paper-and-pencil instrument, consisting of a series of statements concerning an institution, situation, person, event, and so on. Each statement is responded to by endorsing it or indicating one's degree of agreement or disagreement with it.

Balanced scale. A set of response alternatives in which the options above the middle category are balanced by those below it.

Base rate. Proportion of individuals having a specified condition who are identified or selected without the use of new selection procedures.

Base rate scores. Converted scores obtained by weighting raw scores to take into account the incidence of a particular characteristic or disorder in the general population. Raw scores on a psychometric instrument are transformed in such a way as to maximize the ratio of the number of correct classifications (valid positives) to the number of incorrect classifications (false positives).

Bias. Any one of a number of factors that cause scores on psychometric instruments to be consistently higher or lower than they should be if measurement were accurate. See *Leniency error.*

Biographical inventory. Questionnaire composed of items designed to collect information on an individual's background, interests, and other personal data.

Block sampling. See *Area sampling.*

Bogus pipeline. Procedure by which respondents are tricked into believing that their answers to questions can be objectively verified.

CAPI. Computer-assisted personal interviewing.

Case study. Detailed study of an individual, designed to provide a comprehensive, in-depth understanding of personality. Information for a case study is obtained from biographical, interview, observational, and test data.

CATI. Computer-assisted telephone interviewing. The items on the questionnaire are read aloud by the interviewer from a computer monitor, and the respondent's answers are recorded and analyzed by the computer. Depending on the respondent's answer, the computer can skip certain items.

Central limit theorem. Theorem stating that the frequency distribution of the means of large samples of observations selected at random and independently from a population will be approximately normal, that the mean of the distribution of means will be equal to the population mean, and that the standard deviation of the means will be approximately equal to the population standard deviation divided by the square root of the sample size.

Central tendency. Average, or central, score in a group of scores; the most representative score (e.g., arithmetic mean, median, mode).

Checklist. List of words, phrases, or statements descriptive of personal characteristics; respondents endorse (check) those items characteristic of themselves (self-ratings) or other people (other-ratings).

Closed-ended questions. Questions on which respondents select one of several answer options: for example, Yes or No; a, b, c, or d; or Strongly Disagree, Disagree, Undecided, Agree, Strongly Agree.

Cluster. A naturally occurring group of individuals, such as a school, hospital, city, state, or other unit.

Cluster sampling. Sampling procedure in which the target population is divided into clusters, and a sample of the clusters or subclusters is selected at random in one or more stages.

Coding. Assigning a numerical or verbal designation to a questionnaire response according to the particular category in which the response is judged to fall.

Coding frame. Preparing questionnaire data for analysis by indicating what is to be coded and how it is to be done.

Coefficient alpha. An internal-consistency reliability coefficient, appropriate for tests comprised of either dichotomous or multipoint items; the expected correlation of one test with a parallel form containing the same number of items.

Coefficient of equivalence. A reliability coefficient (correlation) obtained by administering a test, questionnaire, or inventory to the same group of people on two different occasions. See *Test-retest reliability.*

Coefficient of internal consistency. Reliability coefficient based on estimates of the internal consistency of a test or other psychometric instrument (for example, Kuder-Richardson coefficients or coefficient alpha).

Coefficient of stability. A reliability coefficient (correlation) obtained by administering a test or other psychometric instrument to the same group of people on two different occasions. See *Test-retest reliability.*

Coefficient of stability and equivalence. A reliability coefficient obtained by administering different forms of a test or other psychometric device to a group of people on two different occasions.

Cohort. A group of people of the same age, class membership, or culture.

Completion item. A statement consisting of one or more blanks to be filled in; an incomplete statement that is to be completed by the respondent.

Concurrent validity. The extent to which scores obtained by a group of people on a particular psychometric instrument are related to their simultaneously determined scores on another measure (criterion) of the same characteristic.

Confidence interval. A range of values within which one can be fairly confident (usually 95 or 99 percent) that the mean of a population, or the difference between the means of two populations, actually falls.

Confounding. A situation in which two measures or characteristics vary in such a way that the independent effect of each cannot be determined.

Construct validity. The extent to which scores on a psychometric instrument designed to measure a certain characteristic are related to measures of behavior in situations in which the characteristic is supposed to have a significant effect on behavior.

Consumer panel. A list, maintained by a number of commercial research firms, of individuals or families who agree to respond to questionnaires that are sent to them. The members of a consumer panel are typically rewarded for their participation with cash, free samples of products, or other incentives.

Consumer psychology. A field of psychology concerned with the identification or segmentation of markets based on the psychological characteristics of consumers; designing, advertising, and selling products and services with respect to consumer characteristics.

Content analysis. Method of studying and analyzing written (or oral) communications in a systematic, objective, and quantitative manner to assess certain psychological variables.

Content validity. The extent to which a group of people who are experts in the material with which a test or other psychometric instrument deals agree that the instrument measures what it was designed to measure.

Convenience sample. A sample limited to individuals who are readily available or easy to contact, but are likely to be biased in their responses to a survey.

Correlation. Degree of relationship or association between two variables, such as traits assessed by a personality inventory and behavioral indications of adjustment problems.

Correlation coefficient. A numerical index of the degree of relationship between two variables. Correlation coefficients usually range from −1.00 (perfect negative relationship) through .00 (total absence of a relationship) to +1.00 (perfect positive relationship). Two common types of correlation coefficient are the product-moment coefficient and the point-biserial coefficient.

Cover letter. Explanatory letter accompanying a mailed questionnaire.

Creative thinking. Original, novel, or divergent thinking.

Criterion. A standard or variable with which scores on a psychometric instrument are compared or against which they are evaluated. The validity of a test or other psychometric procedure used in selecting or classifying people is determined by its ability to predict a specified criterion of behavior in the situation for which people are being selected or classified.

Criterion-related validity. The extent to which a test or other assessment instrument measures what it was designed to measure, as indicated by the correlation of scores on the test with scores on a performance criterion.

Cross-sectional study. Comparisons of the physical and psychological characteristics of groups of people of different ages.

Cross-sequential design. Developmental research design in which two or more successive cohorts are studied longitudinally. For example, the change in attitude or ability from 1970 to 1990 in groups of individuals born in 1920, 1940, and 1960 are compared.

Demographic variable. Variable such as age, sex, socioeconomic status, educational level, income, and political party membership describing characteristics of individuals or groups.

Demography. The science of vital and social statistics (births, marriages, diseases, etc.) of populations.

Dependent variable. Variable in a scientific investigation that changes as a result of changes in the independent variable. Variations in magnitude of a dependent variable, plotted on the Y axis of a graph, can be viewed as an effect of changes in an independent variable.

Descriptive statistics. Measures that are used to summarize and describe a set of data. Illustrative descriptive statistics include: measures of central tendency such as the arithmetic mean, the median, and the mode; measures of variability such as the range, variance, and standard deviation; and measures of correlation such as the Pearson product-moment coefficient and the point-biserial coefficient.

Diary panel. Special type of consumer panel in which respondents keep detailed records of their behavior (e.g., products purchased, coupons used, radio or television stations listened or looked at, newspapers and magazines read).

Dichotomous question. A question having two response options.

Double (double-barreled) question. A question containing more than one query.

Effect size. Magnitude of the difference between an estimated population parameter, usually the mean, resulting from a particular treatment and the mean under the control (no treatment) condition.

EPSEM sample. A sample selected in such a way that every element in the population has an equal probability of being selected for the sample.

Equiprobability sample. See *Random sampling.*

Evaluation. To judge the merit or value of a person's behavior from a composite of scores on psychological assessment instruments, observations, and reports.

Face validity. The extent to which the appearance or content of the materials (items and the like) on a test or other psychometric instrument is such that the instrument appears to be a good measure of what it is supposed to measure.

Factor analysis. A mathematical procedure for analyzing a matrix of correlations among measurements to determine what factors (constructs) are sufficient to explain the correlations.

False consensus effect. Tendency for a person to overestimate the extent to which other people agree with him or her.

False negative error. Prediction error made when the predicted score is below the cutoff score on the criterion but the obtained score is above the cutoff score.

False positive error. Prediction error made when the predicted score is above the cutoff score on the criterion but the obtained score is below the cutoff score.

Filter (skip) questions. Questions on a questionnaire that direct the respondent to the questions that pertain to him or her and permit irrelevant questions to be skipped.

Fixed-alternative question. See *Closed-ended question.*

Focus group. A group-interviewing procedure that may be used to generate ideas for a survey questionnaire and help frame solutions to problems identified in a survey.

Forced-choice item. Item on a personality or interest inventory, arranged as a dyad (two options), a triad (three options), or a tetrad (four options) of terms or phrases. The respondent is required to select an option viewed as most descriptive and perhaps another option perceived to be least descriptive of the personality, interests, or behavior of the person being evaluated. Forced-choice items are found on certain personality inventories; for example, the Edwards Personal Preference Schedule, interest inventories (Kuder General Interest Survey), and rating forms to control for response sets.

Free-response question. See *Open-ended question*.

Frequency distribution. A table of score intervals and the number of cases (scores) falling within each interval.

Funneling. Arranging the items on a questionnaire so the most general questions in a particular topic area are asked first and then followed by more specific questions.

General Social Survey. A nationwide survey, conducted by NORC, which covers a wide range of topics of interest to social researchers.

Grade norm. The average of the scores on a test made by a group of children at a given grade level.

Group interview. Self-administered questionnaire in which a single interviewer presents instruction and sometimes visual information to many respondents at the same time.

Halo effect. Giving a person a high rating on one characteristic merely because he or she rates high on other characteristics.

Hot-decking. Replacing a missing observation with the value of the last observation having similar known characteristics or with a random selection from all available observations with similar characteristics.

Hypothetical question. Speculative question concerning what might happen or what one might do in certain circumstances.

Incident sampling. In contrast to *time sampling,* an observational procedure in which certain types of incidents, such as those indicative of aggressive behavior, are selected for observation and recording.

Independent variable. Variable whose effects (on the dependent variable) are to be determined in a scientific investigation.

Informed consent. A formal agreement made by an individual, or the individual's guardian or legal representative, with an agency or another person to permit use of the individual's name and/or personal information for a specific purpose.

Interest inventory. A self-report, paper-and-pencil instrument, such as the Strong Interest Inventory or the Kuder General Interest Survey, designed to assess an individual's preferences for certain activities and topics.

Interlocking items. Questions or items on which a response to one question is affected by or contingent upon responses to other questions.

Internal consistency. The extent to which all questions or items on a psychometric instrument measure the same variable or construct. The reliability computed by the Spearman-Brown, Kuder-Richardson, or Cronbach-alpha formulas is a measure of the internal consistency of the instrument.

Interobserver reliability. Two observers assign a numerical score to a sample of people. Then the correlation between the two sets of scores is computed.

Interview. A systematic procedure for obtaining information by asking questions and, in general, verbally interacting with a person (the interviewee).

Inventory. A set of questions or statements to which an individual responds (for example, by indicating agreement or disagreement), designed to provide a measure of personality, interest, attitude, or behavior.

Ipsative scores. Scores obtained when the variables being measured are compared with each other; thus, a person's score on one variable is affected by, and hence correlated with, his or her scores on other variables.

Item. One of the units, questions, or tasks of which a psychometric instrument is composed.

Item sampling. Selecting subsets of items from a composite pool of items and administering each subset to a different group of people.

Kuder-Richardson formulas. Formulas used to compute a measure of internal-consistency reliability from a single administration of a psychometric instrument having 0–1 scoring.

Leading question. A question containing cues that suggest what the proper or desirable answer is, producing the response expected by the researcher but not necessarily an accurate response.

Leniency error. Tendency to rate an individual higher on a positive characteristic and less severely on a negative characteristic than he or she should actually be rated.

Letter of transmittal. See *Cover letter.*

Likert scale. An attitude scale consisting of a series of statements with five response categories: Strongly Agree, Agree, Undecided, Disagree, Strongly Disagree.

Loaded question. A question phrased in such a way that the respondent is more likely to give a desired answer.

Loaded word or phrase. Words or phrases contained in a question that, because of prior associations, elicit an emotional reaction in the respondent and bias his or her answer.

Local norms. Percentile ranks, standard scores, or other norms corresponding to the raw test scores of a relatively small, local group of examinees.

Longitudinal investigation. Studying the development of the same individual(s) at different ages over a period of years.

Mail survey. Survey conducted by means of a mailed questionnaire.

Minnesota Multiphasic Personality Inventory (MMPI-2). The most widely administered and researched of all personality inventories. The MMPI was developed originally to diagnose mental disorders in people, and has since been used for many other applied and research purposes.

Multidimensional scaling. Procedure of ordering consumer preferences for particular products on two or more dimensions.

Multiple-choice question. A question consisting of a stem and several response options.

Multistage cluster sampling.   Procedure for selecting a representative sample by dividing the population of interest into a series of groups, elements, or clusters. At the first sampling stage, a set of clusters is selected at random; at the second stage, a random sample of subclusters is selected from each cluster; and so on down to the lowest sampling elements.

National norms.   Percentile ranks, standard scores, or other norms based on a national sample. See *Local norms* and *Norms.*

Nonprobability sample.   Sample selected from a population by a nonprobabilistic procedure; for example, convenience samples, haphazard samples, snowball samples, and quota samples.

Nonrespondent.   Individual who fails to respond or fails to return a completed mailed survey, despite repeated requests.

Nonresponse bias.   Bias in survey results produced by the failure of some members in the sample to respond to the survey.

Nonspecific adjective.   An adjective such as *some, many,* or *most* that has no specific meaning.

Nonverbal behavior.   Any communicative behavior that does not involve making word sounds or signs; includes movements of large (macrokinesics) and small (microkinesics) body parts, interpersonal distance or territoriality (proximics), tone and rate of voice sounds (paralinguistics), and communications imparted by culturally prescribed matters relating to time, dress, memberships, and the like (culturics).

Norm group.   Sample of people on whom a test is standardized.

Normal distribution.   A smooth, bell-shaped frequency distribution of scores, symmetrical about the mean and described by an exact mathematical function. The scores of a large group of people on a psychometric instrument often approximate a normal distribution.

Normalized scores.   Scores obtained by transforming raw scores in such a way that the transformed scores are normally distributed with a mean of 0 and a standard deviation of 1 (or some linear function of these numbers).

Normative scores.   In contrast to *ipsative scores,* scores that are assigned independently of the scores on other variables being measured by a psychometric instrument.

Norms.   A list of scores and the corresponding percentile ranks, standard scores, or other transformed scores of a group of individuals on whom a psychometric instrument has been standardized.

Null hypothesis (H_o).   Hypothesis of no difference between the actual value of a population parameter and its hypothesized value, or a hypothesis of no difference between corresponding parameters in two or more populations.

Objective question.   A question containing a set of possible response options.

Omnibus survey.   A large-scale survey involving many questions on many issues; for example, the semiannual Maryland Poll, the Twin Cities Area Survey, and the Minnesota State Survey.

Open-ended question. A question in which the respondent's answer is not fixed or limited in any way; he or she is free to make any short-answer or essay response.

Opinion. A verbalized judgment concerning a specific occurrence or situation. The meaning of *opinion* is similar to that of *attitude*, but the former term has the connotation of being more specific and based on more thought that the latter. In addition, a person is aware of his or her opinions, but not necessarily of his or her attitudes.

Opinionnaire. Paper-and-pencil instrument designed to measure opinions.

Opinion polling. Questioning a sample of a target population on particular issues and opinions.

Overreporting/underreporting. Tendency on the part of respondents to report that they have bought something or engaged in some other behavior more frequently or less frequently than they actually have.

Panel survey. Survey research procedure in which a group of people is questioned at two or more points in time to study changes in their responses over time.

Parallel forms. Two psychometric instruments that are equivalent in the sense that they contain the same kinds of items of equal difficulty and are highly correlated. The scores made on one form of the instrument are very close to those made on the other form.

Parallel forms reliability. An index of reliability determined by correlating the scores of individuals on parallel forms of a psychometric instrument.

Parameter. A population characteristic, such as the arithmetic mean or standard deviation, having a specific numerical value.

Percentile norms. A list of raw scores and the corresponding percentages of the standardization group with scores below the given percentile.

Percentile rank. The percentage of scores falling below a given score in a frequency distribution or group of scores; the percentage corresponding to the given score.

Personality. Sum total of the qualities, traits, and behaviors characterizing a person and by which, together with his or her physical attributes, the person is recognized as a unique individual.

Personality inventory. A self-report inventory or questionnaire consisting of statements concerning personal characteristics and behaviors. On a true-false inventory, the respondent indicates whether each item is self-descriptive; on a multiple-choice or forced-choice inventory the respondent selects the words, phrases, or statements that are self-descriptive.

Pilot study. See *Pretesting.*

Point-biserial coefficient. Correlation coefficient computed between a dichotomous variable and a continuous variable; derived from the product-moment correlation coefficient.

Population. A group of people, objects, or events of interest and to which one wishes to generalize the results of a survey conducted on a sample.

Power (of a statistical test). The probability of rejecting a false null hypothesis. Power equals 1 minus the probability of a Type II error.

PPS sampling. Sampling procedure in which the probability of an element being selected varies with the number of primary sampling units.

Precoding. Preparation of a key for categorizing and evaluating responses to the items on a survey or inventory.

Predictive validity. Extent to which scores on a psychometric instrument are predictive of performance on some criterion measure assessed at a later time; usually expressed as a correlation between the psychometric instrument (predictor variable) and the criterion variable.

Pretesting. Administering a questionnaire or inventory to a small group of individuals prior to administering it to a large representative sample in order to detect problems with the instrument and characteristics of the sample.

Probability. The chances (odds) of occurrence of a given event.

Probability sampling. Sampling procedure in which the probability that any member of a population will be included in a sample can be specified.

Probe. A question or statement made by an interviewer to elicit further information from a person concerning something; for example: "What do you mean?" or "Tell me more about that."

Proportional reduction in error (PRE). Principle of deriving a statistic by comparing the number of errors made in predicting the dependent variable when the independent variable is taken into account with the number of errors made when the independent variable is not taken into account. Examples are lambda and gamma, which are premeasures of association for nominal and ordinal data, respectively.

Prospective study. Research investigation that follows up, over time, people having different characteristics or lifestyles to determine which ones develop a particular condition or disorder.

Proxy respondent. A person who responds for another person, by answering detailed questions concerning the latter when he or she is unavailable.

Psychometrics. Theory and research pertaining to the measurement of psychological (cognitive and affective) characteristics.

Questionnaire. A paper-and-pencil instrument composed of a set of questions concerning certain issues, events, or other matters of concern.

Quota sampling. Selecting a sample that reflects the numerical composition of various subgroups (by age, sex, socioeconomic status, etc.) in a population. The different groups are contained in the sample in the same proportions as in the population of interest.

Random-digit dialing. Dialing random sequences of digits within working telephone exchanges to ensure the inclusion of unlisted telephone numbers in a telephone survey.

Random sample. A sample of observations drawn from a population in such a way that every member of the target population has an equal chance of being selected in the sample.

Randomized response technique.   A survey research procedure designed to encourage people to respond honestly to sensitive questions. A random procedure is used to determine whether the respondent receives either an innocuous or a sensitive question. Then statistical methods are applied to the responses to determine the proportion of people who actually engaged in the sensitive behavior.

Rapport.   A warm, friendly relationship between an interviewer or examiner and a respondent.

Reliability.   The extent to which a psychological assessment device measures anything consistently. A reliable instrument is relatively free from errors of measurement, so respondents' obtained scores are close in numerical value to their true scores.

Reliability coefficient.   A numerical index, between .00 and 1.00, of the reliability of an assessment instrument. Methods for determining reliability include test-retest, parallel-forms, and internal consistency.

Representative sample.   A group of individuals whose characteristics are similar to those of the population of individuals of interest in a research investigation or test standardization.

Response rate.   Proportion of individuals in a survey sample who actually respond to the questions in a face-to-face interview, telephone, or mail survey.

Response sets (styles).   Tendencies for individuals to respond in relatively fixed or stereotypical ways in situations where there are two or more response choices, such as on personality inventories. Tendencies to guess, to answer true (acquiescence), and to give socially desirable answers are some of the response sets that have been investigated.

Retrospective study.   Comparisons of the incidence of a disorder or other condition in two or more groups of people having different backgrounds, behaviors, or other characteristics.

Sample.   A subset of a target population actually included in a research investigation.

Sampling.   Process by which a sample is selected to represent a designated population.

Sampling distribution.   The frequency or probability distribution of statistics computed on samples selected at random from a particular population. See *Central limit theorem.*

Sampling error.   Error arising from the fact that a sample of subjects is not completely representative of the population of interest.

Sampling fraction.   The fraction of the population elements selected in the sample.

Sampling frame.   The set of people, objects, or events in a population that might be included in the sample, given that the population has been defined and the sampling approach has been determined.

Sampling from lists.   See *Systematic random sampling.*

Sampling unit.   The element (individual, group, etc.) selected from a population by a specified sampling procedure.

Scale. A measure or method of evaluating some attribute.

Self-report inventory. A paper-and-pencil measure of personality traits or interests, comprised of a series of items that the respondent indicates are characteristic (true) or not characteristic (not true) of himself or herself.

Skewness. Degree of asymmetry in a frequency distribution. In a positively skewed distribution, there are more scores to the left of the mean (low scores). In a negatively skewed distribution, there are more scores to the right of the mean (high scores).

Skip instructions. Instructions concerning which question should be asked or answered next on a questionnaire or in an interview.

Skip questions. See *Filter questions.*

Snowball sampling. Sampling procedure used when an adequate list for constructing a sampling frame is not available. It involves identifying persons in the population of interest having the desired characteristics and asking them if they know of other people with these characteristics, and so on.

Social desirability response set. Response set or style affecting scores on questionnaires and inventories. Refers to the tendency on the part of a person to respond in what he or she judges to be a more socially desirable direction, rather than responding in a manner that is truly characteristic or descriptive of him- or herself.

Spearman-Brown formula. A formula for estimating the internal consistency reliability (r_{11}) of a full-length test by correlating separate scores on two split halves of the test $[r_{11} = 2r_{\frac{1}{2}\frac{1}{2}}/(1 + r_{\frac{1}{2}\frac{1}{2}})]$.

Specific determiners. Words such as *sometimes, never, always,* and *occasionally* that may induce a respondent to answer in a particular way.

Split-ballot technique. Splitting questionnaires into groups and assigning alternative questions to each group.

Split-half coefficient. An estimate of reliability determined by applying the Spearman-Brown formula to the correlation between two halves of the same psychometric instrument, such as the odd-numbered items and the even-numbered items. See *Spearman-Brown formula.*

Standard error of the mean. The standard deviation of the distribution of the means of samples selected randomly and independently from a population. For large samples, the standard error of the mean equals the population standard deviation divided by the square root of the sample size.

Standardization. Administering a carefully constructed psychometric instrument to a large, representative sample of people under standard conditions for the purpose of determining norms.

Standardization sample. The subset of a target population on which a psychometric instrument is standardized.

Standardized test. A test that has been carefully constructed by professionals and administered with standard directions and under standard conditions to a representative sample of people for the purpose of obtaining norms.

Standard scores. A group of scores, such as z scores, T scores, or stanine scores, having a desired mean and standard deviation. Other standard scores are computed by transforming raw scores to z scores, multiplying the z scores by the desired standard deviation, and then adding the desired mean to the product.

Stanine. A standard score scale consisting of the scores 1 through 9, having a mean of 5 and a standard deviation of approximately 2.

Statistic. A sample characteristic, such as the sample mean or standard deviation, based on data and having a computed numerical value.

Stratification variable. Demographic or other variable used to divide a survey sample into a series of groups from which individuals or elements can be selected at random.

Stratified random sampling. A sampling procedure in which the population is divided into strata (e.g., men and women; blacks and whites; lower class, middle class, upper class), and samples are selected at random from the strata; the number of elements in the sample is proportional to the number of elements in the corresponding stratum of the population.

Structured questionnaire. Questionnaire on which the wording of questions and the order in which they are to be answered are specified.

Survey method. Popular descriptive research method in which people respond to certain questions or directions orally or in writing. Data are collected on large numbers of people by means of questionnaires, interviews, inventories, and scales to assess the incidence, distribution, and interrelationships of selected variables.

Systematic random sampling. Drawing a sample from a list of elements in a population of interest by selecting every *n*th element on the list. Also known as *sampling from lists.*

Target population. The population of interest in standardizing a psychometric instrument; the norm group (sample) must be representative of the target population if valid interpretations of scores are to be made.

Telemarketing. Advertising and selling procedures conducted over the telephone.

Telephone survey. A survey conducted by telephone, in which the respondent answers a series of questions asked by a questioner or computer.

Test-retest reliability. A method of assessing the reliability of a psychometric instrument by administering it to the same group of people on two different occasions and computing the correlations between the scores obtained on the two occasions.

Threatening questions. Questions that can cause anxiety or uneasiness in respondents.

Time-lag design. Developmental research procedure for examining several cohorts, each at a different time period.

Time sampling. Procedure in which observations lasting only a few minutes are made over a period of a day or so.

Transitional phrases or questions. Words or questions on a questionnaire indicating that the topic of the questions is about to change.

T scores.   Converted, normalized standard scores having a mean of 50 and a standard deviation of 10.

Type I error.   The error, in a research investigation, of rejecting a true null hypothesis; also known as an *alpha error* or *error of the first kind*.

Type II error.   The error, in a research investigation, of retaining (failing to reject) a false null hypothesis; also known as a *beta error* or *error of the second kind*.

Unit of analysis.   A unit or element of the population about which information is to be obtained and conclusions drawn.

Unobtrusive observations.   Observations made without interfering with or otherwise influencing the behavior to be observed.

Unstructured questionnaire.   Questionnaire on which the topics to be covered are listed, but the exact wording of the questions and the order in which they are asked are left up to the interviewer.

Validity.   The extent to which an assessment instrument measures what it was designed to measure. Validity can be assessed in several ways: by analysis of the instrument's content *(content validity)*, by relating scores on a psychometric instrument to a criterion measure *(predictive* and *concurrent validity)*, and by a more thorough study of the extent to which the instrument is a measure of a certain psychological construct *(construct validity)*.

Visual analogue scale.   Psychometric device for measuring subjective experiences such as pain, anxiety, and cravings for certain substances. The patient points to or marks the point on a line corresponding to the intensity of his or her experience.

Vital statistics.   Statistics concerning human life, the conditions affecting it, and the maintenance of the population (e.g., births, marriages, divorces, and deaths) during a specified time period.

World questions.   Doubled-barreled questions that ask two things at the same time, necessitating two separate ideas within a single answer.

z score.   Any one of a group of derived scores varying from $-\infty$ to $+\infty$, computed from the formula $z = $ (raw score $-$ mean)/standard deviation, for each raw score. In a normal distribution, over 99% of the cases lie between $z = -3.00$ and $z = +3.00$.

References

Aiken, L.R. (1962). Frequency and intensity as psychometric response variables. *Psychological Reports, 11,* 535–538.

Aiken, L.R. (1983). Number of response categories and statistics on a teacher rating scale. *Educational and Psychological Measurement, 43,* 397–401.

Aiken, L.R. (1988). The problem of nonresponse in survey research. *Journal of Experimental Education, 56,* 116–119.

Aiken, L.R. (1992). Some measures of interpersonal attraction and group cohesiveness. *Educational and Psychological Measurement, 52,* 63–67.

Aiken, L.R. (1996a). *Assessment of intellectual functioning* (2nd ed.). New York: Plenum.

Aiken, L.R. (1996b). *Rating scales and checklists: Evaluating behavior, personality, and attitudes.* New York: Wiley.

Aiken, L.R. (1997a). *Psychological testing and assessment* (9th ed.). Boston: Allyn & Bacon.

Aiken, L.R. (1997b). *Assessment of adult personality.* New York: Springer.

Allen, S.J. (1995). Review of the Offer Self-Image Questionnaire, Revised. In J.C. Conoley & J.C. Impara (Eds.), *The twelfth mental measurements yearbook* (pp. 710–711). Lincoln, NE: The Buros Institute of Mental Measurements, The University of Nebraska-Lincoln.

Allport, G.W., & Allport, F.H. (1928). *The A-S Reaction Study.* New York: Holt, Rinehart & Winston.

Allport, G.W., & Odbert, H.S. (1936). Trait names, a psycholexical study. *Psychological Monographs, 47* (Whole No. 211).

American Educational Research Association, American Psychological Association, & National Council on Measurement in Education. (1985). *Standards for educational and psychological testing.* Washington, DC: American Psychological Association.

American Psychiatric Association. (1994). *Diagnostic and statistical manual of mental disorders* (4th ed.). Washington, DC: Author.

American Psychological Association. (1986). *Guidelines for computer-based tests and interpretations.* Washington, DC: Author.

American Psychological Association. (1992). Ethical principles of psychologists and code of conduct. *American Psychologist, 47,* 1597–1611.

Andrews, J.V. (1992). Review of the Canfield Instructional Styles Inventory. In J.J. Kramer & J.C. Conoley (Eds.), *The eleventh mental measurements yearbook* (pp. 146–147). Lincoln, NE: The Buros Institute of Mental Measurements, The University of Nebraska-Lincoln.

Ash, P. (1995). Review of the Eating Disorder Inventory-2. In J.C. Conoley & J.C. Impara (Eds.), *The twelfth mental measurements yearbook* (pp. 334–335). Lincoln, NE: The Buros Institute of Mental Measurements, The University of Nebraska-Lincoln.

Beaton, A.E. (1994). Missing scores in survey research. In T. Husén & T.N. Postlethwaite (Eds.), *International encyclopedia of education* (2nd ed., Vol. 7, pp. 3858–3862). New York: Elsevier.

Beck, A.T., Brown, G., & Steer, R.A. (1989). Prediction of eventual suicide in psychiatric inpatients by clinical ratings of hopelessness. *Journal of Consulting and Clinical Psychology, 57,* 309–310.

Bem, S.L. (1974). The measurement of psychological androgyny. *Journal of Counseling and Clinical Psychology, 42,* 165–172.

Ben-Porath, Y.S., & Waller, N.G. (1992). Five big issues in clinical personality assessment: A rejoinder to Costa and McCrae. *Psychological Assessment, 4,* 23–25.

Benton, S.L. (1992). Review of the Canfield Learning Styles Inventory. In J.J. Kramer & J.C. Conoley (Eds.), *The eleventh mental measurements yearbook* (pp. 147–148). Lincoln, NE: The Buros Institute of Mental Measurements, The University of Nebraska-Lincoln.

Binder, D.A. (1983). On the variances of asymptotically normal estimators for complex surveys. *International Statistical Review, 51,* 279–292.

Block, J. (1995). A contrarian view of the five-factor approach to personality description. *Psychological Bulletin, 117*(2), 187–215.

Bolton, B. (1992). Review of the California Psychological Inventory. In J.J. Kramer & J.C. Conoley (Eds.), *The eleventh mental measurements yearbook* (pp. 138–139). Lincoln, NE: Buros Institute of Mental Measurements of the University of Nebraska-Lincoln.

Bowling, A. (1991). *Measuring health: A review of quality of life measurement scales.* Bristol, PA: Open University Press.

Brachter, R.L., Morgan, M.A., & Zimmer, W.J. (1970). Tables of sample sizes in the analysis of variance. *Journal of Quality Technology, 2,* 156–164.

Brams, S.J., & Fishburn, P.C. (1991). Alternative voting systems. In L.S. Maisel (Ed.), *Political parties and elections in the United States: An encyclopedia* (Vol. 1, pp. 23–31). New York: Garland.

Brown, K.W. (1986). Survey research: Determining sample size and representative response. *Business Education Forum,* 31–34.

Burisch, M. (1984). Approaches to personality inventory construction. *American Psychologist, 39,* 214–227.

Butcher, J.N. (1993, June). *MMPI-2, the Minnesota report, adult clinical interpretive system.* Minneapolis, MN: University of Minnesota Press.

Buros, O.K. (Ed.). (1978). *The eighth mental measurements yearbook.* Vols. 1 and 2. Highland Park, NJ: Gryphon Press.

Butcher, J.N., Dahlstrom, W.G., Graham, J.R., Tellengen, A., & Kaemmer, B. (1989). *MMPI-2.* Minneapolis, MN: University of Minnesota Press.

Butcher, J.N., & Rouse, S.V. (1996). Personality: Individual differences in clinical assessment. In J.T. Spence, J.M. Darley, & D.J. Foss (Eds.), *Annual Review of Psychology, 47,* 87–111.

Cattell, R.B. (1965). *The scientific analysis of personality.* New York: Penguin.

Chapman, C.R., Casey, K.L., Dubner, R., et al. (1985). Pain measurement: An overview. *Pain, 22,* 1–31.

Cochran, W.G. (1977). *Sampling techniques* (3rd ed.). New York: Wiley.

Cohen, J. (1968). Weighted kappa: Nominal scale agreement with provision for scaled disagreement or partial credit. *Psychological Bulletin, 70,* 213–220.

Cohen, J. (1988). *Statistical power analysis for the behavioral sciences* (2nd ed.). New York: Academic Press.

Conoley, J.C., & Impara, J.C. (Eds.). (1995). *The twelfth mental measurements yearbook*. Lincoln, NE: Buros Institute of Mental Measurements of the University of Nebraska-Lincoln.

Conoley, J.C., & Kramer, J.J. (Eds.). (1989). *The tenth mental measurements yearbook*. Lincoln, NE: Buros Institute of Mental Measurements of the University of Nebraska-Lincoln.

Daut, R.L., Cleeland, C.S., & Flanery, R.C. (1983). Development of the Wisconsin Brief Pain Questionnaire to assess pain in cancer and other diseases. *Pain, 17*, 197–210.

Davis, J.A., & Smith, T.W. (1994). *General Social Surveys, 1972–1994*. Chicago: National Opinion Research Center.

Dreger, R.M. (1978). Review of State-Trait Anxiety Inventory. In O.K. Buros (Ed.), *The eighth mental measurements yearbook* (Vol. 1, pp. 1094–1095). Highland Park, NY: Gryphon Press.

Drummond, R.J. (1995). Review of the Alcohol Use Inventory. In J.C. Conoley & J.C. Impara (Eds.), *The twelfth mental measurements yearbook* (pp. 65–66). Lincoln, NE: The Buros Institute of Mental Measurements, The University of Nebraska-Lincoln.

Dubuisson, D., & Melzack, R. (1976). Classification of clinical pain descriptions by multiple group discriminant analysis. *Experimental Neurology, 51*, 480–487.

Dupont, W.D., & Plummer, W.D. (1990). Power and sample size calculations: A review and computer program. *Controlled Clinical Trials, 11*, 116–128.

Ehrenberg, R.L., & Sniezek, J.E. (1989). III. Development of a standard questionnaire for occupational health research. *American Journal of Public Health, 79*, 15–17.

Engelhard, G. (1992). Review of the California Psychological Inventory. In J.J. Kramer & J.C. Conoley (Eds.), *The eleventh mental measurements yearbook* (pp. 139–141). Lincoln, NE: Buros Institute of Mental Measurements of the University of Nebraska-Lincoln.

Evans, R.I., Hanson, W.B., & Mittelmark, M.B. (1977). Increasing the validity of self-reports of smoking behavior in children. *Journal of Applied Psychology, 62*, 521–523.

Evans, S.S., & Scott, J.E. (1984). Effects of item order on the perceived seriousness of crime: A reexamination. *Journal of Research in Crime and Delinquency, 21*, 139–151.

Eysenck, H.J. (1981). *A model for personality*. New York: Springer-Verlag.

Fager, J.J. (1995). Review of the Menstrual Distress Questionnaire. In J.C. Conoley & J.C. Impara (Eds.), *The twelfth mental measurements yearbook* (pp. 596–597). Lincoln, NE: The Buros Institute of Mental Measurements, The University of Nebraska-Lincoln.

Fleiss, J.L. (1971). Measuring nominal scale agreement among many raters. *Psychological Bulletin, 76*, 278–382.

Forrest, D.W. (1974). *Francis Galton: The life and work of a Victorian genius*. New York: Taplinger.

Furlong, M., & Karno, M. (1995). Review of the Offer Self-Image Questionnaire, Revised. In J.C. Conoley & J.C. Impara (Eds.), *The twelfth mental measurements yearbook* (pp. 710–711). Lincoln, NE: The Buros Institute of Mental Measurements, The University of Nebraska-Lincoln.

Galton, F. (1883). *Inquiries into human faculty and its development* (2nd ed.). London: Eugenics Society.

Goldberg, L.R. (1972). Parameters of personality inventory construction and utilization: A comparison of prediction strategies and tactics. *Multivariate Behavioral Research Monograph*, No. 72-2.

Goodman, L.A., & Kruskal, W.H. (1954). Measures of association for cross-classification. *Journal of the American Statistical Association, 49*, 732–764.

Greenberg, B.G. et al. (1969). The unrelated question randomized response model: Theoretical framework. *Journal of the American Statistical Association, 64*, 520–539.

Hammill, D.D., Brown, L., & Bryant, B.R. (1992). *A consumer's guide to tests in print* (2nd ed.). Austin, TX: pro•ed.

Haney, R.D. (1995). Public opinion polling. In F.N. Magill (Ed.), *Survey of social science: Government and politics series* (Vol. 4, pp. 1627–1632). Pasadena, CA: Salem Press.

Hartman, B.W., Fuqua, D.R., & Jenkins, S.J. (1985). Problems of and remedies for nonresponse bias in educational surveys. *Journal of Experimental Education, 54,* 85–90.

Hase, H.D. (1992). McGill Pain Questionnaire: Revised format. In L. VandeCreek, S. Knapp, & T.L. Jackson (Eds.), *Innovations in clinical practice: A source book* (Vol. 11, pp. 285–291). Sarasota, FL: Professional Resource Press.

Hastings, E.H., & Hastings, P.K. (1995). *Index to international public opinion, 1993–1994.* Westport, CT: Greenwood Press.

Healey, J.F. (1996). *Statistics: A tool for social research* (4th ed.). Belmont, CA: Wadsworth.

Hinkle, D.E., Oliver, J.D., & Hinkle, C.A. (1985). How large should the sample be? Part 2— The one-sample case for survey research. *Educational and Psychological Measurement, 45,* 271–280.

Hite, S. (1976). *Hite report: A nationwide study on female sexuality.* New York: Macmillan.

Hollingworth, H.L. (1920). *The psychology of functional neuroses.* New York: D. Appleton.

Holt, R.R. (1970). Yet another look at clinical and statistical prediction: Or, is clinical psychology worthwhile? *American Psychologist, 25,* 337–349.

Hoover, D.W. (1993). Community studies. In M.K. Cayton, E.J., Gorn, & P.W. Williams (Eds.), *Encyclopedia of American social history* (Vol. 1, pp. 297–305). New York: Scribner's.

Jackson, D.N. (1971). The dynamics of structured personality tests: 1971. *Psychological Review, 78*(3), 229–248.

Jackson, D.N. (1989). *Basic Personality Inventory manual.* Port Huron, MI: Sigma Assessment Systems.

Jansen, J.H. (1985). Effect of questionnaire layout and size and issue-involvement on response rate in mail surveys. *Perceptual and Motor Skills, 61,* 139–142.

Kearney, K.A., Hopkins, R.H., Mauss, A.L., & Weisheit, R.A. (1984). Self-generated identification codes for anonymous collection of longitudinal questionnaire data. *Public Opinion Quarterly, 48*(1B), 370–378.

Kerr, B. (1995). Review of the Substance Abuse Subtle Screening Inventory. In J.C. Conoley & J.C. Impara (Eds.), *The twelfth mental measurements yearbook* (pp. 1017–1018). Lincoln, NE: The Buros Institute of Mental Measurements, The University of Nebraska-Lincoln.

Keyser, D.J., & Sweetland, R.C. (Eds.). (1984–1994). *Test critiques* (Vols. 1–10). Austin, TX: pro•ed.

Kinnear, T.C., & Taylor, J.R. (1991). *Marketing research* (4th ed.). New York McGraw-Hill.

Kish, L. (1965). *Survey sampling.* New York: Wiley.

Korchin, S.J., & Schuldberg, D. (1981). The future of clinical assessment. *American Psychologist, 36,* 1147–1158.

Kramer, J.J., & Conoley, J.C. (1992). *The eleventh mental measurements yearbook.* Lincoln, NE: Buros Institute of Mental Measurements of the University of Nebraska-Lincoln.

Lanyon, R.L., & Goodstein, I.D. (1982). *Personality assessment* (2nd ed.). New York: Wiley.

Lippa, R. (1991). Some psychometric characteristics of gender diagnosticity measures: Reliability, validity, consistency across domains, and relationship to the big 5. *Journal of Personality and Social Psychology, 61,* 1000–1011.

Lippa, R., & Connelly, S. (1990). Gender diagnosticity: A new Bayesian approach to gender-related individual differences. *Journal of Personality and Social Psychology, 59,* 1051–1065.

McNeely, S. (1995). Review of the Alcohol Use Inventory. In J.C. Conoley & J.C. Impara (Eds.), *The twelfth mental measurements yearbook* (pp. 66–67). Lincoln, NE: The Buros Institute of Mental Measurements, The University of Nebraska-Lincoln.

Meehl, P.E. (1954). *Clinical versus statistical prediction.* Minneapolis, MN: University of Minnesota Press.

Meehl, P.E. (1965). Seer over sign: The first good example. *Journal of Experimental Research in Personality, 11,* 27–32.

Meehl, P.E. (1973). *Psychodiagnosis: Selected papers.* Minneapolis, MN: University of Minnesota Press.

Melzack, R. (1975). The McGill pain questionnaire: Major properties and scoring methods. *Pain, 1,* 1–5.

Melzack, R. (1983). *Pain measurement and assessment.* New York: Raven Press.

Melzack, R. (1987). The short-form McGill Pain Questionnaire, *Pain, 30,* 191–197.

Melzack, R., & Katz, J. (1992). The McGill Pain Questionnaire: Appraisal and current status. In D.C. Turk & R. Melzack (Eds.), *Handbook of pain assessment* (pp. 152–168). New York: Guilford.

Millon, T., Millon, C., & Davis, R. (1994). *Manual for the MCMI-III.* Minneapolis, MN: NCS Assessments.

Mischel, W. (1968). *Personality and assessment.* New York: Wiley.

Mitchell, J.V., Jr. (Ed.). (1983). *Tests in print III.* Lincoln, NE: Buros Institute of Mental Measurements of the University of Nebraska-Lincoln.

Mitchell, J.V., Jr. (Ed.). (1985). *The ninth mental measurements yearbook.* Lincoln, NE: Buros Institute of Mental Measurements of the University of Nebraska-Lincoln.

Murphy, L.L., Conoley, J.C., & Impara, J.C. (Eds.). (1994). *Tests in print IV.* Lincoln, NE: University of Nebraska and Buros Institute of Mental Measurements.

Murray, H.A. (and collaborators). (1938). *Explorations in personality.* New York: Oxford University Press.

Norusis, M.J. (1992). *SPSS/PC+ base system user's guide version 5.0.* Chicago: SPSS.

Ochse, R., & Plug, C. (1986). Cross-cultural investigation of the validity of Erikson's theory of personality development. *Journal of Personality and Social Psychology, 50,* 1240–1252.

Ozer, D.J., & Reise, S.P. (1994). Personality assessment. *Annual Review of Psychology, 45,* 357–388.

Pagano, R.R. (1994). *Understanding statistics in the behavioral sciences* (4th ed.). Minneapolis/St. Paul, MN: West.

Payne, F.D. (1985). Review of Bem Sex-Role Inventory. In J.V. Mitchell, Jr. (Ed.), *The ninth mental measurements yearbook* (Vol. 1, pp. 137–138). Lincoln, NE: Buros Institute of Mental Measurements of the University of Nebraska-Lincoln.

Peterson, C., & Austin, J.T. (1985). Review of Coopersmith Self-Esteem Inventories. In J.V. Mitchell, Jr. (Ed.), *The ninth mental measurements yearbook* (Vol. 1, pp. 396–397). Lincoln, NE: Buros Institute of Mental Measurements of the University of Nebraska-Lincoln.

Peterson, C., Semmel, A., von Baelyer, C., Abramson, L.Y., Metalsky, G.I., & Seligman, M.E.P. (1982). The Attributional Style Questionnaire. *Cognitive Therapy and Research, 6,* 287–299.

Petzelt, J.T., & Craddick, R. (1978). Present meaning of assessment in psychology. *Professional Psychology: Research and Practice, 9,* 587–591.

Powers, D., & Alderman, D. (1982). Feedback as an incentive for responding to a mail questionnaire. *Research in Higher Education, 173,* 207–211.

Pressey, S.L., & Pressey, L.W. (1919). Cross-out test, with suggestions as to a group scale of the emotions. *Journal of Applied Psychology, 3,* 138–150.

Riley, W.T., & McCranie, E.W. (1990). The Depressive Experiences Questionnaire: Validity and psychological correlates in a clinical sample. *Journal of Personality Assessment, 54,* 523–533.

Rorer, L.G. (1990). Personality assessment: A conceptual survey. In L.A. Pervin (Ed.), *Handbook of personality theory and research* (pp. 693–720). New York: Guilford.

Ross, K.N., & Rust, K. (1994). Sampling in survey research. In T. Husén & T.N. Postlethwaite (Eds.), *The international encyclopedia of education* (2nd ed., Vol. 9, pp. 5131–5142). New York: Elsevier.

Ryan, C., & Bradford, J. (1993). The National Lesbian Health Care Survey: An overview. In L.D. Garnets & D.C. Kimmel (Eds.), *Psychological perspectives on lesbian and gay male experiences. Between men—between women: Lesbian and gay studies* (pp. 541–556). New York: Columbia University Press.

Schaie, K.W. (1977). Quasiexperimental research designs in the psychology of aging. In J.E. Birren & K.W. Schaie (Eds.), *Handbook of the psychology of aging* (pp. 39–59). New York: Van Nostrand Reinhold.

Schenke, S. (1995). Review of the Eating Disorder Inventory-2. In J.C. Conoley & J.C. Impara (Eds.), *The twelfth mental measurements yearbook* (p. 335). Lincoln, NE: The Buros Institute of Mental Measurements, The University of Nebraska-Lincoln.

Seligman, M.E.P. (1975). *Helplessness: On depression, development and death.* San Francisco: Freeman.

Seligman, M.E.P. (1992). *Helplessness* (2nd ed.). San Francisco: Freeman.

Selye, H. (1993). History and present status of the stress concept. In L. Goldberger & S. Breznitz (Eds.), *Handbook of stress: Theoretical and clinical aspects* (2nd ed., pp. 7–17). New York: Free Press.

Sewell, T.E. (1985). Review of Coopersmith Self-Esteem Inventories. In J.V. Mitchell, Jr. (Ed.), *The ninth mental measurements yearbook* (Vol. 1, pp. 397–398). Lincoln, NE: Buros Institute of Mental Measurements of the University of Nebraska-Lincoln.

Sigall, H., & Page, R. (1971). Current stereotypes: A little fading, a little faking. *Journal of Personality and Social Psychology, 18,* 247–255.

Sines, J.O. (1970). Actuarial versus clinical prediction in psychopathology. *British Journal of Psychiatry, 116,* 129–144.

Stewart, A.L., Hays, R.D., & Ware, J.E., Jr. (1988). The MOS Short-Form General Health Survey. *Medical Care, 26(7),* 724–735.

Stewart, A.L., & Ware, J.E. (Eds.). (1992). *Measuring functions and well-being: The Medical Outcomes Study.* Durham, NC: Duke University Press.

Stokes, G.S., Mumford, M.D., & Owens, W.A. (1994). *Biodata handbook: Theory, research, and use of biographical information in selection and performance prediction.* Palo Alto, CA: CPP Books.

Sudman, S., & Bradburn, N.M. (1982). *Asking questions: A practical guide to questionnaire construction.* San Francisco: Jossey-Bass.

Sundberg, N.D. (1992). Review of the Beck Depression Inventory (Revised Edition). *The eleventh mental measurements yearbook* (pp. 79–81). Lincoln, NE: Buros Institute of Mental Measurements of the University of Nebraska-Lincoln.

Sundre, D.L. (1995). Review of the Menstrual Distress Questionnaire. In J.C. Conoley & J.C. Impara (Eds.), *The twelfth mental measurements yearbook* (pp. 597–599). Lincoln, NE: The Buros Institute of Mental Measurements, The University of Nebraska-Lincoln.

Sweetland, R.C., & Keyser, D.J. (Eds.). (1991). *Tests* (3rd ed.). Austin, TX: pro•ed.

Taylor, J.A. (1953). A personality scale of manifest anxiety. *Journal of Abnormal and Social Psychology, 48,* 285–290.

Tellengen, A., & Waller, N.G. (1993). Exploring personality through test construction: Development of the Multidimensional Personality Questionnaire. In S.R. Briggs & J.M. Cheek (Eds.), *Personality measures: Development and evaluation.* Greenwich, CT: JAI Press.

Vacc, N.A. (1995). Review of the Substance Abuse Subtle Screening Inventory. In J.C. Conoley & J.C. Impara (Eds.), *The twelfth mental measurements yearbook* (pp. 1017–1018). Lincoln, NE: The Buros Institute of Mental Measurements, The University of Nebraska-Lincoln.

Viglione, D.J., Clemmey, P.A., & Camenzuli, L. (1990). The Depressive Experiences Questionnaire: A critical review. *Journal of Personality Assessment, 55,* 52–64.

Waksberg, J. (1978). Sampling methods for random digit dialing. *American Statistical Association, 73,* 40–66.

Warner, E.L. (1965). Randomized response: A survey technique for eliminating error answer bias. *Journal of the American Statistical Association, 60,* 63–69.

Weller, L., & Livingston, R. (1988). Effect of color of questionnaire on emotional responses. *The Journal of General Psychology, 115,* 433–440.

Wewers, M.E., & Lowe, N.K. (1990). A critical review of visual analogue scales for the measurement of clinical phenomena. *Research in Nursing and Health, 13*(4), 227–236.

Willerman, L. (1975). *Individual and group differences.* New York: Harper's College Press.

Winer, B.J., Brown, D.R., & Michels, K.M. (1991). *Statistical principles in experimental design* (3rd ed.). New York: McGraw-Hill.

Wolfe, R.N. (1993). A commonsense approach to personality measurement. In K.H. Craik, R. Hogan, & R.N. Wolfe (Eds.), *Fifty years of personality psychology* (pp. 269–290). New York: Plenum.

Wunsch, D.R. (1986). Survey research: Determining sample size and representative response. *Business Education Forum, 40*(5), 31–34.

Zuckerman, M. (1994). *Behavioral expressions and biosocial bases of sensation seeking.* New York: Cambridge University Press.

Zuroff, D.C., Quinlan, D.M., & Blatt, S.J. (1990). Psychometric properties of the Depressive Experiences Questionnaire in a college population. *Journal of Personality Assessment, 55,* 65–72.

Author Index

Subject Index

Instruments Index

313